Fitzgerald and Gould have consistently raised the difficult questions and inconvenient truths about western engagement in Afghanistan. While many analysts and observers have attempted to wish a reality on a grim and tragic situation in Afghanistan, Fitzgerald and Gould have systematically dug through the archives and historical record with integrity and foresight to reveal a series of misguided strategies and approaches that have contributed to what has become a tragic quagmire in Afghanistan. I suspect that many of their assessments while presently viewed as controversial and contentious, will eventually be considered conventional wisdom.

—**Thomas Johnson**, Department of National Security Affairs
and Director, Program for Culture and Conflict Studies,
Naval Postgraduate School, Monterey, California

Americans are now beginning to grasp the scope of the mess their leaders made while pursuing misguided military adventures into regions of Central Asia we once called "remote." How this happened—and what the U.S. can do to extricate itself from its entanglements in Pakistan and Afghanistan—is the story of *Crossing Zero*. Based on decades of study and research, this book draws lines and connects dots in ways few others do. It is clear, sober and methodical—an ideal handbook for anyone seeking to understand how the U.S. became the latest imperial power to blunder into this turbulent and fascinating region.

—**Stephen Kinzer**, author of *All the Shah's Men* and *Reset:
Iran, Turkey and America's Future*

An extraordinary contribution to understanding war and geo-politics in Afghanistan that will shock most Americans by its revelations of official American government complicity in using, shielding, sponsoring and supporting terrorism. A devastating indictment on the behind-the-scenes shenanigans by some of America's most respected statesmen. I loved it.

—**Daniel Estulin**, investigative journalist and author of *The True Story of the Bilderberg Club, The Secrets of Club Bilderberg,* and *Shadow Masters: An International Network of Governments and Secret-Service Agencies Working Together with Drugs Dealers and Terrorists for Mutual Benefit and Profit*

Gould and Fitzgerald have identified the triumphalist strain that has marked American foreign policy over the past 100 years and documented President Obama's failure to introduce change to American national security policy. The war in Afghanistan is consistent with previous failures in U.S. policymaking over the past 50 years as well as with the misuse of military force. This book should be required reading at the National Security Council and the Pentagon.

—**Melvin A. Goodman**, CIA Senior Soviet Analyst, 1966–1990; Professor of International Security at the National War College,1986–2004; Senior Fellow, Center for International Policy, Washington, DC.

After several decades of facile and destructive answers from Washington policymakers, the authors deploy a phalanx of incisive questions about U.S. policies in Afghanistan and Pakistan. The result is a book that shatters the key myths promoted by American news media and the last six presidents. *Crossing Zero* is a searing exposé of distortions that have fundamentally warped U.S. perceptions and actions in the "AfPak" region. Fitzgerald and Gould provide crucial antidotes to poisonous assumptions and bromides of conventional wisdom that continue to delude the USA into further lethal follies. This book deconstructs and dismantles a deadly formula of ignorance and deceit.

—**Norman Solomon**, author of *War Made Easy: How Presidents and Pundits Keep Spinning Us to Death*

In *Crossing Zero*, Paul Fitzgerald and Elizabeth Gould provide a much needed antidote to mainstream accounts of the AfPak war by documenting in detail the disastrous consequences of United States and NATO military intervention in the region. Drawing from a wide range of sources, and written in crisp, clear prose, the book will be useful to students, researchers, policy makers, and anyone interested in knowing the truth.

—**Julien Mercille**, lecturer in U.S. foreign policy
at University College Dublin

Crossing Zero is much more than a devastating indictment of the folly of U.S. military intervention in Afghanistan. Paul Fitzgerald and Elizabeth Gould demonstrate that the U.S. debacle in Afghanistan is the predictable climax of U.S. imperial overreach on a global scale. Like their earlier work documenting the origins of U.S. involvement in Afghanistan during the Cold War, *Crossing Zero* deserves the attention of all serious students of U.S. foreign policy.

—**Selig S. Harrison**, co-author with Diego Cordovez of *Out of Afghanistan: The Inside Story of the Soviet Withdrawal*

PRAISE FOR *INVISIBLE HISTORY*

★ Journalists Fitzgerald and Gould do yeoman's labor in clearing the fog and laying bare American failures in Afghanistan in this deeply researched, cogently argued and enormously important book. The authors demonstrate how closely American actions are tied to past miscalculations—and how U.S. policy has placed Afghans and Americans in grave danger.

—*Publishers Weekly* (starred review)

A probing history of the country and a critical evaluation of American involvement in recent decades. . . . A fresh perspective on a little-understood nation.

—*Kirkus*

Invisible History shows us that we now have an opportunity to transform ourselves through an honest confrontation with our past: a confrontation that would lead us to reorient our national policies around the tabernacle of our professed moral values. If we choose to ignore this opportunity, and once again turn a blind eye to history and its lessons, then we may find ourselves in grave danger, not just from the threat of terrorist attacks, but from falling victim to the same folly that has toppled empires throughout history.

—*Tikkun*

The fog obscuring U.S. policies in Afghanistan is thicker than elsewhere in the region. The authors cut through it meticulously, exposing layers of cultural arrogance and myopia. They demonstrate with painful clarity how these traits helped push our would-be ally into the Soviet orbit, causing us to arm and promote the violent extremists we're fighting today. When confronted with al-Qaeda's nihilism on 9/11, our response was "wildly exaggerated, dangerously reckless, and . . . ineffective."

—*Dallas Morning News*

CROSSING ZERO

The AfPak War at the Turning Point of American Empire

Paul Fitzgerald and Elizabeth Gould

 Open Media Series | City Lights Books

The Open Media Series is edited by Greg Ruggiero and archived by
the Tamiment Library at New York University.

Cover design by Pollen, New York

Library of Congress Cataloging-in-Publication Data

Fitzgerald, Paul.
 The AfPak war at the turning point of American empire / by Paul Fitzgerald and
Elizabeth Gould.
    p. cm. — (Open media series)
 Includes index.
 ISBN 978-0-87286-513-6
1. Afghanistan—Strategic aspects. 2. Pakistan—Strategic aspects. 3. Asia,
Central—Strategic aspects. 4. Afghanistan—Military relations—United States.
5. United States—Military relations—Afghanistan. 6. Pakistan—Military
relations—United States. 7. United States—Military relations—Pakistan. 8.
Imperialism—History. 9. Afghan War, 2001– 10. Terrorism—Afghanistan. I.
Gould, Elizabeth. II. Title.
 DS371.4.F58 2011
 958.104'7—dc22
                                    2010049891

City Lights Books are published at the City Lights Bookstore,
261 Columbus Avenue, San Francisco, CA 94133.

www.citylights.com

For Alissa and Devon
The future is yours to make real.

CONTENTS

INTRODUCTION

I

In the age of airport full-body security scans, underwear bombers, bulging no-fly and person-of-interest watch lists, it's not every day that a U.S. citizen gets an unsolicited email from the representative of a notorious terrorist stating that they may face legal action for writing well-documented criticisms of his boss. But that is exactly what happened to these two authors on Monday, January 25, 2010. On that day Los Angeles resident Mr. Daoud M. Abedi of the Hesb-i-Islami Afghanistan (HIA) emailed us on behalf of Afghanistan's longest-running warlord, drug trafficker and terrorist, Gulbuddin Hekmatyar.

Abedi's email followed the posting of our essays "Apocalypse of the American Mind,"[1] on Sibel Edmunds' *Boiling Frogs* and "In Afghanistan: Embracing Gulbuddin Hekmatyar Is No Method at All" on *Huffington Post*.[2] Our online essays addressed the insane possibility, recently reported in the media,[3] that in Washington's growing desperation, a known terrorist like Gulbuddin Hekmatyar might be considered a "sane" solution to the U.S. quagmire in Afghanistan. Under Executive Order 13224,[4] since February 18, 2003 Hekmatyar has been listed as a global terrorist by both the United States State Department and the United States Treasury (which freezes his assets and criminalizes any U.S. support for him). He has also been the intended object of at least one Predator drone attack[5] and has most recently claimed credit for a deadly assault on French NATO forces fighting in Afghanistan.[6] So it came as a great surprise that Gulbuddin Hekmatyar and his political party Hesb-i-Islami are not only operating out in the open in the United

States, but are issuing threats (just the way they do in Afghanistan) to anyone who tries to get the word out about the atrocities he is known to have committed.

The order of Abedi's complaints is a window into the mind of one of the world's most notorious terrorists. It is not Hekmatyar's well-documented record as a murderer, terrorist and major drug kingpin that disturbs him. The terrorist-strongman label actually appeals to Mr. Abedi, who in one email asserts that he is "happy he is called a terrorist because what he does for Afghanistan is what George Washington did for the US." Abedi's primary concern is for published reports that "His Excellency" might once have been a member of the nominally communist People's Democratic Party of Afghanistan (PDPA) as a student in the late 1960s and early 1970s.[7] He is willing to bend time and dozens of well-documented facts in order to protect Gulbuddin Hekmatyar's reputation as a pure, messianic Islamist, lay blame for his bad deeds on communists, Maoists, Afghanistan's King Zahir Shah and assorted foreigners, while denouncing his chief rival, Ahmed Shah Massoud as "the biggest traitor of Afghan politics."

To Mr. Abedi, other people's facts accumulated over the last forty years and compiled by experts are not facts. They are lies. Gulbuddin Hekmatyar's critics are wrong because Gulbuddin Hekmatyar is always right, and if he and his Hesb-i-Islami Afghanistan someday come to power, "I promise you, the HIA will call on all these so called experts, and knowledgeable sources to come up and clean what they have written, prove it or apologize to the Afghan and international communities for misleading them, or we will not allow their feet in Afghan soil so they don't do this kind [of] stupidity in the future against other Afghans."[8]

Abedi has been actively negotiating on Hekmatyar's behalf at least since the Obama administration came to power. A May 10, 2009, report in the London *Sunday Times* stated that a representative of Richard Holbrooke, President Barack Obama's regional envoy, had met with "Daoud Abedi, an Afghan-American businessman close to Hekmatyar," and that "the U.S. administration will fund an

Afghan government department to conduct negotiations with the Hesb-i-Islami and the Taliban."[9] In the interim, with the help of Abedi, he has begun to rebrand himself as a "moderate fundamentalist with Afghanistan's best Islamic interest at heart."[10]

But Hekmatyar's coercive brutality is not moderate. According to published reports, during the 1980s Hekmatyar's Hesb-i-Islami developed a reputation for attacking moderates and raiding caravans of arms and supplies of other forces as well as relief organizations such as Doctors Without Borders.[11] According to author Steve Coll, Hekmatyar attacked his rival Ahmed Shah Massoud so often during his climb to power as the CIA's favorite in the 1980s that Washington "feared he might be a secret KGB plant whose mission was to sow disruption within the anti-communist resistance."[12] According to press reports, Hekmatyar was not viewed as the most aggressive anti-Soviet guerrilla and "not feared so much by the communists as by his allies," who believed his commanders were saving their men and weapons to establish Hesb-i-Islami as the dominant organization once the Soviets departed.[13] That analysis proved correct.

The history of attempting to work with warlords like Hekmatyar has consistently proven to be nothing but bad for the Afghan people, the region and the United States as well. A 1988 report by Henry Kamm for the *New York Times* summed up what was then common knowledge about the potential for a government run by Hekmatyar. "He advocates a radical program that rejects a return to the traditional ways of Islam that dominated Afghanistan during the monarchy that was overthrown in 1973. . . . 'We want a pure Islamic state in Afghanistan,' said 'Brother' Hekmatyar as his associates refer to him. 'Before 1973? That was never an Islamic system. It was completely against Islam.'"[14]

Nick Grono and Candace Rondeaux of the International Crisis Group in Belgium wrote in January 2010:

> One of the warlords who may soon star in the new U.S. efforts to rebrand fundamentalists as potential government partners is Gulbuddin Hekmatyar, a brutal Afghan insurgent commander

responsible for dozens of deadly attacks on coalition troops. As a mujahedeen commander during the civil war in the 1990s Hekmatyar turned his guns on Kabul, slaughtering many thousands of Afghans, with his militias raping and maiming thousands more. . . . Doing deals with Hekmatyar, or others like him, is a mistake. . . . Instead of entering into alliances of convenience with the most undesirable of local powerholders, the international community, and the Afghan government, would gain by holding warlords like Hekmatyar accountable for past abuses, and ending the climate of impunity that has allowed so many of them to flourish within and outside the government.[15]

On March 23, 2010, Carlotta Gall reported in the *New York Times* that Afghan President Hamid Karzai had welcomed a delegation of Hekmatyar's Al Qaeda– and Taliban-connected Hesb-i-Islami in Kabul, headed by his representative, Mohammed Daoud Abedi. "Though the insurgent group Hesb-i-Islami or Islamic Party operates under a separate command from the Taliban, it has links to the Taliban leadership and Al Qaeda and has fought on a common front against foreign forces in Afghanistan."[16]

The delegation was reported to have presented Karzai with a fifteen-point peace plan that included the withdrawal of foreign troops, to which Abedi claimed the Taliban would agree. According to the report, "Mr. Abedi described their reception in Kabul as 'fabulous' and said 'the president was very, very gentle, very, very friendly.'"[17]

In the final analysis, Gulbuddin Hekmatyar has never been successful at anything other than creating chaos and bloodshed. For over forty years, through his ruthlessness, brutality, foreign financial backing and unceasing public relations campaigns, he has clung to his messianic dream of a "pure Islamic state" while most of his contemporaries have perished. If he and his agents assume a role in the Afghan government, with the volumes of deeds that are known about him, it is certain that he will demand more than just apologies from the people on whom he calls. Should he come to power and gain his dream as part of Obama's AfPak strategy, the administration will have opened Afghanistan, as well as itself, to a very dark messiah.

II

The year 2011 marks ten full years since the United States invaded Afghanistan and overthrew the uncooperative Saudi- and Pakistani-backed government of the Taliban. It has been over thirty years since the former Soviet Union overthrew a quasi Marxist-Maoist-oriented regime in Kabul. For many who have followed the course of developments in Afghanistan and know something of its complicated history, the 2001 U.S. invasion was seen as the opportunity for the international community to give Afghanistan the chance at democracy, peace and independence that it had been denied following the 1989 withdrawal of the U.S.S.R.'s Red Army and the 1992 collapse of the Marxist government of the People's Democratic Party of Afghanistan (PDPA).

It would be impossible to exaggerate the conceptual, managerial, political, military, moral and ethical failures that characterized the war orchestrated under President George W. Bush. Had the administration set out to design a plan that would fail at every juncture, radicalize the entire region, protect and even strengthen the Pakistan military's link to terrorism and establish the requisite conditions for a Taliban–Al Qaeda resurgence, it would look no different than it does today. Afghanistan's potential for peace, stability and development was the Bush administration's to squander, and they squandered it.

From the outset, Washington's Afghan problem was largely threefold. First there was the absence of an adequate understanding of Afghanistan's history, its people, their needs and how to provide for them. Prior to the Soviet invasion of 1979, Afghanistan had been one of the poorest countries on earth, with a per capita income of under $200 dollars a year and an infant mortality rate of almost 50 percent. After nearly thirty years of war, Afghanistan had been reduced to a Stone Age subsistence, its already impoverished population traumatized, displaced and occupied by an army of savage religious extremists exported by Pakistan, calling themselves the Taliban—"seekers of the light."

In 2001, the solutions appeared simple and straightforward. Security, food, irrigation and electricity topped the list of needs, followed by roads and housing. Despite its poverty, prior to the Soviet invasion of 1979 Afghanistan had been largely self-sufficient in food production.[18] A few hundred million dollars shrewdly managed and carefully distributed at a grassroots level could have provided a solid foundation for recovery. Instead, the rapacious and incompetent mishandling of the country's reconstruction monies, the confused misapplication of counterinsurgency/counterterrorism doctrine and a telltale weakness for ignoring Pakistan's open support for the Taliban, spelled disaster. After eight years and billions spent, the Bush administration's efforts by 2009 had amounted to the virtual collapse of governance in much of Afghanistan and Pakistan, the spread of religious violence throughout the region and the ascent of a narco-funded criminal enterprise global in scope. This is the legacy that has become President Obama's war.

Washington's second major issue regarding Afghanistan is Pakistan. Originally carved from British India in 1947 with two wings, West Pakistan (Punjab, Baluchistan, Sindh and the North West Frontier) and East Pakistan (Bengal, today's Bangladesh),[19] the country has suffered an identity crisis from its inception. The name itself derives from initials of the various states from which it was composed: Punjab, Afghania, Kashmir, Sindh, Tukharistan and the suffix -stan, from Baluchistan.[20] The Persian word *pak*, which means "pure," was also said to have influenced the meaning, rendering the concept of Pakistan to its adherents as a "land of the pure." With a northern border within a stone's throw of Soviet Central Asia and adjoining Communist China as well as the strategic port of Karachi on the Arabian Sea, Pakistan's purity was of less importance than its strategic location, and the country was quickly brought into the fold of the U.S. Cold War machine.

But instead of putting Pakistan at an advantage relative to its South Asian neighbors India and Afghanistan, America's military embrace had the effect of freezing Pakistan into a special relationship that discouraged the nation's democratization and secular development while at the same time encouraging a radical pan-Islamization that now threatens to tear both Pakistan and Afghanistan apart.

Most analysis of Pakistan's seemingly schizophrenic behavior toward the U.S. mission in Afghanistan has focused mainly on the Pakistani military's support for the Taliban's Islamic extremism. But the struggle with Afghanistan's Pashtun tribes for control of Central Asia precedes Russian, U.S. and British involvement, the Cold War, the Great Game and even the creation of Islam itself.

India's ethnic Punjabis and Afghanistan's Pashtuns have been warring enemies for more than 2,000 years. Their historical relationship is one of abiding hatred, as the Punjabis aspire to their former glory as Mughal overlords and the Pashtuns seek the reunification of their national tribal lands denied to them by the British in the nineteenth century. Today they fight the same war under different flags, with political Islam acting as the vector, but the deadly and destructive drama has taken on new dimensions.

According to an analysis put forward on the Web site of India's Cinema Rasik,[21] the growing upheaval in Pakistan isn't about Islam but about the rising anger of the Pashtun tribes who have been forced to live under the rule of Pakistan's Punjabi military since 1947.

> The Af-Pak situation began in 1893 when the British-led Indian Army conquered South Afghanistan (the part of Afghanistan below the Khyber Pass) and forced the partition of Afghanistan into North and South. . . . The main aim of the Pashtun Taleban used to be to reconquer North Afghanistan and unite all of Afghanistan under Pashtun rule. The American presence in North Afghanistan and the determination of the Obama administration have convinced the Taliban that America will not leave Kabul. So the Pashtun Taliban

have decided to move south towards the plains of Pakistani Panjab, a much richer prize than impoverished Afghanistan.[22]

Pakistan's humiliating defeat in its 1971 war against East Pakistan continues to haunt Pakistan's predominantly Punjabi military establishment. Born as a Bengali struggle for more autonomy and political rights, the conflict elicited a brutal response from Pakistan that transformed it into a war with India, severed East Pakistan from Pakistan and created the independent nation of Bangladesh. Following the war against the Soviet Union in the 1980s, Pakistan used the Mujahideen and subsequently the Taliban to settle old scores with India and control Afghanistan. But as the state of Pakistan becomes increasingly weak and the Taliban movement grows increasingly strong, the relationship becomes dangerously unstable.

By setting the poorly trained, poorly equipped Pashtun Frontier Corps against the Pakistani Taliban after 9/11, Pakistan's generals temporarily avoided a direct Punjabi/Pashtun confrontation like the one that created Bangladesh. But as Taliban cells recruit and multiply inside the Punjab—setting up their own Pashtun-controlled "Punjabi Taliban" among the Punjab's disillusioned youth—a new dynamic has taken hold that threatens to redefine the rules of the game. Cinema Rasik notes:

> The racial contempt of the Pakistani Panjabi Generals is making them blind to the realities on the ground. The Pashtun Taliban are getting recruits and building a Panjabi Taleban sub-movement. This combination is rapidly making inroads into rural Panjab and seems poised to take over some semi-urban areas in Panjab. When they succeed, the Pakistani Panjabi Generals will find that their soldiers are not willing to fire on their rural Panjabi brothers.[23]

Washington's third major issue regarding Afghanistan is Washington itself. In fact, the politics of both Afghanistan and Pakistan over the last sixty years have been so entwined in Washington's vast web of special interests that the Obama administration's new AfPak policy could just as easily be termed WaAfPak. Burdened by a hulking bureaucratic structure created at the outset of the Cold War, Washington moved onto the politically complex, multi-ethnic, sectarian South Asian stage in 2001 with all the grace, speed and sophistication of a lumbering 1947 Buick Roadmaster. In its dealings with the complexities of Central and South Asian politics, it continues to exhibit an inability to negotiate even the most rudimentary twists and turns of the new Great Game.

In recognition of the crisis created under the Bush administration's auspices, the Obama administration immediately named veteran diplomat Richard Holbrooke the new special envoy for Afghanistan and Pakistan, while for the first time allocating more money to the Afghan war than to the war in Iraq.[24]

A team of experts, headed by Brookings Institution Fellow and retired CIA expert on South Asia Bruce Riedel, was tasked with developing a workable new strategy for expanding the war from Afghanistan into Pakistan. In a radio interview with the *Philadelphia Inquirer*'s Trudy Rubin on September 9, 2008, Riedel gave voice to the concerns that would lead the Pakistan side of the Afghan equation to take precedence in any new administration's thinking.

> I think Pakistan is the most dangerous country in the world today, because all of the nightmares of the twenty-first century that should concern Americans come together in Pakistan in a unique way. This is a country with nuclear weapons. This is a country with a history of proliferating nuclear technology. This is a country that has fought four wars with its neighbor, and at least one of those wars went very close to becoming a nuclear war. This is a country that has been the host of numerous terrorist organizations and is today the safe haven and stronghold of the Al Qaeda terrorist organization. This is a country also awash in drugs—narcotics—and this is a country where the clash between reactionary Islamic extremism and democracy is being fought out literally in front of us. All of

those issues come together in this one place like nowhere else in the world. That's why it's so important to Americans.[25]

Following the election of Barack Obama, the resulting policy—formed with the help of Council on Foreign Relations (CFR) expert Barnett Rubin—emerged as "AfPak" (classic bit of Washington-acronym-speak). But no sooner had the outlines of this much-awaited strategy emerged than criticism arose from both left and right over just how this new policy would play out.

Before the new President had even set foot in the oval office a chorus of American voices emerged warning that Afghanistan would soon become Obama's Vietnam and calling for the United States to immediately withdraw its forces. They questioned whether the United States ought to be pursuing an Afghan-Pakistan war at all.

In keeping with the old Cold War business-as-usual approach, Riedel's plan actually reflected earlier British preferences for shifting the balance of concern away from Afghanistan to Pakistan altogether[26] while calling for Afghanistan's government to accommodate Pakistan's security concerns.[27] This came despite the fact that Pakistan, with the CIA's assistance,[28] had created the Taliban as an Afghan invasion force in 1992, and for eight years Al Qaeda and the Taliban had maintained Pakistan as a refuge and relied on its military to sustain the insurgency against U.S. and NATO troops.

Other voices, once again mainly British, sought to re-institute a failed Clinton-era policy of separating "moderate" Taliban from "extremist" Taliban or to establish an "acceptable" Afghan dictator[29] such as noted drug lord and admitted terrorist Gulbuddin Hekmatyar.

This, it was argued, would appease the Islamic right wing and gain Saudi Arabian support[30] while allowing the United States to focus on doing the only thing it apparently did well: decapitating Al Qaeda's suspected leadership with Predator drone missile strikes.

Employing Afghanistan's drug-dealing warlords was nothing new for Washington. It had elevated Pakistan's drug-warlords to Beltway cult status vis-à-vis *Charlie Wilson's War* during the Soviet occupation and insisted on including them in the new Afghan government in 2002.[31] Numerous observers, including Pakistan's president, Asif Ali Zardari, maintained that Washington had a hand in the Taliban's creation as well,[32] standing by as they rolled over Afghanistan in league with Al Qaeda and Pakistan's Directorate for Inter-Services Intelligence (Inter-Services Intelligence or ISI) in the late 1990s.

America's multitude of policy mistakes in Afghanistan have mystified many from the beginning. In a February 2, 2009, article in the online edition of the *Times* of London, the international community's High Representative in Bosnia, Paddy Ashdown, accepted responsibility for the Afghan fiasco, admitting that "we are trying to win in Afghanistan with one twenty-fifth the troops and one fiftieth of the aid per head in Bosnia. . . . [T]he real problem is not President Karzai, it's us."[33]

None of these voices reflected the deeper historical and political issues that made the Afghanistan-Pakistan war unique. They also disregarded a responsibility on the part of the United States to undo the damage it had created by seeding the region with terrorism in its anti-Soviet war of the 1980s. In fact, little of the political dialogue surrounding Washington's growing obsession with the Afghan-Pakistan war was based on an agenda-free assessment of the situation. It was instead grounded in a well-financed campaign of special interest politics, K Street lobbying efforts[34] and a resurgence of anti-Russian Reagan-era disinformation, kept on life support by a hard core of aging Cold War bureaucrats[35] and their embedded media acolytes.

The Soviet invasion of Afghanistan in 1979 initiated a golden era for Washington. It diverted U.S. citizens' attention from the cultural introspection made necessary by the social upheavals surrounding the Vietnam War. It wrongly vindicated a corps of neoconservative defense intellectuals whose reputations had been deservedly tarnished by the U.S. defeat in Vietnam and paved the road for the Reagan Agenda and the rise of the New Right. In a heartbeat, the U.S.S.R.'s invasion of Afghanistan restored the Cold

War and justified the introduction of World War II–size increases in the defense budget. But most of all, Afghanistan helped to re-establish a simplistic, good-vs.-evil mythology that had been laid waste by Vietnam.

As the Soviets settled into their long war against terrorism on their southern border, a propaganda campaign aimed at the American public was set up to keep the "evil empire" pinned down in its own Vietnam and the United States rooting for the people who were doing it; the fiercely religious "freedom fighters."[36]

As seen from this 1930s Hollywood perspective, one grafted straight from Britain's nineteenth-century colonial experience (U.S. officials in Kabul in 1981 jokingly referred to Dan Rather as Gunga Dan), Afghanistan was and is an untamable land, filled with wild and irrepressible tribes whose codes and traditions have stood un-changed since medieval times.

Seen from this perspective, men such as Ahmed Shah Massoud were and are still lionized as Afghan heroes,[37] despite a wealth of historical evidence revealing their philosophical grounding in a very un-Afghan, antimodernist, misogynist extremism, massive narcotics trafficking and an extensive history of horrific war crimes against fellow Afghans. From this perspective, the people of Afghanistan reject the modern world and long to remain a strictly conservative fundamentalist society, making any efforts to introduce a Western-style democracy a senseless waste of U.S. taxpayers' money.

Missing from this picture is any hint that a modern Afghanistan was emerging before the Soviet invasion, that its secular second-ary schools graduated over twenty thousand students each year[38] and that a growing number of its women worked alongside men in government and business to bring Afghanistan into the twentieth century. Missing from the argument is the abundance of evidence that Afghanistan's drive toward modernity was thwarted not by the backwardness of its rural tribes (which, if it were true, would ap-ply equally to U.S. ally Pakistan), but by outside forces from the United States, Saudi Arabia, Pakistan, Iran and China, who were bent on subduing the country and bending it to their purposes. The

Afghanistan of today is a product of the policies of those countries and the globalist geopoliticians who framed them, not the internal policies of any pre-Soviet Afghan government. Yet the Afghan and Pakistani people continue to bear the blame for it, and to this day suffer the consequences.

It can be assumed that somehow, in the swamp of human rights violations, terror and counterterror, violations of international law, military-corporate ambitions and the expanding numbers of civilian casualties brought on by it, in the massive heroin trade that now leads the world and in the resurgence of the Taliban and Al Qaeda in both nuclear-armed Pakistan and fragile Afghanistan, some species of outside plan or "Great Game" is still at work. Afghanistan, the crossroads of ancient civilizations and trade, remains a coveted crossroads for oil and gas pipelines from the Caspian basin to India, Pakistan and China. Texas oilmen, Saudi sheiks and Islamist jihadis found common cause with the Taliban as the shock troops for energy conglomerates in the 1990s and most likely still do. But should the current political situation in these two countries continue to erode, new levels of violence and instability will make the past seem only a mild prologue to the crisis that is to come.

At the time of this writing, the term AfPak has shifted from being a catchword to being the official designation for an expanded war that cannot be won militarily. Whether the United States can achieve success will depend on whether Washington can realign its objectives to meet the needs of the Afghan and Pakistani people. If, however, AfPak is another thinly disguised effort to maintain an imperial presence in South Central Asia by working with a status quo of Afghan warlords, corrupted police and an extremist-compromised Pakistani military, it will be another predictable link in a long chain of legendary Washington miscalculations.

Prologue: Fort Del Oro

In 1577, one ship of an Elizabethan fleet—piloted by a notorious English pirate and slave trader named Martin Frobisher—filled with what was thought to be gold bullion brought back from North America, smashed on the isolated, rocky western coast of Ireland at a place known as Smerwick. According to author Benjamin Woolley, the mission was intended to find the fabled Northwest Passage to China as part of a "Protestant adventure that would rival the Catholic quest as well as enrich the queen's treasury."[1] The "gold"—which was soon revealed to be nothing more than iron pyrites (fool's gold)—spilled from the broken ship's hull, littering the base of the cliffs. An Irish rebel captain by the name of James Fitzmaurice raised a fort at the summit of the cliffs and named it Fort Del Oro, (Fort of Gold) to mock the Queen's greed and her vain quest to challenge Rome for wealth and power beyond the seas. Fitzmaurice's family, the Geraldines, had been in conflict with London over land and authority since initiating the Anglo-Norman invasion of Ireland in the twelfth century.[2]

The coming of the Reformation to England earlier in the sixteenth century had turned 400 years of border disputes and jurisdictional feuding into holy war. In 1580, the Holy See in Rome sent an army of Italians and Spaniards to help the Geraldines, under the authority drafted by the "Just War Doctrine,"[3] to help fight the Queen's Protestant forces. By some strange serendipity, this "army" soon found itself with its back to the sea at Fort Del Oro, and after the soldiers surrendered, the entire group was massacred and the bodies thrown onto the rocks below by an army commanded by Walter Raleigh. A few years later, Raleigh would attempt to establish the first British colony in the New World, Virginia, in honor of Queen

Elizabeth, his virgin queen. Along with the sinking of the Spanish Armada in 1588, Fort Del Oro turned the tide for the English and their quest for colonies, wealth and power. But Frobisher's failure to find gold in the West encouraged London to turn to the East. And in the final day of the year 1600, a company was chartered by Queen Elizabeth I and granted a monopoly to compete with Portugal by bringing goods acquired in India back to England.

The East India Company's ships arrived at the Indian port of Surat in 1608. As an emissary of King James I, Sir Thomas Roe reached the court of the Mughal Emperor in 1615. Trading posts were established along the east and west coasts of India, with Calcutta, Bombay and Madras becoming major centers. But the more the Company expanded into the interior of India, the more rapacious it became.

In 1717, the Company acquired a royal dictat or *firman* from the Mughal Emperor that exempted the Company from the payment of custom duties in Bengal. Then, in 1757, the Company transformed into something new and unusual when one of its private military officials, Robert Clive, defeated Prince Siraj-ud-daulah of Bengal at the battle of Plassay.[4] Author Nick Robins writes:

> The turning point came in 1757, when one of its more un-scrupulous executives, Robert Clive, deployed the company's private army, a healthy dose of bribes and ingenious fraud to defeat the nawab of Bengal at the battle of Plassay. In the loot-ing that followed, Clive netted £2.5 million for the company, and £234,000 for himself, equivalent today to a £232 million windfall for his employers and a cool £22 million success fee for himself. Historical convention views Plassay as the first step in the creation of the British empire in India. But it is per-haps better understood as the company's most successful busi-ness deal.[5]

A few years later the Company gained control of the Mughal Emperor's *diwani* (tax system)—"a bit like Wal-Mart running the Internal Revenue Service in today's United States. With this acquisition began the systematic drain of wealth that would continue under corporate control until 1858, and thereafter under the British Raj until 1947."[6]

The draconian transformation from mercantile enterprise to freewheeling corporate state in India meant a windfall for the Company and its London stockholders, but it spelled disaster for the people of Bengal. Company agents plundered the formerly wealthy Indian province and left it destitute. A famine in 1769–70 took the lives of one-third to half of the population, which the company did nothing to prevent or alleviate.[7]

Despite its growing expertise at wealth extraction through trade, taxation and the assumption of state powers, the company's massive military expenditures caused it to seek a bailout from London. The India Bill, also known as the Regulating Act of 1773, placed the Company's authority under greater parliamentary control and established the office of Governor-General. Over time, the East India Company absorbed the whole of India, either through military conquest or simply the power of indirect rule. Scholar Vinay Lal writes, "Lord Dalhousie's notorious doctrine of lapse, whereby a native state became part of British India if there was no male heir at the death of the ruler, was one of the principal means by which native states were annexed; but often the annexation, such as that of Awadh [Oudh] in 1856, was justified on the grounds that the native prince was of evil disposition, indifferent to the welfare of his subjects."[8]

From the outset, the East India company's success in India was a source of devastation for Afghanistan. Historian Vartan Gregorian writes:

> The cultural and economic isolation of Afghanistan was aggravated by the discovery of maritime routes between Europe and the East. The opening of these routes, which were safer, cheaper, and in many respects faster, greatly undermined the monopolistic position of Central Asia and Afghanistan as transit trade centers and the region was soon reduced to a secondary position in world trade. The prosperity of many urban

centers in Afghanistan was permanently threatened and the cause of feudalism strengthened by the consequent weakening of the merchant class.[9]

The East India Company's impact on Afghanistan was often a source of public and political outrage in London as well. The Company's outrageous practices were attacked by Adam Smith in his *An Inquiry into the Nature and Causes of the Wealth of Nations*,[10] as well as by the philosopher Edmund Burke, who argued that "Indian governmental corruption had to be resolved by removing patronage from interested parties," which led to impeachment proceedings against Warren Hastings, the Governor-General of Bengal.[11] The Company was often excoriated for its out-of-control behavior, and the British government was unwilling or unable to stop it. A report by the East India Committee in London written during the First Anglo-Afghan war in 1839 states, "This war of robbery is waged by the English Government through the intervention of the Government of India (without the knowledge of England, or of Parliament and the Court of Directors); thereby evading the checks placed by the Constitution on the exercise of the prerogative of the Crown in declaring war. It presents therefore a new crime in the annals of nations—a *secret war!*"[12] (emphasis in the original).

The Great Game for Central Asia
—Then and Now

1. Crossing Zero

The region today delineated as Afghanistan and Pakistan has been populated by many peoples, contested by numerous empires and divided by many borders over the millennia, yet no border has been more artificial or contentious than the one today separating Pakistan from Afghanistan, known as the Durand line but referred to by the military and intelligence community as Zero line. Much of what the United States does in Afghanistan and Pakistan remains a military secret. A report issued by the Center for Strategic and International Studies by Anthony H. Cordesman in September 2008[1] stated the case alarmingly:

> No country or international organization provides useful unclassified overview data on the developments in the fighting [in Afghanistan] in anything like the depth that the U.S. Department of Defense provides in its quarterly reports on the Iraq war. There are also significant differences in the limit[ed] amount of data that the U.S. government does provide. . . . The reporting that is available also decouples the fighting in Afghanistan from that in Pakistan. Accordingly, public official reporting on the growing intensity of the war since 2006 ignores one of the most critical aspects of the conflict.[2]

The United States has fought on both sides of the Durand line—on the side of militant-political Islam from Pakistan during the 1980s and against it from Afghanistan since the events of September 11, 2001. But, like the Durand line itself, the border between those two now seemingly incompatible objectives haunts Washington as the administration struggles to reconcile its policy with conditions in Pakistan and Afghanistan that may in the end prove irreconcilable.

It is therefore appropriate to think of Zero line as the vanishing point for the American empire, the point beyond which its power and influence disappears or simply ceases to exist. It is the line where America's intentions face themselves, the alpha and omega of nearly sixty years of American policy in Eurasia. The Durand line separating the two countries is visible on a map. Zero line is not.

The Durand/Zero line, originally named after British India's Foreign Secretary Sir Henry Mortimer Durand, was established as a boundary between British India and Afghanistan in 1893 after two Anglo-Afghan wars (1839–1842 and 1878–1880) and a southward Russian expansion resulted in a virtual stalemate for both sides.

By 1893, the relentless territorial expansion and acquisition of the imperial era had reached its limits for both Britain and Russia, and both wished to avoid a direct confrontation. Following over half a century of regional competition for control of Central Asia known as the Great Game, the Durand/Zero line represented a compromise solution by establishing Afghanistan as a buffer between rival empires.

Seen from the map rooms of imperial Britain's nineteenth-century strategists, the line made perfect sense. Seen from the perspective of the Afghan Pashtuns and Baluch tribes living on both sides of this arbitrary border, Durand/Zero was a horrific division of "territories and peoples who since time immemorial had been considered part of the Afghan homeland and nation."[3]

The territory surrounding the Indus River valley, now situated within the borders of Pakistan, Afghanistan and India, is home to one of the four most ancient urban civilizations.[4] It is considered by Afghans to have been their ancient tribal homeland for more than 3,000 years. Its origins, populations and influence on the ancient world have been the source of heated controversy within the archaeological community since the first excavations began in the nineteenth century. Its writing, known as Indus Civilization script, remains a much debated 4,500-year-old mystery that increasingly pits historians, Indologists and linguists in the West (who claim the writings were never developed as a language) against native-born scholars (who maintain they were).[5]

Such arguments over ethno-linguistics are no small matter in a region where territorial claims by India's Hindu nationalists, Afghanistan's Pashtun nationalists and Baluch separatists compete with those of pan-Islamic militants and Pakistani nationalists. According to Vartan Gregorian in his landmark 1969 study *The Emergence of Modern Afghanistan*, Afghan nationalist historians faced a similar resistance from Soviet, Iranian and Arab scholars in their efforts at pegging the origins of an Afghan kingdom at 3,000 to 5,000 years. They welcomed the work of the French archaeological team in the 1930s "who had uncovered the richness of the country's Bactrian and Kushan heritage. The Afghan nationalists took great pride in the fact that Kushan rule had had a far-reaching impact on the destinies of the peoples of eastern Iran and India, especially in the fields of religion and art."[6]

Far from denigrating Afghan society and minimizing its importance, Gregorian's exhaustive study, which he completed a full decade before the Cold War finally subsumed Afghanistan, paints a vivid picture of a once vital country in the brutal throes of modernization and change—from the genesis of the modern Afghan state in the 1880s under Amir Abdur Rahman Khan until the end of World War II.

But the movement for progressive change and modernization was well known to Afghanistan long before the rise of Amir Abdur Rahman and can be traced to the sixteenth century and the rise of the Roshaniya movement.

Led by Sufi poet Bayezid Ansari, also known as Pir (saint) Roshan, the revolt against the Mughal empire is a major chapter in the region's ethnic Pashtun history as well as indicative of the broadly progressive nature of Afghan Islam. Ansari fought against both the oppression of the Mughals and the feudal practices of his own Pashtun nobles. His primary goal as a political and religious leader was said to be the achievement of equality between men and women. According to Gregorian, since Ansari's "aim, among other things was to establish a national religion, the movement encouraged the Afghans in the tribal belt to struggle against Moghul rule. The Roshaniya movement thus promoted the first political formulation of the concept of Afghan nationality."[7]

Prior to British military invasions of the mid-nineteenth century, the Afghans were not hostile to the European powers. In 1809, Scottish statesman and historian Mountstuart Elphinstone and his "retinue of some 400 Anglo-Indian soldiers were well received by the Afghans."[8] So too were others in 1810, 1815 and 1826, when Sunni Afghans were reported to express an open tolerance toward Christians. Gregorian writes of British explorer Charles Masson, who although robbed by Baluchis "was well treated by Muslim religious men and Afghan tribesmen. Of his stay in Kabul in 1832, he reported: 'It is a matter of agreeable surprise to anyone acquainted with Mahommedans of India, Persia, and Turkey, and with their religious prejudices and antipathies to find that the people of Kabul are entirely [devoid of] them. . . . The Christian is respectfully called a 'Kitabi' or 'one of the Book.'"[9]

Renowned adventurer and East India Company political officer Alexander Burnes wrote home to his mother in May of 1832, "The people of this country are kind hearted and hospitable. They have no prejudice against a Christian and none against our nation."[10]

Yet this openness and inclination towards hospitality changed abruptly when 15,000 British and Indian troops—"The Army of the Indus"—crossed the Zero line at the Bolan pass in Baluchistan in the spring of 1839 in the first of three attempts to forcibly incorporate Afghanistan into the British empire.

The invasion had been preordained by the actions of the Governor-General of India, Lord Auckland, whose Simla Manifesto issued on October 1, 1838, set out the reasons and the rationale for a preemptive British takeover of Afghanistan.

Known as the first Anglo-Afghan war, the expedition was haunted from the start by bad planning and insufficient reconnaissance. It was also doomed by the hubris, incompetence and bloated excesses of its planners. According to author Peter Hopkirk in his book *The Great Game*, the army "was followed by an even larger force, a raggle-taggle army of 30,000 camp-followers—bearers, grooms, dhobi-wallahs, cooks and farriers—together with as many camels carrying ammunition and supplies. . . . One brigadier was said to have had no fewer than sixty camels to transport his own camp gear, while the officers of one regiment had commandeered two camels just to carry their cigars."[11]

Fatally misjudging the Afghans' resentment, skill and determination to expel any and all invaders, by 1841 the British mission was no longer sustainable. As predicted by Alexander Burnes, the British-installed puppet, Shah Shuja, commanded no loyalty from the Afghans. When cash payments to tribal chieftains were curtailed, the Ghilzai, one of the major Pashtun tribes, rebelled.[12]

On January 1, 1842, the British signed an agreement that provided for the retreat of their army and all noncombatants with a guarantee of safe passage. In a final and fatal blunder the British departed from Kabul before an Afghan escort could be assembled. Having failed to include the Ghilzai tribal leaders and their allies in the final agreement, the British were attacked and slaughtered down to the last man as they fled through the snow.

The outright foolishness of the British invasion was recognized at the time. In 1842, the government of India issued a proclamation condemning Lord Auckland. In a description that applies as much to the Washington of today as it did to the London of 1842, author John H. Waller writes in his book *Beyond the Khyber Pass*, "Auckland's manifesto of October 1, 1838, had not only been flawed in its logic, but was conspicuously contrived to justify his actions. Yet Auckland's correspondence in August 1838 elicited from the India Office and the British government only tepid reservations as to the wisdom of the policy he intended to follow."[13]

Despite the official rebuke, that wisdom was to be repeated by another British government nearly forty years later. Hawkish advocates of Britain's so called "Forward Policy" had been pushing for the breakup and seizure of Afghanistan and on November 21, 1878, sent a hastily assembled army of 35,000 British soldiers across the Zero line at three locations, seizing the Khyber pass, Kandahar and Jalalabad.

The British attack avoided the disaster it had seen in 1842, and despite a devastating defeat at Maiwand, the invasion initially appeared successful.

Setting the Stage for Crisis: The Treaty of Gandamak

A hasty agreement, which was repudiated by successive Afghan governments, was imposed on Afghan Amir Yaqub Khan as British soldiers occupied Kabul in 1879. Known as the treaty of Gandamak, it forced the Afghans to surrender a number of Afghan districts bordering India and gave the British the authority to negotiate borders and foreign policy on Kabul's behalf.

But by March of 1880 even the more aggressive advocates of Afghanistan's dismemberment began to fear that their initial success was slipping away and that they were confronting a repeat of the first Anglo-Afghan war. Conquering Afghanistan was one thing, holding it was another. The defeat of the conservative government in the election sealed the issue.

Acting before conditions worsened, the new British government invited a popular Afghan leader and nephew of a previous amir then in exile in Russia, Abdur Rahman Khan, to assume the throne. Known as the "Iron Amir," as much for his iron will as his iron rule, Abdur Rahman set the foundations for a modern Afghan state and brought the country into the twentieth century, ruling until 1901.

Under protest, Abdur Rahman Khan accepted the new British-imposed Afghan borders, the most notable of which was the 1893 Durand/Zero line. In doing so he repeated a warning voiced by East India Company officer Alexander Burnes prior to the first Afghan war but repeatedly ignored by those who covet the control of Central Asia, i.e., that a strong Afghanistan was a better strategic ally than a weak and divided one. According to Afghan experts Barnett Rubin and Abubakar Siddique, "The amir always contended that excluding the tribal territories from Afghanistan was a mistake, as he could control the tribes better than the British could."[14]

The Durand line deprived the Afghan amir of all real estate east of the Hindu Kush and of the most strategic mountain passes west of it. It disallowed the return of Peshawar, a city long identified with Afghanistan, and cut Afghanistan's access routes to the Arabian sea through adjacent Baluchistan, leaving the country landlocked and dependent.

Durand's Lasting Impact

The heart of today's Afghanistan-Pakistan dilemma is the legacy of this colonial decision-making. It is the legacy of divide-and-rule, a policy imposed upon Afghanistan by the British regime in India. Following Abdur Rahman's reluctant acceptance of the Durand line in 1893, Britain created a "threefold frontier" of separation from Russia's South Asian khanates. Rubin and Siddique describe the layout:

> Five tribal regions were placed under the direct control of the central government in Delhi. After the creation of Pakistan in 1947, three new agencies were carved out of the other tribal districts. . . . The first frontier was the outer edge of the directly administered territory (the river Indus in the nineteenth century and the settled districts of NWFP [North West Frontier Province] in the mid-twentieth century); the second was the Pashtun tribal area between Afghanistan and the settled districts of NWFP, which was placed under indirect rule; and the third comprised the protectorates of Nepal and Afghanistan on the outer edge of the sphere of influence.[15]

The British then reenacted a set of legal rules known as the Frontier Crimes Regulations (FCR). The FCR were imported and adapted from the Irish penal codes, a series of laws and rules introduced by the British into Ireland beginning in 1366 (Statutes of Kilkenny),[16] for the purposes of keeping the Anglo-Norman population from intermarrying with the native Irish. After centuries of legal evolution, the FCR had transformed from a severe code developed by a Protestant Christian empire to subjugate the Catholic Irish into a set of harsh rules selectively applied to Muslim Pashtuns and Baluchs.[17] These racially and religiously keyed controls over the conquered people of the Federally Administered Tribal Areas (FATA) were then administered by a political "agent," who continues to this day to retain absolute feudal powers. In *Resolving the Pakistan-Afghanistan Stalemate*, Rubin and Siddique write:

> The political agent is the judge, jury, police chief, jail warden, district magistrate, and public prosecutor. He collects and disburses revenue with virtually no accountability . . . [He] may impose an economic blockade or siege of "hostile" or "unfriendly" tribes or inflict fines on whole communities. . . . He can prohibit the construction of houses and raze houses of tribal members as punishment for not meeting the agent's demands and an entire tribe can be held responsible for crimes committed by a single member or occurring anywhere within the tribe's territory. The law empowers the political agent to deliver multiyear jail sentences without due process or right of appeal to any superior court.[18]

British policy maintained the border areas under their control by employing 70,000 tribal scouts to battle Pashtun resistance. This practice encouraged ethnic and tribal divisions. In 1897 they succeeded in squelching a major Pashtun rebellion east of the Durand line. The FCR intentionally maintained the tribal region of the North West Frontier and Baluchistan as lawless backwaters by severely restricting education and political participation. After the 1947 partition of India and the creation of Pakistan, the FCR were applied on an even broader scale. Pakistani journalist Ahmed Rashid writes, "Even after 1996, FATA remained a backwater, as under the FCR, Pakistani political parties were banned from operating in the area, thereby giving the mullahs and religious parties a monopoly of influence under the guise of religion. Development, literacy, and health facilities in FATA therefore remained at a minimum."[19]

Rubin and Siddique see a direct line of policy decisions between Britain's nineteenth-century colonial policies and practices and Pakistan's support for the anti-Soviet jihad of the 1980s and the rise of the Taliban in the 1990s. "The similarity of the threefold frontier to [Pakistan's] quest in Afghanistan illustrates the continuity of strategic policy in the region."[20]

The Anglo-Russian Entente

The Anglo-Russian Entente of 1907 ended the Great Game for Central Asia, as it was then known, by dividing Persia into three zones—British in the south, Russian in the north and a neutral buffer zone in between. Russia accepted Afghanistan as a British protectorate and abandoned efforts to establish direct relations between the two nations while Britain accepted Tibet as a buffer state and agreed "to deal with Lhasa only through China, the suzerain power."[21]

The Amir of Afghanistan, Habibullah Khan, Abdur Rahman's eldest son, protested the entente and declared it illegal because Afghanistan was not represented. His calls went unheeded. But the political climate in Europe and the coming of the Great War would soon expand Afghanistan's options while involving it deeper in European intrigues.

In the fall of 1915, Habibullah was visited by a delegation of Turks and Germans intent on provoking an uprising in the Afghan tribal regions on the other side of the Durand line and waging war on British India. Habibullah entertained the delegation and the idea, but remained true to his commitment of an enforced neutrality.

By the time the First World War ended, it was clear the tide had turned for all the European colonial powers. Germany had been defeated. Imperial Russia had ceased to exist and Britain's hold on its colonies was severely weakened.

In 1919, Afghanistan's new and aggressively modernist Amir, Amanullah Khan, declared a holy war of independence from Britain.

His call provoked an uprising on both sides of the border and re-sulted in the third Anglo-Afghan war.

The Treaty of Rawalpindi

After only one month of fighting, the Treaty of Rawalpindi, signed on August 8, 1919, officially ended the war and guaranteed Afghanistan's independence in both its internal and external affairs. It did not alter Britain's iron-clad refusal to renegotiate the Durand line, which it considered strategically necessary, nor did it redress the damage done to the country's efforts at creating a modern econ-omy or Afghan state. Gregorian writes:

> The Anglo-Afghan wars also contributed to the consolidation of Afghan feudalism and tribalism. The loss of Peshawar and the Punjab to the Sikhs on the eve of the First Afghan war de-prived the Afghan monarchy of an important economic asset. That loss, together with the weakness of the urban sectors and the feudal character of the monarchy itself, forced the Afghan rulers to become increasingly dependent on the Durrani clans and the other tribes for the defense of the country and the maintenance of the dynasty. . . . Tribalism was thus preserved at the expense of the Afghan monarchy and the growth of na-tionalist institutions.[22]

King Amanullah, bent on escaping Afghanistan's feudal her-itage, moved to make up for lost time and quickly embarked on major reforms. He instituted Afghanistan's first constitution in 1923, which guaranteed universal suffrage, granted civil rights to all of Afghanistan's minorities and established a legislative assem-bly, courts, and penal, civil and commercial codes. He prohibited revenge killings and abolished subsidies for tribal chieftains as well as the royal family. His support for women's equality and the rapid modernization of Afghan society was an open and consistent theme. He also denied Afghan mullahs the right to study at the orthodox Deoband school in India.[23]

But Amanullah's reforms were doomed, not so much by the resistance of the conservative clergy and powerful landowners, as certain Western commentators stubbornly hold, but by poor planning, a lack of adequate financial resources and a dearth of the technical skill and manpower necessary to carry out the transformation. In the end, Afghanistan's meager and underdeveloped economy lacked the basic capacity to meet the needs of almost any social, political or economic growth. Contained geographically and thus economically by British and Russian nineteenth-century expansion and forced to choose between foreign occupation, dismemberment or enforced neutrality, Afghanistan throughout the 1920s and beyond remained severely restricted in its options.

Afghan expert David B. Edwards writes in his 2002 book, *Before Taliban: Genealogies of the Afghan Jihad:*

> Hated by many as a tyrant, Abdur Rahman nevertheless forged the basis of governance in Afghanistan and the understandings that the people have retained of the natural and proper duties, role and comportment of its leaders. Amanullah provides an illuminating secondary point of reference for this analysis because he anticipated many of the reforms that the Marxists would later try to put in place, though he did so from his position as a member of the royal family. The transformations that he sought to bring about before his overthrow in 1929 were in many respects forerunners of those of the Marxists and were particularly revealing of the problems they later encountered.[24]

Very little about Afghanistan can be separated from this reality even today.

Following the overthrow of the progressive Amanullah and a brief period of rule by a Tajik bandit, Habibullah Kalakani, Afghanistan was returned to a more conservative footing due in large part to the intervention of the British once again. But the 1930s saw Afghanistan turning away from the influence of both Britain and the Soviet Union toward Europe.

Prior to World War II, Afghanistan looked to Italy, France

and Germany for economic development and by 1941 had engaged Germany as its largest trading partner. Following Germany's surprise attack on the Soviet Union on June 22, 1941, Afghanistan once again found itself surrounded by allied armies and was forced to return to an enforced neutrality to avoid occupation.

The partition of India and the creation of the state of Pakistan in August 1947 marked the end of the colonial period for British India, but the not the end of Britain's neocolonial ambitions in the region or its strategies for maintaining its interests.

The creation of the state of Pakistan itself was a continuation of the British colonial policy that divided and ruled the region by pitting tribe against tribe while establishing artificial boundaries that would be subject to constant conflict. When the maharaja of Kashmir declared his accession to India in 1947, Pakistan raised a tribal army from Pashtun tribes on both sides of the Durand line. This first Indo-Pakistan war failed to resolve the border dispute over Kashmir and established an unending source of conflict. For over sixty years this dispute has formed the foundation of Pakistan's forward policies toward neighboring Afghanistan, its pursuit of nuclear parity with India and its support for jihadist terrorism.

In an address at the Center for International Policy on June 9, 2009, Afghanistan-Pakistan authority Selig Harrison cited Narendra Singh Sarila's book *The Shadow of the Great Game: The Untold Story of India's Partition* to emphasize that it was Britain's long-term security goals and not the needs of India's Muslims that formed the foundation of Pakistan's state. "[A]s early as March 1945, Winston Churchill and the British General Staff decided that Partition was necessary for strategic reasons. They deliberately set out to create Pakistan because [Mohammad Ali] Jinnah had promised to provide military facilities and Nehru refused to do so."[25]

Harrison continued:

This is the key to understanding why Pakistan is so dysfunctional. It's an artificial political entity. The British put together five ethnic groups that had never coexisted in the same body politic historically. The Bengalis were the biggest. They out-numbered all the other four combined—the Punjabis, the Pashtuns, the Baluch and the Sindhis. Five became four, of course, when Bangladesh seceded.

As the United States assumed Britain's responsibility for Pakistan following World War II, the region's strategic importance as a listening post and landing pad for U2 spy planes became of primary importance during the Cold War against the Soviet Union and China. On May 1, 1960, the United States launched a U2 spy plane from a secret base at Badaber near Peshawar in Pakistan to spy on the Soviet Union. The flight was shot down and the pilot captured, thereby destroying the chances for a U.S.-Soviet entente at an upcoming summit in Paris. In a top-secret mission in 1965 the CIA attempted to place a plutonium-powered transceiver in direct line of sight to China's Xinjiang Province, atop India's second-highest peak, Nanda Devi.[26]

The Durand line had been devised in the nineteenth century to provide imperial Britain with a buffer zone against the territorial advances of imperial Russia. Harrison's emphasis makes clear that the modern state of Pakistan was created intentionally by Britain fifty years later for the exact same purpose of maintaining a strategic military zone for use during the Cold War and little else.

Britain Leaves, but the Line Remains

In July 1949, the Afghan government convened a *loya jirga* or tribal council. The council voted in agreement with the Afghan government that Pakistan was not a successor state to India but was in fact a new entity and that all treaties agreed to prior to 1947 were null and void. Looking back to the 1893 Durand line division of the Pashtun tribal homeland, Royal Prime Minister Mohammed Daoud wasted no opportunity in using it to pressure Pakistan. But though his Pashtun nationalism strengthened his popularity on both sides of the border, it played perfectly into Pakistani and U.S. Cold War theorems, allowing them to paint Daoud as a troublesome nationalist or even worse, a Soviet puppet. Rethinking the Durand line also challenged Afghanistan's allies and neighbors. Were Pakistan to agree to renegotiate pre–World War II treaties and borders established by the imperial powers for the benefit of the imperial powers, not only would the map of Pakistan change, but so would the territories of India, Iran and the Soviet Union. Rubin and Siddique write:

> For Pashtun nationalists in Pakistan and Afghanistan, Pashtunistan meant different things, ranging from an independent country to an autonomous province of Pakistan to an integral part of Afghanistan. The Soviet Union and India paid lip service to Pashtunistan for decades. The Soviets wanted to prevent Afghanistan from joining any Western military alliance and to pressure Pakistan: India wanted to divert Pakistan's military resources by cultivating the fear of an unstable western border.[27]

By the early 1960s, Pakistan's "fear" drove Afghanistan even closer to the Soviet Union and nearly destroyed Afghanistan's economy when Pakistan closed the border to Afghan shipping. The resulting impasse by 1963 caused Prime Minister Daoud to step down and his cousin, King Zahir Shah, to assume direct control of the government. Zahir Shah's rule is remembered as a golden age for Afghanistan, and his "experiment in democracy" was considered by U.S. observers at the time to be irreversible.

But the legacy of Afghanistan's colonial boundaries, together with its inability to satisfy the needs of its rapidly modernizing population and its lack of both the political and economic infrastructure to manage the country's advancement, hobbled Zahir Shah's efforts as it had Amanullah's. While the king's political liberalization had opened the country for the first time to multiple political parties, it had also opened the door to the political extremes of both the communist left and the religious right.

When, in 1973, former Prime Minister Mohammed Daoud staged a palace coup with members of Babrak Karmal's Parcham faction of the progressive People's Democratic Party of Afghanistan (PDPA) against his cousin, the king, there was little surprise and less protest from the public.

Daoud publicly based his justification for the coup on a number of issues. The failed economy and the gridlocked political system were central while he accused Zahir Shah of reneging on Pashtunistan to curry favor with Pakistan and the United States. Rubin and Siddique write:

> Zahir's government was accused of not responding forcefully to the firing of the National Awami Party provincial governments in NWFP and Baluchistan by Pakistani Premier Zulfiqar Ali Bhutto in 1973. These governments were composed mainly of Pashtun and Baluch nationalists. . . . After the creation of Bangladesh in 1971, the Pashtun and Baluch nationalist movements along the western borders posed the most activist threats to the remainder of Pakistan.[28]

Zulfiqar Ali Bhutto and the Islamists shared a common cause in the Pashtunistan issue. Both opposed Baluch and Pashtun nationalism as well as Afghan territorial claims. Bhutto supported the Islamists and their goal of unseating Afghanistan's progressive pro-socialist government only so far as it served his own efforts to undermine an independent Pashtunistan movement. According to Harrison, Bhutto did not share the Islamists' opposition to the partition of Pakistan and Bangladesh. In fact, he desired it. His narrow compromise with the extremists over such issues would eventually cost him his life. Pakistan expert Selig Harrison observed:

> I was in Dacca during the Bangladesh crisis of 1971 when the Army moved in to crush the independence movement. I had a memorable conversation with Zulfiqar Ali Bhutto in which he said it would be best if the Bengalis did secede, because Pakistan would be more manageable without them. What he meant was that he would have a better chance of running Pakistan in cooperation with the Punjabis if he could get rid of

the Bengalis. And that's what happened, except that the Army, as you know, eventually executed him.[29]

Bhutto's death marked an abrupt end to an era of secular, Western influence on Pakistan and the beginning of a Punjabi-dominated military theocracy that pitted Punjabis and their Arab allies against Baluchis, Sindhis and Pashtuns on both sides of the Durand line.

Harrison recounted, "With the Bengalis gone the Baluch, Pashtuns and Sindhis have faced a cruel historical irony. For centuries they had resisted the incursions of the Moghuls into their territories, but now they find themselves ruled by Punjabis who invoke the grandeur of the Moghuls to justify their power."[30]

Following his return to power in 1973, Mohammed Daoud offered Baluchi nationalist insurgents a cross-border sanctuary from Pakistan's military.[31] Pakistan responded by harboring and training 5,000 Islamist guerrillas including Ahmed Shah Massoud and Gulbuddin Hekmatyar for a campaign of violent destabilization. Together with Daoud's progressive bent and his regular calls for the independence of the Pashtun tribal homelands in NWFP and FATA, Pakistan's interests in Afghanistan and U.S. Cold War aims became fused. The Pakistan-trained guerrilla network would grow into a full-blown counterrevolutionary force supported by the United States following the 1978 Marxist coup of Nur Mohammed Taraki and Hafizullah Amin.

The 1947 creation of the state of Pakistan and the fate of the various tribal regions institutionalized deep ethnic divisions that would never be resolved by Pakistan's internal political processes. In a perverse way, ethnic tension and the growth of leftist parties served Pakistan's geopolitical interests during the Cold War. Internal dissent supplied Pakistan's military with the pretexts to overthrow its own civilian governments, while Baluch and Pashtun tribal rebellions were sold to Washington as the product of Soviet agitation. The issue came to a head with the Soviet invasion of 1979. But unlike other well-known points of confrontation created by the Cold

War, unqualified support from the U.S. for Pakistan's interests obscured the pre-existing ethnic and political time bomb created by the Durand line.

The United States competed peacefully with the Soviet Union in Afghanistan during the 1960s and early 1970s by providing aid and supporting moderate pro-democracy advocates to counter a shifting mix of emerging leftist parties. But following the 1978 overthrow of Mohammed Daoud, the U.S. policy of extending Pakistan's military exclusive control over billions of dollars in aid, cast these pro-democracy Afghans out of the equation and into the hands of their Pakistani enemies. Long before there was a communism or a Soviet Union, the divided Pashtun tribal homeland plagued Britain's India policy. In the province of Waziristan alone the British maintained 50,000 soldiers well into the 1930s, the largest contingent of forces in India.[32] U.S. support for the anti-Soviet war would only carry British India's unsuccessful policy to a new extreme. Rubin and Siddique write, "The country's ruling military virtually had a free hand to shape the Afghan resistance based in the refugee camps along the Durand Line. Pakistan wanted to prevent the establishment of Afghan nationalist guerrillas on its soil and thus refused to recognize parties and exiles associated with the old regime."[33]

By 1984, after a fierce battle inside the Central Intelligence Agency between the "Bleeders" and the "Dealers,"[34] the bleeders (ideologues) in the Reagan administration saw the lack of the Soviet retaliation against Pakistan as an invitation to up the ante. Bleeders blamed their own dealers for conducting the covert war with too much restraint, even though the Soviets had sent clear signals before the invasion and during the war that a multiparty nonaligned coalition government was the best solution for the politically and ethnically diverse country.[35] In the fall of 2008, Charles Cogan, the CIA's chief of the Near-East South-Asia Division in the Directorate of Operations from 1979 to 1984, explained the Dealers' reluctance to over-antagonize the Soviets. "Washington feared air or land attacks into Pakistani territory and sponsored terrorist activities carried out by Afghan refugees or by Pakistanis themselves. In any event, Western arms, notably the efficient anti-aircraft Stinger missile, were supplied. And the Soviets, after all, did not retaliate."[36]

Throughout the 1980s, as U.S. and Saudi aid increased and the military government of Pakistan's Zia-ul-Haq grew more extreme in its support for Islamization, the United States declined any effort to help establish a broad-based Afghan government. Selig Harrison recalled numerous exchanges with Charles Dunbar, the State Department's Coordinator of Afghan Affairs, regarding the efforts of Afghan moderates to establish a government in exile.

> In July 1987 I confronted [Dunbar] with the results of a random sample poll conducted by the Afghan Information Center in Peshawar among 2,287 Afghan refugees in 108 refugee camps representing twenty-three of the twenty-eight provinces in Afghanistan. The poll showed 71.6 percent in favor of the King as the leader of postwar Afghanistan. Soon after its publication, assassins believed to be identified with the fundamentalist [Gulbuddin Hekmatyar's] Hesbe Islami murdered the respected director of the Afghan Information Center, Bahauddin Majrooh, former dean of Kabul University. . . . Dunbar told me, "The resistance is the only game in town, and you know how the ISI feels about Zahir Shah."[37]

Following the Soviet pullout in February 1989, rebel groups funded by the United States and Saudi Arabia—most notably the Pashtun Gulbuddin Hekmatyar's Hesb-i-Islami and the Tajik Ahmed Shah Massoud's Northern Alliance—continued to battle both the remnants of the Marxist Afghan government and each other. But even after the fall of Kabul's Marxist government in the spring of 1992, Pakistan's involvement with the conquest of Afghanistan and U.S. support for it rested solely on its function as a base for strategic military operations. The Institute of Peace report stated:

> Pakistan's support for the Islamist parties (especially for the Islamic Party of Gulbuddin Hekmatyar) and then for the

Taliban constituted attempts to impose on Afghanistan a government that would never allow an Indian presence on its territory, giving the Pakistani military a secure border and strategic depth. . . . This policy was a continuation under different conditions of the British policy of treating Afghanistan as part of the security buffer zone of South Asia.[38]

2. Creating the Taliban

To this day, media sources in the United States continue to echo the Pakistani Intelligence service, the ISI, by maintaining that the Taliban emerged from the city of Kandahar as an indigenous Afghan student movement in 1994, and therefore is a representative element of Afghan society. This line was held to tightly by Pakistan's general Pervez Musharraf to disavow Pakistan's central role in Afghan terror until he switched his line in August of 2007. As reported by M. K. Bhadrakumar in the *Asia Times*, "There was no acrimony over Musharraf's dramatic turnaround from his consistent plea that the Taliban is an indigenous Afghan force. Musharraf added, 'There is no doubt Afghan militants are supported from Pakistani soil. The problem that you have in your region is because support is provided from our side.'"[1] Yet on a February 2009 episode of the *Rachel Maddow Show* Jimmy Carter's national security advisor Zbigniew Brzezinski seemingly justified Taliban involvement in Afghan affairs, saying, "Taliban is a medieval movement, very negative in its social values from our standpoint, but it is an Afghan movement."[2]

According to Brzezinski's own Near East, South Asia Chief at the CIA, Charles Cogan, the Taliban "was created initially as a wholly owned subsidiary of the Pakistani ISI in 1992."[3] According to the BBC, "The Taliban emerged in the early 1990s in northern Pakistan following the withdrawal of Soviet troops from Afghanistan."[4] In a September 10, 2002, interview on CNN, Democratic Representative Jim McDermott of Washington stunned conservative *Crossfire* co-host Tucker Carlson by stating bluntly, "But you've got to remember that of American policy, we put the Taliban there. We gave the money. . . . We funded the Taliban through the Pakistanis, and all that money—we could have cut off that money and stopped what was going on. We knew what was going on there. All we wanted was a stable, quiet Afghanistan so we could put a pipeline down through there. That's really what we were up to."[5] Carlson insisted on labeling McDermott's assertion "quite a theory." But CIA assistance in the creation of the Taliban had been openly attested to by region expert Selig Harrison long before 9/11.[6]

Pakistani President Asif Ali Zardari brushed aside lingering doubts in a May 10, 2009, interview on *Meet the Press*, when he asserted of the extremist group "the ISI and the CIA created them together."[7] Information from other sources suggests that the problem goes even deeper than a CIA-ISI collaboration.

Former Pakistani ISI Director General Hamid Gul was cited in an interview published by Pakistani Lt. General Kamal Matinuddin in 1999 as saying that former United Kingdom High Commissioner to Pakistan Sir Nicholas Barrington "inducted both former royalists and erstwhile communists into the Taliban movement."[8] Pakistan left the British Commonwealth of Nations in 1972 under Zulfikar Ali Bhutto but rejoined in 1989 when Barrington was ambassador, transforming him automatically from an ambassador to a High Commissioner.

According to his biography, Barrington served in both Afghanistan and Pakistan for many years. He recounted his travels through the Afghan countryside in the early 1960s in his book *A Passage to Nuristan*, and was formally accredited to the first post-Marxist Mujahideen government of Burhanuddin Rabbani before his final departure. According to his biography, "He had contacts with all the mujahideen leaders, one of whom he had known from his earlier days in Kabul."[9]

Matinuddin's interview with Gul, published long before Americans paid close attention to the Taliban as a strategic threat, may explain why the full story of the group's creation has yet to be told. According to author Melanie Phillips, London has been the home to the largest collection of Islamic extremists since the war against the Soviets in Afghanistan began. "Indeed, one could say that it was in Britain that al-Qaeda was actually formed as a movement. . . . Yet the bizarre fact is that the British authorities allowed all this extremist activity to continue with impunity for more than a decade—even after the ostensible 'wake-up' call of 9/11."[10]

The United States and Britain had long maintained relations with militant Islamic organizations in and out of the Middle East and Central Asia through covert intelligence connections like the Safari Club,[11] refugee assistance programs like the Committee for a Free Afghanistan and the International Rescue Committee, as well as through friendly journalists. In Afghanistan particularly, the United States worked in the early 1970s directly through the Shah of Iran's intelligence service, Savak, as well as through Pakistani General Nasrullah Babar to fund the efforts of extremist Gulbuddin Hekmatyar and Ahmed Shah Massoud to destabilize the government of Mohammed Daoud. Selig Harrison writes:

> On the one hand, Teheran used its aid leverage to press Daoud for the removal of suspected Communists. At the same time, Savak channeled U.S. weapons, communications equipment, and other paramilitary aid to anti-Daoud groups. Some of this assistance was given directly by Iran to tribal dissidents operating in adjacent Afghanistan; some was channeled through Pakistan to the underground fundamentalist groups. . . .
> Savak, the CIA, and Pakistani agents were also involved in the abortive, fundamentalist-backed coup attempts against Daoud in September and December 1973 and June 1974.[12]

The U.S. semi-official Freedom House sponsored Jamaat-i Islami spokespersons in the United States during the early 1980s.[13] The United States Information Agency worked closely with the seven extremist groups in Pakistan to train Afghan refugees in journalism.[14] When the Boston University-based program proved too controversial, it was handed over to a member of Gulbuddin Hekmatyar's Hesb-i-Islami to manage.[15] Afghan Aid UK was established by Romy Fullerton,[16] wife of British journalist John Fullerton. According to CBS stringer Kurt Lohbeck, Afghan Aid worked closely with MI-6 and later Britain's SIS, Secret Intelligence

Service.[17] On his bio page at The Royal Literary Fund, Fullerton admits to working for MI-6 "undercover for two years against the Soviets in Afghanistan."[18]

Prompted by Gulbuddin Hekmatyar's failure to secure Afghanistan from Ahmed Shah Massoud's Northern Alliance, the Taliban arose as the product of the collective interests of Saudi Arabia, Pakistan, the United Kingdom and the United States. And there is no reason to think that the Taliban are any less connected to their ultimate goals today than they were in 1992. But the question remains, what are those goals? How do they work? What is the policy, who are the people pushing it and will the American public continue to back another growing and costly AfPak agenda that has yet to be fully explained?

3. AfPak: What Is It?

Although it is often compared to the British and Russian involvements and even Alexander the Great's fourth-millennium B.C.E. campaign, the U.S. war in Afghanistan and Pakistan today is nothing like the wars conducted there or in fact anywhere in the past. There are no Macedonians with white horses and chariots, British red coats with brass buttons or dour, olive-drab Russians fighting another great patriotic land war for the homeland. Although superficially similar, it is nothing like America's war in Vietnam, where the United States threw its seemingly unlimited resources against a determined indigenous force that had been fighting against foreign occupation for centuries and was determined to unite its divided nation under one socialist flag. In many ways, the U.S. war in Afghanistan is unrecognizable. To grasp it, one must think *Star Wars* or *Dune* with imperial storm troopers dropped onto a ravaged planet of ruined cities, white-capped mountain peaks, vast deserts and internecine warfare. It is the place where bubble economics, blatant corruption and oil politics meet rank poverty and radical Islam in a high-tech, high-profile duel for the dominance of Asia and conversely the future of the American empire.

Following the U.S. invasion of Afghanistan in 2001, Al Qaeda and its Taliban hosts fled over the Durand line to Pakistan and found safe haven. From here they have regrouped, reorganized and grown stronger.

Since World War II and the invention of strategic bombing, the United States has relied increasingly on the threat of high-tech weaponry, "death from above," "shock and awe" as a way to dominate in the wars it wages. After initially abandoning its Afghan war to fight in Iraq in 2003, the United States overly relied on this kind of warfare to compensate for a lack of troops, using high-tech unmanned Predator drones and F-16s to deal with a deteriorating military situation.

While focused on Iraq, the U.S. paid Pakistan's President Pervez Musharraf $15 billion[1] to root out, kill or capture Al Qaeda leaders and stop Taliban infiltration over the Durand line into Afghanistan. But instead of fighting the terror organizers known to reside in the country, like Osama bin Laden, Mullah Omar, Beitullah Massud, Gulbuddin Hekmatyar and the Haqqani network, Musharraf played a "double game," bolstering the Taliban's insurgent networks while diverting billions of U.S. tax dollars to Pakistan's perpetual military preparations for a war with India.

Ahmed Rashid described the campaign of deception:

> Pashtun bureaucrats in Islamabad and Peshawar told me of the ISI's internal debates, whose subjects included some officers' intentions to create a broad "Talibanized belt" in FATA that would keep pressure on Karzai to bend to Pakistani wishes, keep U.S. forces under threat while maintaining their dependence on Pakistani goodwill, and create a buffer zone between Afghan and Pakistani Pashtuns.[2]

The practice of radicalizing the Pashtun population of the North West Frontier Province (NWFP) as a threat to Kabul and its foreign backers was nothing new to Pakistan. Britain and Afghanistan had been playing a game of mutual destabilization of the tribal areas since the culmination of the First Anglo-Afghan war in 1842. This tactic had formed the core of the U.S. covert war against the Soviet Union in the 1980s. But during the Bush-era "war on terror," the process took on an absurdist Catch-22 dimension as Washington proceeded to finance a Pakistani army that was not only undermining its efforts in Afghanistan but supporting attacks against its own soldiers.

Rashid comments:

The growth of Taliban sympathies in FATA [Federally

Administered Tribal Areas] was also a direct result of gravely misguided policies by Rumsfeld and the Pentagon. . . . Rumsfeld forced the U.S. military to become captive to Islamabad's whims and fancies. There was no U.S. political strategy for dealing with the army's support to the Taliban or with the real problems of FATA. Pakistan asked for weapons and helicopters, diverting the real issue of its lack of political will to a supposed lack of weapons capability.[3]

Looking back, it is hard to fathom exactly what the Bush administration plan was, as Rumsfeld heaped weapons, money and praise onto Pakistan's president, General Musharraf for the "war on terror" while receiving little but empty gestures in return. The Obama administration's decision to actively engage Pakistan on an equal footing in the Afghan war emerged only after Washington's military-intelligence community reluctantly accepted proof that Pakistan's ISI was in fact aiding Taliban actors such as Malawi Jalaluddin Haqqani in their ongoing cross-border war with the U.S. and NATO forces.[4] It also emerged, after years of accumulated evidence, that the United States was not merely losing the war against the Taliban and its Al Qaeda allies in Afghanistan, but Pakistan itself was on the verge of caving in to Taliban extremism.

Made public on March 27, 2009, the Obama administration's much anticipated AfPak plan was a work in progress, as Washington grappled awkwardly with a complex set of irreconcilable problems.

According to the White Paper describing its new policy, the primary objectives were fivefold.[5]

1. Disrupting terrorist networks in Afghanistan and especially Pakistan to degrade any ability they may have to plan and launch international terrorist attacks.

2. Promoting a more capable, accountable, and effective government in Afghanistan that serves the Afghan people and can eventually function, especially regarding internal security, with limited international support.

3. Developing increasingly self-reliant Afghan security forces that can lead the counterinsurgency and counterterrorism fight with reduced U.S. assistance.

4. Assisting efforts to enhance civilian control and stable constitutional government in Pakistan and a vibrant economy that provides opportunity for the people of Pakistan.

5. Involving the international community to actively assist in addressing these objectives for Afghanistan and Pakistan, with an important leadership role for the United Nations.

Obama's White Paper satisfied the immediate need to articulate its aim of shifting the war in Afghanistan from counterterrorism to counterinsurgency. But within the community of Beltway critics there was little to no agreement over whether the President's plan offered a solution, whether a solution could be found or even whether the assumptions on which the new policy were based were credible.

Before the paper had even been issued, questions were raised about whether U.S. and European troops ought to be there at all.

Boston University professor and best-selling author Andrew Bacevich had set the tone for the de-escalation, non-nation-building argument in a December 31, 2008, *Newsweek* article titled "Winning in Afghanistan," by limiting U.S. goals in Afghanistan to an effort "to ensure that terrorist groups like Al Qaeda can't use it as a safe haven for launching attacks on the West."[6]

On February 3, 2009, visiting scholar Gilles Dorronsoro, in a panel discussion at the Carnegie Endowment billed as "An Alternative Strategy for the Afghan War," argued for a change in "the political dynamic in Afghanistan by withdrawing U.S. forces to strengthen the Afghan government."[7] Dorronsoro blamed the presence of foreign troops for the resurgence of the Taliban, while maintaining that neither a military victory nor a negotiated settlement with "moderate Taliban" was possible.

Within weeks, the March 2009 White Paper was drawing fire from Washington's foreign policy establishment. April 2009 the

CFR's Daniel Markey responded sharply by recommending a set of alternatives that rejected the bulk of the plan. He endorsed the fight against Al Qaeda in Pakistan but labeled the recommendations for expanding U.S. armed forces, diplomatic corps and U.S. Agency for International Development (USAID) assistance to Afghanistan, as ill advised. Instead, Markey proposed that the entire burden of the plan either be drastically downsized and off-loaded to other donors or be shifted away from Afghanistan altogether and back towards U.S. ally Pakistan in an aptly titled document, "From AfPak to PakAf."[8]

As evidence of the kind of old thinking the new president was going to get from old Washington, Markey's set of solutions sounded astonishingly like the history of solutions that destroyed Afghanistan and rewarded Pakistan for over sixty years and for the same reasons: "A fractured or incapacitated Pakistan would threaten core U.S. interests, not least because its nuclear weapons would be vulnerable to al-Qaeda or similar terrorist groups."[9]

Markey's thinking reflected Washington's proclivity toward creating prophecies that once set in motion proved self-fulfilling. It had been Washington's policy to look the other way while Pakistan developed its nuclear arsenal in the early 1970s, and it was Washington's decision to grant Pakistan's military carte blanche in supporting Islamist terror groups in the 1980s and early '90s that created Al Qaeda and the Taliban. It was then Washington's policy to ignore these terror groups for a decade as they grew and networked inside and outside of Afghanistan. It had even been Washington's policy to look the other way when these terror groups fled Afghanistan following 9/11[10] and Washington's policy to ignore their resurgence as their influence grew with the help and direction of Pakistan's military government.[11] As the final assault on Taliban strongholds raged in eastern Afghanistan during the last week of November 2001, a half-dozen or more Pakistani air force planes landed in the northern Taliban-controlled city of Kunduz and evacuated hundreds of non-Afghan soldiers who had been fighting U.S. and alliance forces.[12] Dubbed the "airlift of evil" by dozens of witnesses in the press and

denied by Secretary of Defense Donald Rumsfeld and the chairman of the Joint Chiefs of Staff, Gen. Richard Myers, the incident
hinted at the increasingly strange and secret relationship between
the United States and Pakistan's military establishment.

Yet here was Markey, an influential Washington opinion mak-
er, recommending from the platform of one of Washington's most
prestigious organizations, the CFR, that instead of fixing a notoriously failed Afghan policy, the United States should go back to
maintaining the kind of "generous defense assistance" to Pakistan
that had got it into so much trouble in the first place. This assistance
even included an existing commitment to bribe Pakistan with F-16s
"as a means to retain the confidence of officers who have bought
into partnership with the United States."[13]

Swat Offensive

As if to put Washington to the test, the Obama administration immediately found itself forced to make impossible decisions on a host
of perennially complex and unresolvable issues.

In February, following a two-year campaign of terror in
Pakistan's Swat Valley that saw the closing of dozens of girls' schools,
the murder of women who refused to stop working and the public
beheadings of civilians, Islamabad capitulated to the Taliban and
agreed to make peace. Formerly known as the Malakand Accord,[14]
the agreement with Sufi Mohammed, leader of the radical Tehrik-
e-Nifaz-e-Shariat-e-Mohammed (TNSM, the Movement for the
Enforcement of Mohammed's Law), allowed for the establishment
of a rival Islamic court system (Sharia), an end to the Pakistan army's
campaign and a release of Taliban prisoners.[15]

Originally defended by Pakistan's Ambassador to Washington,
Husain Haqqani, as "a local solution to a local problem that was
being exploited by Taliban and al-Qaeda supporters outside the region,"[16] others, like Pakistan author Shuja Nawaz, criticized the size
of the area ceded to Taliban control.[17] Athar Minallah, the leader
of a Pakistan lawyers' movement, addressed the problem with the
truce more bluntly. "This means you have surrendered to a handful

of extremists. . . . The state is under attack; instead of dealing with them as aggressors, the government has abdicated."[18]

Whatever its merits, by early April the Malakand Accord was breaking down as the Taliban used the lull in fighting to press into the neighboring district of Buner with a renewed offensive.[19]

By May 1, 2009, events in Swat were already diverting Obama's plan for unifying American strategy toward Afghanistan and Pakistan from one acronym, AfPak, to another acronym, PakAf, to a sublimely ridiculous acronym, AllPak, while pushing the administration towards the traditional views articulated by Markey and other influential Washington insiders. As reported in the *New York Times*, "The key to stabilizing Afghanistan, the White House concluded five weeks ago, is a stable and cooperative Pakistan. That calculation has been utterly scrambled by the Taliban offensive in western Pakistan, which has forced the United States to concentrate on the singular task of preventing further gains in Pakistan by an Islamic militant insurgency that has claimed territory just 60 miles from Islamabad."[20]

The size and ferocity of the Pakistani Taliban's renewed offensive in the Swat Valley and the Pakistan army's response to it was a clear indication of the daunting task Obama faced in salvaging anything from the eight-year-old war. Accompanied by a mass migration of 2.5 million people away from the fighting, the refugee crisis alone rivaled the partitioning of India sixty years before. But instead of provoking Washington to reassess its core reliance on Pakistan, the emergency only provided AfPak critics with another excuse to ignore the core problem that had been plainly visible to analysts outside the Beltway for decades.

Boston University anthropologist Thomas Barfield summed up the problems with Washington's blind reliance on Pakistan's military in a *Mother Jones* magazine interview prior to the Taliban surge in Swat.[21]

Thomas Barfield: They [Pakistan] have trained their troops to fight conventional warfare on the plains with tanks, with missiles, against India. So in places like Swat where you've got guys with guns fighting in the mountains, and who are experts on ambush, they have just trounced the Pakistani army. The army is able to take back the major roads, the major towns, but its people are not trained and they don't seem to have much stomach for taking these guys on in essentially a counterinsurgency.

Mother Jones: Yet we've given the Pakistanis more than $10 billion, some $6 billion for the Federally Administered Tribal Area and the border, ostensibly to fight jihadis. Has Pakistan taken us for a ride?

Thomas Barfield: Oh sure. But they took us for a ride during the Soviet War, too. They feel they're experts at playing us for suckers. A lot of these problems were evident, three, four, even six years ago, but nobody, including the Bush administration was particularly interested. All the attention has been on Iraq. So this gave the Pakistanis a lot of flexibility to cause mischief.

Despite this understanding, the administration's attention continued to be pulled away from even addressing Afghanistan's problems and to underwriting an emergency financial and military bailout of Pakistan. Retired CIA expert Bruce O. Riedel weighed in on the need to go soft on Pakistan in an interview with the Council on Foreign Relations (CFR).

CFR: You used the expression when we spoke that this was the "Frankenstein monster that was created by the Pakistan army and the Pakistan intelligence service." Is there any sign that they're realizing what they've created and willing to do something about it?

RIEDEL: There are a few tentative signs, but it is far from clear that they acknowledge the existential threat to Pakistan's freedoms comes from within. I think the army remains focused on the external threat posed by India. Of course, here the "Frankenstein" [monster] is a self-fulfilling prophecy because extremist groups, in this case the Lashkar-e-Taiba [Army of the Righteous], attacked India last November [2008] in Mumbai. . . . In that sense, the "Frankenstein" [monster creates] the conditions for the army to be focused on India. . . .[22]

Despite Riedel's sensitivity to what Thomas Barfield described as Pakistan's expertise at playing the United States for suckers, the mood in Pakistan lurched from melancholy to resentment to outright anger. Riedel had started out by making a dangerous diplomatic faux pas in a September 2008 interview with the CFR by suggesting the Afghan government should be pressured to accept the Durand line as an international border. [23]

Pakistani public opinion expressed outrage at the very idea of being lumped together with Afghanistan in one policy. Public policy advisor Mosharraf Zaidi wrote in *The News*:

In 100 days on the job, President Obama's response to the growing crisis in Pakistan has been defined by three C's: confused, confounded and contrived.

Confused, because let's face it. Nobody really knows who's running the show in Pakistan. Is it Joe Biden? After all, the Veep is no foreign policy slouch. . . . Or is it Hillary Clinton, who has more Pakistani friends and donors than probably any other U.S. politician. . . . Or maybe it's Richard Holbrooke. . . ?

Confounded, because when you have a dozen cooks, you don't just spoil the broth, you damn near kill it. There must be very little accountability in DC for someone to have been as arrogant and ignorant as to have proposed lumping together countries as diverse and difficult as Pakistan and Afghanistan, and to then openly and brazenly refer to them as Af-Pak. . . .

Contrived, because American attention for Pakistan is so explicitly temporal and myopic that it has no chance of being taken seriously. . . . The blunt reality is that today's Pakistan is a lot closer to being a model of U.S. foreign policy failure, than it is of Taliban success. Failure here will stain every last speck of achievement by the Obama administration at home and elsewhere. This is not Talibanistan, it is Obamistan.[24]

As Washington juggled its old illusions with stark new realities, the growing list of irreconcilables stretched the spreading patchwork of policy goals to the breaking point. By mid-May 2009, intensifying attacks by Predator drones in the border region of Pakistan and Afghanistan, the failure to hold and protect territory already seized and the lack of reconstruction had turned public opinion against the United States and NATO.[25] Widespread civilian casualties undermined whatever meager "success" the U.S. could claim with its massive technological advantage.

In Afghanistan's Farah province, 147 people from two villages were killed in an air attack by U.S. forces, the deadliest since 2001.[26] Despite repeated claims by the U.S. military command that not all the casualties were civilian, the incident and others like it fueled a growing propaganda windfall for the Taliban.

Citing the need for a "new approach," within days of the latest debacle, Secretary of Defense Robert Gates fired the U.S. Commander in Afghanistan, General David McKiernan, and replaced him with Iraq veteran Lieutenant General Stanley A. McChrystal.

"We have a new strategy, a new mission and a new ambassador. I believe that new military leadership is also needed,"[27] Gates said. But whether the U.S. military was up to the new strategy was the leading question of the day.

For over a year, the Pentagon had made it clear that there was no military solution to the war in Afghanistan.[28] Chairman of the Joint Chiefs of Staff Admiral Michael Mullen's remark on September 10, 2008, that "We can't kill our way to victory, and no armed forces anywhere—no matter how good—can deliver these keys alone . . ."[29] had become a virtual mantra for the incoming Obama administration.

But the reality on the ground told a different story. The facts of the matter were hard and cold. Despite a desperate desire and need to shift policies and tactics after eight years of grueling, budget-breaking combat, the U.S. war-making apparatus was not structured to do much other than what it was already doing.

According to investigative historian Gareth Porter, despite the hundreds of billions of dollars already poured into a failing war effort, "U.S. military and civilian agencies lack the skills and training as well as the institutional framework necessary to carry out culturally and politically sensitive socio-economic programs at the local level in Afghanistan, or even to avoid further alienation of the population. . . . The U.S. government does not even have enough people capable of speaking Pashto," the language of 42 percent of the population.[30]

The problems facing Obama's AfPak strategy were system-wide and struck deep into the Beltway's legendary capacity for special-interest decision-making without regard for the consequences. Testifying before Congress in May 2009, special representative Ambassador Richard Holbrooke spoke of the shift in U.S. policy from counterterrorism to counterinsurgency embodied in AfPak as a move toward "Smart Power." But Holbrooke failed to explain how a counterinsurgency strategy that required a ratio of 80 percent political and 20 percent military could be obtained when 90 percent of the new administration's war supplemental bill was allocated to military expenditures.[31]

Katrina Vanden Heuvel of *The Nation* writes, "The simple fact is that the funding ratio will not approach what the counterinsurgency strategy calls for, and one senior staffer told me this: 'The bottom line is that [the bill] is the same funding, for the same military efforts, it's just coming from a State Department account instead of DoD.'"[32]

Even if Congress provided an adequate amount of money to make Obama's "Smart Power" plan more than just a new slogan, pacifying Afghanistan required a military commitment that it was not capable of making.[33] In Afghanistan the United States and NATO forces combined never amounted to more than a woefully inadequate 1.6 soldiers per thousand inhabitants.[34] There was little to no coordination or even shared objectives between the American military, the embassy and the White House, let alone NATO and U.S. military operations. There was no effort to protect the local population from the depredations of U.S.-sponsored criminal warlords and no coordinated, systematic effort to hold onto territory once it had been reclaimed. Milt Bearden, the CIA's station chief in Pakistan during the 1980s, wrote of American prospects under Obama, "The Soviet Union had 120,000 troops in the country for most of the decade-long occupation, from 1979 to 1989. In the end, it lost. After-action assessments conducted in the Soviet Union and the United States of the Soviet failure concluded that about 500,000 troops would have been needed to 'pacify' Afghanistan. And even if the Red Army could have mustered some extra troops, the country's terrain would have blocked their deployment."[35]

Despite these glaring discrepancies and verbal commitments from the U.S. military, there was little evidence that the military's shift from counterterrorism to counterinsurgency represented anything more than just a shift in public relations strategy. In an interview with Inter Press Services in September 2008, Colonel David Lamm, former chief of staff to Lieutenant General David Barno, the U.S. top commander in Afghanistan from 2003 to 2005, said, "The institutional army doesn't want this. . . . There isn't a lot of money in counterinsurgency. It isn't a high-tech war—it's a low-tech humint [human intelligence] operation."[36] Lamm went on to emphasize that the U.S. army simply wasn't interested in fighting a counterinsurgency in Afghanistan. It "wanted to roll in, round up terrorists, drive them out of the country, kill them."[37]

Defense Secretary Robert Gates's abrupt firing of General David McKiernan and the appointment of Lieutenant General Stanley McChrystal to replace him as the new U.S. commander in Afghanistan was reported to address this resistance. In his introduction of McChrystal and his second in command, Lieutenant General David Rodriguez, Gates emphasized their "unique skill set in counterinsurgency." But the kind of counterinsurgency represented by McChrystal and Rodriguez and the cult-like aura surrounding the ascension of their new "intellectual movement"[38] left some experts worried.

Referred to by the acronym COIN, the counterinsurgency movement's reputation rested on the military's single achievement in Iraq known as the "surge." In a May 17, 2009, commentary in the *Washington Post*, Celeste Ward, the former political advisor to General Peter Chiarelli, operational commander of U.S. forces in Iraq in 2006, expressed deep concern.

> The story of the surge has developed into a tidy narrative—bordering on mythology—that overlooks several critical factors. Many questions remain about what really happened in Iraq. To be sure, violence rose and then ebbed significantly following the arrival of surge forces in 2007. But why?[39]

Upon her return to the Pentagon in 2007, Ward grew increasingly uneasy with the disconnect between what she experienced first hand of U.S. strategy in Iraq, "and the way it was characterized and interpreted back in Washington."[40] She feared that instead of being a genuine solution to the thorny 8-year-old conflict in Afghanistan, COIN was merely another example of a perpetually out-of-whack Washington system grasping desperately for an answer without understanding or even knowing the question.

> Washington's ultimate objectives in Afghanistan remain unclear," said Ward. "The United States has spent six years, more than 4,000 American lives, mass quantities of psychic and political energy, and untold billions on the effort in Iraq—a project that has to date yielded little in a strategic sense.[41]

It also seemed the tidy narrative on which General Stanley McChrystal's reputation stood did little to reveal what Obama's twenty-first-century counterinsurgency army was evolving into. A June 26, 2006, article in *Newsweek* magazine had thrown a warm glow on the deep blackness surrounding the qualifications of the new U.S. commander for Afghanistan. "Lt. Gen. Stanley McChrystal,

West Point '76, is not someone the Army likes to talk about. . . . That's not because McChrystal has done anything wrong—quite the contrary, he's one of the Army's rising stars—but because he runs the most secretive force in the U.S. military. This is the Joint Special Operations Command [JSOC], the snake-eating, slit-their-throats 'black ops' guys who captured Saddam Hussein and targeted Abu Mussab al-Zarqawi."[42]

In a hats-off to Star Wars and the Bush administration's efforts at bringing an out-of-this world quality to U.S. foreign policy, *Newsweek* described JSOC as "part of what Vice President Dick Cheney was referring to when he said America would have to 'work the dark side' after 9/11. To many critics, the veep's remark back in 2001 fostered his rep as the Darth Vader of the war on terror and presaged bad things to come. . . . But America also had its share of Jedi Knights who are fighting in what Cheney calls, 'the shadows.' And McChrystal . . . and other elite teams he commands are among them."[43]

To the American media, McChrystal represented exactly the kind of Jedi Knight Obama needed to turn a losing enterprise around by improving security and building institutions of self-governance for the Afghan people.

But the record showed that McChrystal's ascent to number one derived almost exclusively from his expertise at killing people suspected of terrorism—not from any proven ability at nation-building.[44]

As a close friend and protégé of Bush's defense secretary, Donald Rumsfeld, McChrystal came more to embody the dark side of the "war on terror" than the light. He was ruthless, independent, secretive and above the law. Despite a supposed mandate to plan, synchronize and conduct global operations against terrorist networks in coordination with other commanders, McChrystal was generally believed to have taken the authority to act unilaterally wherever and whenever he pleased.[45]

Pulitzer Prize–winning reporter Seymour Hersh went even further by calling McChrystal's Joint Special Operations Command an "executive assassination ring. . . . They do not report to anybody, except in the Bush Cheney days, they reported directly to the Cheney office. . . . Under President Bush's authority, they've been going into countries, not talking to the ambassador or the CIA station chief, and finding people on a list and executing them and leaving."[46]

Despite a ritual grilling over reports of torture under his command in Iraq, the Senate unanimously confirmed McChrystal on June 10, 2009, to serve as commander of U.S. forces in Afghanistan. But however great his Beltway popularity, the legacy of his style of targeted raids remained painfully emblematic of the self-destruction inherent in the U.S. operation. One incident alone in the spring of 2007 had left fifty-seven villagers dead, at least half of them women and children. The United States defended its action by claiming 136 Taliban fighters had been killed as it scoured the area for weapons and a local tribal commander.[47] Few took the U.S. denials seriously.

One foreign official remarked of the incident that "the Americans went after one guerrilla commander and created a hundred more."[48]

By the middle of 2009 the United States was faced with not hundreds of new guerrillas, but thousands, in both Afghanistan and Pakistan. In June, under the terms of the Kerry-Lugar bill, the Senate Foreign Relations committee voted unanimously to triple non-military aid to Pakistan to $7.5 billion over five years. But the number of dollars barely approached the number of issues the increase in foreign aid was intended to address. Worst of all, after eight years of fighting there was still no consensus as to what exactly the problem was in Afghanistan and Pakistan, and consequently what exactly should be done to correct it.

With Afghan policy finally out of the back rooms of Washington's K Street lobbyists and with General McChrystal's much heralded summer surge confronting the Taliban's monopoly in Helmand Province, a crop of panicked Pakistani military officials suddenly emerged to cry foul.

On July 17, 2009, senior analysts and officials at Pakistan's

Directorate for Inter-Services Intelligence presented a two-hour briefing for the *New York Times*. According to the report, one of the first briefing slides was directed straight at Washington's worst fears: "The surge in Afghanistan will further reinforce the perception of a foreign occupation of Afghanistan. It will result in more civilian casualties; further alienate the local population. Thus more local resistance to foreign troops."[49]

According to a *New York Times* article on the presentation, Pakistan's major concern was that the American offensive would push Taliban militants back over the border with Afghanistan into Baluchistan, but, the analysts insisted, Pakistan didn't have enough troops to take on an insurgency and still protect its border with India.[50] Another opinion, by *Time* magazine correspondent Omar Waraich, one week later came more directly to the point; not only did American ally Pakistan not expect the United States to win, it did not *want* the United States to win.[51]

Citing independent Pakistani analyst Ayesha Siddiqa, Waraich suggested that Pakistan's policy of covertly supporting the Taliban remained unchanged; that sooner or later the United States would be forced to abandon Afghanistan and be driven to the negotiating table:

> The deeper Pakistani fear about the U.S. offensive is that the more it succeeds, the less chance Pakistan will have of influencing events in Afghanistan after the Americans and their allies leave. "Pakistan will find itself in a fix," says analyst Siddiqa. "What Pakistan doesn't want is a U.S. military victory in the short-term without securing its own long-term strategic interests." It is for this reason, many suspect, that Pakistan has not broken with the Afghan Taliban and other Pakistan-based militant groups fighting in Afghanistan.[52]

The very idea that Pakistan never wanted the United States to win in Afghanistan raised troubling issues about the future of any American involvement and the potential self-interest of other regional powers. If the United States couldn't persuade an ally of sixty years to stop shooting at U.S. troops, root out insurgent training camps and work towards a regional settlement, what chance did it have of working with such disparate players as Iran, China, Russia and India? In the United States, the issue of Pakistani responsibility constantly resulted in contentious debates. Juan Cole, a high-profile commentator on Middle Eastern and South Asian history, saw the Taliban threat as overblown or merely a Western invention to justify a military intervention and the removal of Pakistan's nuclear weapons.[53] Others, like the *New York Times*' Nicholas Kristof, saw the viability of the Pakistani state to protect that nuclear capacity as something to fear.[54] That fear was realized when a suicide bomber attacked a bus coming from the headquarters of Pakistan's nuclear program, the Kahuta Research Laboratories in Rawalpindi, in early July 2009, injuring thirty workers. "It showed that their intelligence is current," said Talat Masood, a retired general and a military analyst. "It was deliberate strike. They are trying to give a hint that they can strike the personnel who are working for the nuclear facilities."[55]

Kristof's July 2009 commentary cited a recent poll of Pakistanis[56] that indicated that one-third believed the Taliban intended to take control of all of Pakistan, while 81 percent believed Islamic militants constituted a "critical threat," up from 34 percent only two years before.

The complexities of Pakistan's ethnic, religious and political makeup were, in and of themselves, an enigma, barely understood and rarely addressed by Washington's policy makers for over sixty years. But the growing contradictions of poverty, inequality, secularization and extremist militancy, fostered by a succession of Pakistani military governments with a history of support and blessing from the United States, were at last reaching critical dimensions.

Hidden from public scrutiny by mutual security agreements forged with the United States during the Cold War, the Pakistani military's continued suppression of ethnic independence and democratic political movements, under the cover of the Bush administration's "war on terror," lay at the heart of the Obama administration's confusion over policy. Added to that was Pakistan's obsession with archrival India, which drove a paranoid internal political agenda. The findings of an exhaustive investigation by Amnesty International were detailed in an April 2009 special report by Selig Harrison for the Center for International Policy. "[T]he Pakistani government has used the rhetoric of fighting 'terrorism' to attack its internal critics," writes Harrison "and to justify large-scale 'enforced disappearances' in which 'activists pushing for greater regional and ethnic and regional rights . . . and greater access to provincial resources' in Baluchistan and Sindh were branded as terrorists and 'arbitrarily detained, denied access to lawyers, families and courts and held in undeclared places of detention run by Pakistan's intelligence agencies, with the government concealing their fate or whereabouts.'"[57]

According to the report, the United States "'condoned, or acquiesced in, these enforced disappearances' as part of ongoing intelligence cooperation in which Pakistani intelligence agencies round up and incarcerate alleged terrorists identified by the two governments."[58]

Yet despite Washington's increased technical support for Islamabad's internal ethnic and religious warfare, further evidence that Pakistan continued to play the United States for a sucker began to surface. Daphne Benoit wrote for the *Kuwait Times* in late June 2009, "Having pressed Pakistan to take on Islamist militants on its soil, Washington has hailed Islamabad for its anti-Taliban military campaign launched in April. But Islamabad has not targeted Washington's main enemies—Afghan Taleban and Al Qaeda leaders on the Pakistani border—and instead has directed its assault on Pakistani Taleban."[59]

Benoit continued by citing Malou Innocent of the Cato Institute, who states, "It appears as though Pakistan still has the same policy as before and continues to differentiate between the 'good Taleban,' being the ones who attack U.S. and NATO forces . . . and the 'bad Taleban,' like Baitullah Mehsud, being the ones who attack the Pakistani government."[60]

As General McChrystal took up his new command he faced a

legacy of U.S. political and military failure not seen since Vietnam. But despite the many similarities and the repeated allusions to America's Southeast Asian quagmire of the 1960s, the consequences of failure in Vietnam paled in comparison to what the United States stood to lose in Afghanistan.

4. Obama's Vietnam?

To summarize their analysis, professor Thomas H. Johnson of the Naval Postgraduate School and M. Chris Mason, senior fellow at the Center for Advanced Defense Studies in Washington, D.C., reported in 2009:

> In both Vietnam and Afghanistan a guerrilla war defeated a European power. Insurgents in both countries enjoyed the advantage of a trackless border and sanctuary beyond it. Both were land wars in Asia with harsh terrain and bad roads that nullified any U.S. advantage. In both countries, the United States military sought to create an indigenous army modeled in its own image, grossly misled the American people about the size of the indigenous force, supported an incompetent and corrupt government that was seen as illegitimate by its own people, and consistently and profoundly misunderstood the nature of the enemy. The United States lost in Vietnam because its politicians and its military failed to adapt and they are doing the exact same thing in Afghanistan.[1]

From a purely American perspective, Johnson and Mason's comparison of Afghanistan to Vietnam was strikingly accurate. What the United States did in World War II and Korea it did in Vietnam, and what it did in Vietnam it did in Afghanistan. Everywhere the United States went with its army it brought the same baggage, while the instruments of U.S. government had no institutional memory for failure or success. The standard tools of American corporate-military statecraft—its Congressional supporters and legions of lobbyists, its government-supported think tanks and universities—were intended to produce a corporate-friendly American client. Where they worked, the United States got partners and allies, and where they didn't, the United States got quagmire.

From a U.S. political-military perspective, the United States *was* repeating its war in Vietnam. But from a Taliban and Al Qaeda perspective, from the perspective of every teenage boy who looked to Osama bin Laden as a role model, and in the mind of every jihadi who planted an improvised explosive or pointed a Kalashnikov, the United States was repeating *Russia's* Vietnam. The more U.S. troops that were sent and the deeper it was drawn in, the closer the United States came to making their dream come true.

In Vietnam, the United States suffered a devastating military and political humiliation. But the "domino effect"—the feared chain of events that U.S. policy was intended to prevent—never occurred.[2] Yet, by spreading radical Islam into Afghanistan in order to create a Vietnam-style quagmire for the U.S.S.R. as payback for its own nightmare in Vietnam,[3] the United States had inadvertently set the stage for an Islamic domino effect.

According to Mark LeVine, a professor of modern Middle Eastern history at the University of California–Irvine, "The problem is that Pakistan's leaders were viewing NWFP and FATA [North West Frontier Province and Federally Administered Tribal Areas] through the same distorted lens as the British did before them, seeing the region as a bastion of backward tribes who could be manipulated and cajoled into preserving a status quo that left most of the people living in the region among the most underdeveloped in the world."[4]

While this distorted image of the political situation in the Pashtun tribal areas served Pakistan's purposes during the 1980s and '90s, its blind embrace by U.S. political and media elites undermined any chance that the United States could ever formulate an effective policy regarding Afghanistan or Pakistan. Says LeVine:

> The views of journalists, commentators and the public at large have been even more problematic. By and large, most people

have simplistically assumed that any society that possessed tribes was technologically, politically and morally "inferior" to and "backwards" with regard to Europe and the United States. This view has changed little in mainstream policy-making or journalism, as demonstrated by the writings of many well-known commentators, who have often had a disproportionate influence on the formation of U.S. foreign policy in the Muslim world.[5]

The forced Islamization of Afghanistan through Pakistan did more than just eradicate the secular administration of the country and bleed the Red Army, it broke down the traditional Pashtun tribal structure on both sides of the Afghan-Pakistan border that had for centuries defined politics in Afghanistan. Selig Harrison writes:

> The traditional supremacy of the malik [tribal elder] over the mullah [religious leader] in tribal society was weakened when the United States,[6] together with Islamist groups in Saudi Arabia and the Persian Gulf, channeled weapons and funding for the anti-Soviet struggle to favored Islamist clients in Afghanistan. This was at the behest of the Pakistan Directorate of Inter-Services Intelligence. The ISI's objective was to build up surrogates opposed to the Pashtunistan concept. When these surrogates proved unable to consolidate their power after Soviet forces left, the ISI turned to the Taliban, which had a Pashtun base but was dominated by clerical leaders with a pan-Islamist ideology.[7]

According to LeVine, "What is particularly dangerous about this dynamic is that the coming together of the Taliban and the tribesman brought into synergy two seemingly contradictory positions: the anti-nationalist and pan-Islamic identity of the Taliban, many of whom came from outside Pakistan, and the particularistic and locally rooted identity of the region's tribal groups."[8]

By marrying its war on terror to the Northern Alliance's political agenda and Pakistan's anti-Pashtun ethnic politics following its 2001 invasion, Washington had stepped into a hornet's nest of long-standing anticolonial resentment as well as a hybridized Afghan tribal politics of its own making. By 2008 the traditional system of genuine *secular* tribal authority that the population had once trusted and relied on, had been replaced by warlords and foreign-sponsored radical religious extremists.

Complicating matters further was the apparent failure of the U.S. command to come to grips with longstanding Pashtun and Baluchi separatist sentiment inside Pakistan, which fueled the Taliban's resistance and simultaneously undermined the American effort. Harrison writes:

> The newly-politicized and radicalized Pashtuns of the Federally Administered Tribal Areas, known as FATA, now see themselves as political brethren of the Pashtuns in the Northwest Frontier Province and northern corner of Baluchistan. They want economic development, but development under Pashtun control, not under the control of the Punjabi-dominated central government. More important, by arousing a Pashtun sense of victimization at the hands of outside forces, the conduct of the "war on terror" in FATA has strengthened the very Jihadi forces that the U.S. seeks to defeat.[9]

On August 6, 2009, the head of the White House homeland security office, John Brennan, officially declared that "war on terrorism" was finally over. Instead, he said, "we are at war with al Qaeda. . . . We are at war with its violent extremist allies who seek to carry on al Qaeda's murderous agenda."[10] Also in August 2009, Defense Secretary Robert Gates announced at a press conference that it would take "a few years" to defeat the Taliban and Al Qaeda. "In the intelligence business, we always used to categorize information in two ways, secrets and mysteries. . . . The secrets were things that were knowable. Mysteries were those where there were too many variables to predict. And I think that how long U.S. forces will be in Afghanistan is in that area."[11]

But the bigger, more immediate mystery still was whether U.S. forces were going to be helped by the upcoming 2008 Afghan presidential election or hurt by it. As the day approached Washington held its breath.

The Election

As the long-awaited presidential election arrived, everything the United States had done since the overthrow of King Zahir Shah in 1973 hung in the balance. The Obama administration had shown its displeasure early on by inviting a handful of candidates to the inauguration in Washington while leaving Afghan President Hamid Karzai off the list.[12] Washington's overtures to former Afghan Foreign Minister Abdullah Abdullah; Governor of Nangarhar province Golagha Sherzoy; former Finance Minister Ashraf Ghani Ahmadzai; and former Interior Minister, Ali Ahmad Jalali, were intended to send a loud signal to Karzai about Washington's displeasure.

Indeed, Karzai's government—where it exercised authority at all—was legendary for its corruption. In February 2008, then–U.S. Senator Joseph Biden and two other senators stormed out of a formal dinner with Karzai after he refused to accept accountability for actions Biden maintained were corrupt.[13] By late March 2009, the anti-Karzai campaign had been twisted into bypassing him altogether and threatening to create a new office of prime minister or chief executive who would carry out U.S. and European orders directly.[14] But the anti-Karzai campaign was a tricky game, which Karzai knew well how to play. By the time the Obama administration realized the error of its ways, the damage had been done.[15]

Karzai posed a dilemma for Washington, but just as the Soviet Union had had to rely on an unpopular Afghan communist leader thirty years before, the Obama administration had nowhere else to turn. For many Afghans, the election was seen as just another example of foreign meddling in their country, which in the end wouldn't make life easier, safer or more democratic. Says scholar Jawied Nawabi:

> The Afghan election is just a farce democracy and there is absolutely NO sovereignty in Afghan politics. No matter who wins the election, they are not independent from the influence and pressures of Western powers cajoling them to accept the increase of troop presence or military bases without a clear and crisp term limit for when they will leave.[16]

Ahmad Shah Ahmadzai—one of Afghanistan's richest men and the former interim prime minister—posed the rhetorical question to the *Asia Times*, "Will this [election] change the situation on the ground, which is that this is not a democratic election process but a pure occupation agenda? Will this gimmick legitimize the occupation?"[17]

Ahmadzai bluntly demystified America's involvement: "Even during the Soviet invasion, Soviet troops never knocked on the doors of people after dusk, but these 'friends' of ours not only raid houses in the night with sniffing dogs, they don't even spare women."[18]

In the final days, a series of political deals assured that Karzai would come out ahead of his rivals, supported by a cast of warlords that read like a demon's registry.[19]

As summarized by *GlobalPost*'s election correspondent Jean MacKenzie, "To a large extent, the elections seem to have been reduced to a feel-good exercise for the foreign community. . . . No one speaks any longer of 'free and fair,' elections. . . . For many Afghans, the whole idea was absurd from the beginning. . . . 'Everyone knows the next president will be chosen in Washington,' . . . Most observers expect large-scale fraud, especially in the more remote areas of the country."[20]

And a large-scale fraud it was, with as much as a third of the vote subjected to a recount.[21] In late September 2009, the UN-backed Independent Election Commission awarded President Hamid

Karzai 54.6 percent of the vote,[22] putting him over the critical 50 percent necessary to secure victory without a runoff. But the controversy over voter fraud would ramble on amid charge and countercharge for over a month.

It wasn't supposed to be this way. According to Afghan human rights expert and King Zahir Shah's representative at the Bonn Conference, Sima Wali, the process of building a new Afghanistan was doomed from the beginning by Islamist opposition to the king's traditional role and his promotion of a moderate form of Islam. The king was traditionally referred to by Afghans as Baba, the father. Historically, Afghans considered the role of the king as "God's shadow on earth" to be an elemental part of the Afghan nation. Islamist opposition to women having equal rights under the constitution ran counter to long-held principles advanced by Afghan rulers beginning with Amanullah in the 1920s. Wali personally fought the Islamist agenda and succeeded, but she was shocked by the challenge to such a fundamental principle of Afghan history. [23]

In addition to placing former Taliban madrassa students in positions of authority, the Bush administration brought warlords into the tribal Loya Jirga that established the new government, a decision that had an instant and irreversible effect. Pakistani journalist Ahmed Rashid cited a European diplomat's shock at the American strategy. "'Giving the warlords a front seat was a blow to the Afghans and a negative symbol of U.S. influence,' said one ambassador. However, the Americans, with their pro-warlord policy, were anxious to show that the warlords supported the political process."[24]

Operating under the false assumption that warlords had always been a fundamental aspect of governance in Afghanistan, few in the media or Washington policy establishment questioned the thinking behind such onerous decisions. The Saudi- and Egyptian-based extremism of the so-called "Peshawar Seven" jihadi groups, which the United States insisted be implanted into the Karzai government, was as alien to Afghan governance as any European colonial ideology.[25] But the fatal moment arrived when the Bush administration made the unilateral decision to sideline the one person who could have pulled the country together after his thirty years in exile—King Zahir Shah.

Commentator William Pfaff wrote, "Washington manipulated the Loya Jirga (national assembly of tribal leaders) called in June 2002, so as to put Karzai in office. This was despite the will of the majority of the assembly to bring back the royal family, and the ex-king, as nonpartisan and traditionally legitimate influences in the country's affairs. By acting as it did, the Bush administration robbed Karzai of legitimacy, making him a foreign puppet."[26]

5. **Metrics**

It is only now, after some eight years of warfare, that NATO-ISAF [International Security Assistance Force] is truly beginning to shift its strategy to fight the war necessary to win, and focusing on control of key population centers. This shape, clear, hold, and build strategy seeks to defeat the Taliban and insurgents in the war they have actually been fighting by:

Shape: Create the military conditions necessary to secure key population centers; limit the flow of insurgents;

Clear: Removing insurgent and anti-government elements from a given area or region, thereby creating space between the insurgents and the population;

Hold: Maintaining security, denying the insurgents access and freedom of movement within the given space; and

Build: Exploiting the security space to deliver humanitarian relief and implement reconstruction and development initiatives that will connect the Afghan population to its government and build and sustain the Afghanistan envisioned in the strategic goals.

—Anthony H. Cordesman, *The New Metrics of Afghanistan*[1]

Whatever value Anthony H. Cordesman's strategy represented for establishing an AfPak Metric, it was still going to be 400,000 troops short and eight years behind schedule. With political opposition to the war rising in Afghanistan, Pakistan, China and the U.S., with the security situation rapidly deteriorating and the administration reeling from the election blowback, by September 2009, support for Obama's shifting AfPak plan was evaporating. In order to succeed at the new counterinsurgency strategy, General Stanley McChrystal needed a reasonably stable and legitimate government, an adequate number of troops and a minimum of one year to try to turn the situation around. The odds were increasing that he wasn't going to have any of them.

A big part of Washington's ongoing problem in Afghanistan was the issue of metrics—how to measure performance. Despite eight years and billions spent, the Beltway's best and brightest still could not agree on what success in Afghanistan actually meant or how it was to be attained. Cordesman's study found the situation to be unprecedented.

> No one who works with the unclassified data on Afghanistan can fail to be aware of how poor and contradictory much of the data are now. In general, no NATO-ISAF government— including the United States—has yet provided an honest and meaningful picture of the war. Far too often, official reporting has been tailored to report success when the Taliban, Hekmatyar, and Haqqani were actually scoring major gains. In other cases, key problems in the Afghan government, the NATO-ISAF effort, and the economic aid effort were ignored or disguised as successes.[2]

Washington's involvement in Afghanistan was largely a product of its own creation, yet it seemed strangely confounded by the challenges it posed. Despite vehement Pakistani denials, Afghanistan's Taliban military commander and religious leader, Mullah Mohammed Omar, had been left unmolested in the Pakistani city of Quetta since his escape in 2001, free to organize and coordinate attacks on American and NATO forces.[3]

Considering that the Taliban and Al Qaeda had been central to justifying wars in Afghanistan and Iraq; had caused unprecedented national security strictures in the United States, the application of torture on captured suspects, and the suspension of key civil liberties guaranteed by the U.S. constitution; and had upended a host of legal precedents dating back to 1215 and the Magna Carta,[4] the U.S. government appeared profoundly indifferent to rooting them out. Now, Mullah Mohammed Omar's return to the forefront of the Taliban's 2009 resurgence was viewed as nothing short of miraculous by Washington's premier intelligence experts. The *New York Times* reported:

> "This is an amazing story," said Bruce Riedel, a former Central Intelligence Agency officer who coordinated the Obama administration's initial review of Afghanistan policy in the spring. "He's a semiliterate individual who has met with no more than a handful of non-Muslims in his entire life. And he's staged one of the most remarkable military comebacks in modern history."[5]

So, how did Mullah Mohammed Omar—a dogged, semiliterate fundamentalist— make such a comeback right under the nose of the largest and most expensive high-technology military-intelligence establishment in the history of civilization? In terms of metrics, until the change in policy represented by AfPak, the Pentagon's reporting on the war in Pakistan, where Al Qaeda and the Taliban were based, had not even been coupled with the fighting in Afghanistan.[6]

In his study, Cordesman pointed out the glaring contradictions in the U.S. military's conduct.

> The war has not been a purely Afghan conflict since 2002. Al Qai'ida and Afghan insurgent groups, increasingly mixed with Pakistani Deobandi and 'Taliban,' have established major sanctuaries and operational centers in the FATA and Baluchi areas of Pakistan. NATO-ISAF does not cover these developments. The war mysteriously has stopped at the Afghan border, and such reporting is inherently misleading and dishonest.[7]

Even more mysterious was the missing role that Pakistan's military continued to play, even as the country accepted billions in military and civilian assistance without the accounting necessary to track whether it still supported the expanding Taliban operation. Cordesman continued:

> These critical shortfalls in reporting have been compounded by the fact that elements of the Pakistani military and ISI have continued to support Al Qa'ida and Afghan Pashtun insurgents in both FATA and especially Baluchistan (The Omar-led Taliban operates freely in the Quetta area). Metrics which do not show the actual level of Pakistani military operations and border activity to deal with them, are equally misleading and dishonest.

Cordesman offered a set of sweeping reassessments and recommendations designed to put the president's AfPak plan on a solid factual foundation.[8] But whether they would or could be implemented was increasingly doubtful. In fact, by mid-September 2009 it appeared the ground had shifted underneath the entire post-Cold-War-global-U.S. project.

Commenting on the annual report of the International Institute for Strategic Studies (IISS) in London, the BBC announced the dawning of the new era politely: "Stand by for some new buzz phrases to describe what is going on in international relations as the first year of the Obama administration unfolds. 'Bundles of co-operation,' 'coalitions of the relevant,' and 'minilateralism' are some key ones. 'Engagement' is another."[9]

After eight years of neoconservative disengagement from the world community, with a unilateral military program for "full spectrum dominance,"[10] America's new jargon more resembled the plaintive language of a recovering alcoholic's encounter group than a virile economic and military empire on the verge of world conquest.

In analysing how a "weakened" United States should lower its sights and try to form regional groupings to help it, the IISS Director General Dr. John Chapman said: "Domestically, [President] Obama may have campaigned on the theme 'yes we can'; internationally he may increasingly have to argue 'no we can't.'"[11]

According to Associated Press reporter Raphael G. Satter, the IISS study laid the blame squarely at the door of Washington's imperial overreach and Wall Street's financial malfeasance. "The report said the U.S. struggles against insurgent groups in Iraq and Afghanistan had exposed the limits of the country's military muscle, while the near collapse of the world financial markets sapped the economic base on which that muscle relied."[12]

That U.S. capacity to project unilateral authority would some-day be in decline was no surprise to Washington. In November 2008, the National Intelligence Council (NIC) of the Central Intelligence Agency prepared a projection for the next administration, titled *Global Trends 2025*. The report predicted that over the next fifteen years American preeminence as a world power "even in the military realm—will decline and U.S. leverage will become more constrained."[13] The report even accepted that in terms of "size, speed, and directional flow, the transfer of **global wealth and economic power** [emphasis theirs] now under way—roughly from West to East—is without precedent in modern history."[14] Yet, in only one year, the fifteen-year timetable for the shift in global power predicted in the NIC report had evaporated.

The speed with which the United States had declined and the unforeseen consequences of its sudden loss of influence was indeed unprecedented. Said military expert Michael Klare:

> Countries that once looked to the United States for guid-ance on major international issues are ignoring Washington's counsel and instead creating their own autonomous policy networks. . . . No one seems to be saying this out loud—yet—but let's put it bluntly: less than a year into the 15-year GlobalTrends 2025, the days of America's unquestioned global dominance have come to an end.[15]

But what did America's rapid fall from grace mean to its plans in Afghanistan, its involvement in Central Asia and its traditional post–World War II relations to its European allies?

6. NATO

In Geneva, former national security advisor Zbigniew Brzezinski issued a somber warning at a gathering of military and foreign policy experts. The *New York Times* quoted him: "'We are running the risk of replicating—obviously unintentionally—the fate of the Soviets'. . . . The presence of so many foreign troops underpins an Afghan perception that the Americans and their allies are hostile invaders and 'suggests transformation of the conflict is taking place.'"[1]

Brzezinski's trepidations were caused by more than just the realization that, after his greatest victory as Jimmy Carter's national security advisor, the United States was mirroring the fate of the Soviet Union. Brzezinski now feared that the stresses posed by AfPak were taxing the U.S.-European relationship to the breaking point.[2] Afghanistan presented the Western alliance with its greatest paradox since World War II. Not only was the United States mimicking the Soviet invasion and subsequent long-term occupation, but the ongoing U.S. plan to peel "moderate" elements of the Taliban away from the hardcore Islamists was instead peeling Europe away from the United States and threatening the NATO alliance with dissolution.

Afghanistan had been testing NATO's cohesiveness from the inception of its commitment. In 2005, Bush Defense Secretary Donald Rumsfeld described it in terms of a basketball team that practiced together but refused to play at game time.[3] Central to Rumsfeld's complaint was the issue of national caveats, where a member country was allowed to write its own rules of engagement given that country's specific legal requirements regarding the use of its troops.[4] These caveats meant that U.S., British and Canadian forces doing much of the fighting in the eastern border region of

Afghanistan, while German, French, Spanish and Italian troops faced less hostile opposition in quieter provinces.

In addition to trivializing the deeper legal reasons for the caveats, Rumsfeld's basketball metaphor disguised the growing rift between NATO's military leadership and the European population. Civilian restrictions on the conduct of Europe's militaries were a direct social consequence of the devastating effect of twentieth-century European militarism.[5] But a lengthy article in the German magazine *Der Spiegel* made it clear that the German military harbored plans to change that. "About 70 percent of Germans are currently in favor of a rapid withdrawal. In reality, the opposite is taking place. The Bundeswehr is becoming more entrenched in this war and it is also gradually going on the offensive. . . . This shift is another move towards the normalization of Germany's feelings about itself as a nation. It's something that German governments have been working toward for 60 years."[6]

Although German resurgence as a unified European power was inevitable, the continuation of NATO power in a partnership with the United States as a player in Afghanistan, was not. In October 2009, in a book titled *A Soldier First: Bullets, Bureaucrats and the Politics of War*, the former head of the Canadian armed forces, General Rick Hillier, angrily asserted that Afghanistan had exposed an inner rot that was tearing the alliance apart. "Afghanistan has revealed that NATO has reached the stage where it is a corpse decomposing and somebody's going to have to perform a Frankenstein-like life-giving act by breathing some lifesaving air through those rotten lips into those putrescent lungs or the alliance will be done."[7]

Hillier predicted that NATO could not last long in its present form and that any further setback in Afghanistan "will see it off to the cleaners."[8] That setback came only days later when the respected Afghan minister of counter-narcotics, General Khodaidad Khodaidad announced that NATO troops from the United States, the United Kingdom and Canada were profiting from the drug trade.[9] Rumors of Western involvement in the Afghan opium trade had been building for some time. Some pundits referred to it as

Afghanistan's best-kept secret.[10] But having the charge erupt into the open during the final moments of the post-election furor between Afghan president Hamid Karzai and his main contender, former Afghan Foreign Minister Abdullah Abdullah, was a fatal omen.

Only two weeks before, Senator John Kerry had intervened with Karzai in an attempt to salvage the election. Press reports hailed Kerry, declaring that he had achieved a diplomatic triumph when Karzai agreed to fast-track an early runoff.[11] President Obama praised Kerry's actions, calling them "extraordinarily constructive and very helpful."[12] But the delicate campaign to work with Karzai was blown sky high by the *New York Times* on October 27, 2009, when the paper accused Karzai's brother, Ahmad Wali Karzai, of being "a suspected player in the country's booming heroin trade" who had received regular payments for a variety of services from the CIA "for much of the past eight years."[13]

Seen as Karzai's counterattack, Khodaidad's announcement of NATO drug dealing sent power-sharing negotiations with Abdullah Abdullah into a tailspin. On Sunday, November 1, 2009, Abdullah withdrew from the runoff, declaring that he could not take part because of the risk of fraud.[14] The next day Afghan election officials declared Hamid Karzai the winner.

But the real story of Abdullah's abdication had passed far beyond ongoing concerns for election fraud. Facing a lack of political support at home for a long-haul military commitment, the White House had gambled its last cards on a quick fix and lost. Now it had to work with Karzai on Karzai's terms, leaving Washington with no leverage and Abdullah with no choice but to back out.[15]

Even before the fateful weekend, Senator Kerry had signaled that the United States was backing away from a full-blown commitment to Afghanistan both civically and militarily. In a major foreign policy speech to the CFR on October 23, 2009, Kerry said, "Achieving our goals does not require us to build a flawless democracy, defeat the Taliban in every corner of the country, or create a modern economy—what we're talking about is 'good-enough' governance."[16]

Kerry's speech was clearly aimed at rebuffing General Stanley McChrystal's desire to mount a full-blown no-holds-barred counterinsurgency campaign and supporting the traditional opinions of Daniel Markey[17] and other CFR members who wanted America's sympathies, money and effort shifted to Pakistan where—in their opinion—America's real interests lay.

Kerry's presentation was warmly received by a war-weary defense-intelligence community that had nothing to show for its multi-decade involvement in Central Asia but chaos and instability.[18] Graham Allison of Harvard University's Belfer Center for Science and International Affairs set the tone for how Americans should think of Kerry's position in a *Boston Globe* op-ed. "Kerry's analysis begins with the most important consideration: U.S. national interests. What should Americans care about here? What matters *more* [emphasis his] than other things that matter? Kerry says: Pakistan—not Afghanistan."[19]

But Kerry's suggestion that, in order to lessen the burden on the United States, the brunt of the military campaign could somehow be shifted to America's Tajik, Uzbek, Turkmen and Hazara allies[20] raised several unsettling questions about what the Obama administration might be up to. For those familiar with Afghanistan's history, Afghanistan meant Pashtun. Historians Richard F. Nyrop and Donald M. Seekins write: "The term Afghan usually referred specifically to a Pashtu (or Pakhtu) speaker who is recognized as a member of one of the several Pashtun tribes."[21]

Selig Harrison writes of the existing imbalances, "Tajiks constitute only about 24 percent of the population, yet they largely control the armed forces and the intelligence and secret police agencies that look over the daily lives of the Pashtuns."[22] The very idea that the United States, Britain or Russia would further organize Afghanistan's minority populations against "Afghans" was reason enough in itself to infuriate Pashtuns on both sides of the Durand line. Fighting them for eight years, bombing their villages and isolating them from the political process, while building up a corrupt government stacked with former Northern Alliance warlords, amounted to a recruiting campaign for the Taliban. Harrison continued, "The psychological cement that holds the disparate Taliban factions together is opposition to Tajik dominance in Kabul. Until the power of the Panjshiris is curbed, no amount of American money or manpower will bring the insurgency to an end."[23]

Redrawing the map of Central Asia had been on the European colonial agenda for much of the last 200 years. In the late nineteenth century, London's advocates of "Forward Policy" wanted Afghanistan subdued and dismembered. Britain had already once partitioned Pashtun tribal homelands with the creation of the Durand line in 1893.[24]

Was Washington's plan to partition the country again, by backing Pakistan's Punjabi military to squeeze it from the east while a coalition of tribes pressed it from the west? A new map of Afghanistan and Pakistan had already been drawn up by U.S. military thinkers. In a controversial article in the June 2006 *Armed Forces Journal*, retired U.S. Army Lieutenant Colonel Ralph Peters suggested that not just Afghanistan but the entire Middle East would look a lot better if realigned around ethnic, cultural and sectarian preferences.

> A root cause of the broad stagnation in the Muslim world is the Saudi royal family's treatment of Mecca and Medina as their fiefdom. . . . Imagine how much healthier the Muslim world might become were Mecca and Medina ruled by a rotating council representative of the world's major Muslim schools and movements in an Islamic Sacred State. . . . Iran, a state with madcap boundaries, would lose a great deal of territory to Unified Azerbaijan, Free Kurdistan, the Arab Shia State and Free Baluchistan, but would gain the provinces around Herat in today's Afghanistan. . . . What Afghanistan would lose to Persia in the west, it would gain in the east, as Pakistan's Northwest Frontier tribes would be reunited with their Afghan brethren (the point is not to draw maps as we would like them but as local populations would prefer them). Pakistan, another unnatural state, would also lose its Baluch

territory to Free Baluchistan. The remaining "natural" Pakistan would lie entirely east of the Indus, except for a westward spur near Karachi.[25]

The chance that Pakistan's Punjabi-dominated military would ever go along with a plan to relinquish its "unnatural" boundaries was highly unlikely. If anything bonded Pakistan's ethnically disparate civilian population to its generally despised military establishment, it was the omnipresent fear of external pressure from India and the United States to undermine and dissolve the Pakistani state. On his brief stop in Islamabad in October 2009, Senator Kerry, then chairman of the Senate Foreign Relations Committee, was confronted by Pakistan's military chiefs. They believed that the conditions applied by the U.S. Congress to the $7.5 billion dollar U.S. aid package threatened Pakistan's national security. [26]

7. **U.S.-Pakistan —A History**

When it came to dealing with Pakistan, the United States had a long history of narrowly self-interested, expedient and ultimately self-defeating decisions. Created in 1947 out of the remains of the British Empire in India, Pakistan had by 1955 aligned itself firmly with the West, joining the Southeast Asia Treaty Organization and the Central Treaty Organization (or "Baghdad Pact").[1] In return, Pakistan received $2 billion in aid between 1953 and 1961.[2] The United States suspended military assistance during and after the Indo-Pakistani wars of 1965 and 1971, leading to criticism that the United States was an unreliable ally. Following the loss of East Pakistan in its 1971 war with India, Zulfiqar Ali Bhutto, then the Minister for Fuel, Power and Natural Resources, established Pakistan's nuclear weapons program. U.S. aid was again suspended in 1979 over the discovery of a covert uranium-enrichment program, but was restored following the Soviet invasion of Afghanistan in December of that year. In 1985 the Solarz Amendment prohibited aid to countries that attempted to import nuclear commodities from the United States. Also in 1985, the Pressler amendment was added to the Foreign Assistance Act requiring the president to certify to Congress that Pakistan did not possess a nuclear weapon. That same year Pakistan crossed the threshold of weapons-grade uranium production and by 1986 is believed to have produced enough material to produce a bomb.[3] Despite having full knowledge of Pakistan's growing nuclear capabilities, the United States government largely ignored Pakistan's nuclear program given the continuing occupation of Afghanistan by Soviet troops.[4] In 1990 President George H.W. Bush again suspended all military and most economic aid over Pakistan's refusal to destroy the cores of its nuclear weapons.[5]

According to K. Alan Kronstadt of the Congressional Research Service,

> U.S. disengagement from Pakistan (and Afghanistan) after 1990 had serious and lasting effects on Pakistani perceptions. Former Pakistani Army Chief and President Musharraf himself repeatedly voiced a narrative in which Pakistan joined the United States to "wage a Jihad" in Afghanistan in the 1980s, only to see "disaster" follow when the "military victory was bungled up" and the United States then left the region "abandoned totally."[6]

Following the events of 9/11, the United States resumed a military relationship with Pakistan in the Bush administration's "war on terror." Yet, even as the Obama administration tried to move the emphasis of its AfPak program from Afghanistan to Pakistan by building up the country's civilian sector, the United States continued to find itself caught between a distrustful civilian population and a double-dealing Pakistani military that skillfully manipulated both.

Karin Brulliard of the *Washington Post* wrote of Pakistani civilian resentment over the Kerry-Lugar aid grant, "Even moderate voices said the terms—which demand civilian oversight of military promotions and a commitment to dismantling terrorist bases in Pakistan—were insensitive. Polls show the public is increasingly queasy about its government's cooperation with U.S. anti-terror efforts."[7]

Central to Pakistan's objections to any U.S. oversight was the Pakistani military's thinly veiled support for Islamist groups seen as acting in defense of their long-range interests. Pakistan's Inter-Services Intelligence Directorate had helped to found the Taliban as a vanguard for conquering Afghanistan in the 1990s and was reported to still be directly helping to facilitate their operations.[8]

For years, U.S. policy makers had been debating how to incorporate the Taliban into a grand, global resolution for Afghanistan, separating them from Al Qaeda and bringing them into a power-sharing arrangement with the Karzai government,[9] and still keeping

Pakistan as an ally. That the Taliban's very purpose was rooted in the overthrow of any form of democracy or participatory secular government was just another in a series of glaring inconsistencies that Washington's military-intelligence elite continued to ignore. Taliban commander Mullah Mohammed Omar was even said to have opposed a traditional Afghan Loya Jirga to choose an Afghan leader on the grounds that such a native practice of democracy was un-Islamic.[10] But all this aside, after nearly ten years, no two experts could even agree on who exactly the Taliban were or what their relationship to Al Qaeda was, in either Pakistan or Afghanistan. By 2009, the only thing experts could agree on was that they were winning and Washington was not.[11]

Prior to the announcement of the AfPak strategy in March 2009, U.S. Director of National Intelligence Dennis Blair complained about the lack of understanding of Afghanistan's regional dynamics. Blair told the *Los Angeles Times*, "We know a heck of a lot more about Iraq on a very granular basis than we do in Afghanistan."[12] According to the report, the overall strategy differed little from the Clinton-era plan and would focus on "separating factions that can be induced to support the U.S.-backed government from those seen as irreconcilable."[13]

But who were these irreconcilables? And who were the factions that were going to be convinced to work within a government that represented no one, rigged its own elections and lined its own pockets?

8. **Warlords, the Taliban and Al Qaeda**

There is little agreement in the West today over who exactly the Taliban are, the extent of their links to Al Qaeda, whether they are a unified force, how many are hardcore "irreconcilables" and whether the Afghan Taliban and the Pakistani Taliban share the same Islamic goals and philosophy. David Rohde, a *New York Times* journalist who escaped from Taliban captivity in June 2009 after being held hostage for seven months, saw the link between the Afghan Taliban and Pakistani Taliban as seamless. U.S. envoy for Afghanistan and Pakistan Richard Holbrooke disagreed vehemently, insisting that various Taliban groups have different goals, presenting "a uniquely complicated problem."[1]

Ziauddin Sardar, a writer and visiting professor at City University, London provides an account of how the Taliban have evolved since their origin.

> A new generation of militants is emerging in Pakistan. Although they are generally referred to as "Taliban," they are a recent phenomenon. The original Taliban, who ruled Afghanistan briefly during the 1990s, were Afghan fighters, a product of the Soviet invasion of their country. They were created and moulded by the Pakistani army, with the active support of the United States and Saudi money, and the deliberate use of madrasas [fundamentalist Islamic schools] to prop up religious leaders. Many Taliban leaders were educated at [Darul Uloom] Haqqania by Maulana Sami ul-Haq.[2]

According to numerous sources, the Darul Uloom Haqqania religious school, south of Peshawar in Pakistan, is where many top

Taliban leaders, including Mullah Mohammed Omar attended. It continues as one of the largest madrassas in Pakistan, graduating 3,000 students a year, mostly from exceptionally impoverished backgrounds, dedicated to joining jihad (holy war).[3]

Ziauddin Sardar continues,

> The new generation of militants are all Pakistani; they emerged after the U.S. invasion of Afghanistan and represent a revolt against the government's support for the U.S. . . . They are led by young mullahs who, unlike the original Taliban, are technology- and media-savvy, and are also influenced by various indigenous tribal nationalisms, honouring the tribal codes that govern social life in Pakistan's rural areas. "They are Taliban in the sense that they share the same ideology as the Taliban in Afghanistan," says Rahimullah Yusufzai, Peshawar-based columnist on the *News*. "But they are totally Pakistani, with a better understanding of how the world works."[4]

Pakistan's new breed of Taliban differed not only from their original lineage as refugees, but also in their goals. According to Sardar, their jihad was not just about the "infidels occupying Afghanistan," it was also about the "infidels" running Pakistan and "the secular values of Pakistani society." According to Rashed Rahman, executive editor of the Lahore-based *Post* newspaper, "They aim at nothing less than to cleanse Pakistan and turn it into a pure Islamic state."[5]

Jayshree Bajoria of the CFR broke down the many Islamic combat groups now operating out of Pakistan into five categories by citing Ashley J. Tellis, a senior associate at Carnegie Endowment for International Peace and Rohan Gunaranta of the International Centre for Political Violence and Terrorism Research in Singapore.

> **Sectarian:** Groups such as the Sunni Sipah-e-Sahaba and the Shia Tehrik-e-Jafria, which are engaged in violence within Pakistan; **Anti-Indian:** Terrorist groups that operate with the alleged support of the Pakistani military intelligence agency

Inter-Services Intelligence (ISI), such as the Lashkar-e Taiba (LeT), the Jaish-e-Muhammad (JeM), and the Harakat ul-Mujahadeen (HuM). **Afghan Taliban:** The original Taliban movement and especially its Kandahari leadership centered around Mullah Mohammad Omar, believed to be now living in Quetta; **Al-Qaeda and its affiliates:** The organization led by Osama bin Laden and other non-South Asian terrorists believed to be ensconced in the Federally Administered Tribal Areas (FATA). Rohan Gunaratna of the International Centre for Political Violence and Terrorism Research in Singapore[6] says other foreign militant groups such as the Islamic Movement of Uzbekistan, Islamic Jihad group, the Libyan Islamic Fighters Group and the Eastern Turkistan Islamic Movement are also located in FATA; **the Pakistani Taliban:** Groups consisting of extremist outfits in the FATA, led by individuals such as Hakimullah Mehsud, of the Mehsud tribe in South Waziristan, Maulana Faqir Muhammad of Bajaur, and Maulana Qazi Fazlullah of the Tehrik-e-Nafaz-e-Shariat-e-Mohammadi (TNSM).[7]

Experts disagree on what unites the groups, which in many ways behave more like a drug-funded international mafia than a rural insurgency. But all agree the dynamic that holds them together is rapidly evolving into something never seen before—driven by a whole new generation of terrorists. Don Rassler of the Combating Terrorism Center at the U.S. military academy at West Point believes Al Qaeda now acts as a mediator and coalition builder among the groups, unifying factions and resolving conflicts.[8] Ashley J. Tellis believes that the coordination between these groups is driven by necessity, but that the most important development is that coordination now "takes place through the entire spectrum of jihadi groups . . ."[9] and that they are now more flexible in their cooperation than at any time in history.

Nothing about the U.S. war in Afghanistan and Pakistan was as complex or had been so intentionally misinterpreted as the web of interconnected tribal, sectarian and foreign insurgents that composed the Taliban and Al Qaeda. Dozens and perhaps hundreds of armed groups, tribal militias, armed criminal gangs and foreign fighters vie for control of the countryside against or sometimes in collaboration with thousands more hired by the Karzai government to fight the insurgents in various parts of the country. Says Thomas Ruttig from the Afghanistan Analysts Network (AAN), a Kabul-based research group, "In Afghanistan, military logic drives the conflict, and armed groups for hire turned that into a system of political economy, i.e. they profit from the fighting and are not interested for it to stop."[10] According to Ruttig, foreign intelligence agencies, powerful warlords and even government officials run illegal armed groups for security, economic and political purposes.[11] According to the UN office for the Coordination of Humanitarian Affairs, the Kabul government has armed and paid at least 10,000 men to fight the insurgents in their villages with little to no control over how they will be deployed or whom they will fight.[12]

The three main groups responsible for most of the fighting in Afghanistan are the Quetta Shura Taliban (QST) of Mullah Mohammed Omar, who controlled most of Afghanistan from 1996 until 2001; the Haqqani Network (HQN), originally run by Jalaluddin Haqqani but now controlled by his son, Sirajuddin Haqqani; and the Hesb-i-Islami Gulbuddin (HIG) of Gulbuddin Hekmatyar, the Mujahideen commander made notorious by his exploits during the anti-Soviet war.[13]

The Quetta Shura

Mullah Mohammed Omar's credentials as a legendary fighter date back to late in the war against the communist Najibullah regime and his efforts at the futile 1989 battle of Kandahar, in which he is reported to have lost an eye.[14] *Newsweek*'s Ron Moreau writes, "Omar, who lost an eye in the fighting, became renowned for his prowess at knocking out Russian tanks with rocket-propelled grenades."[15] According to the popular narrative, during the chaos following the defeat of the Soviet-backed regime in 1992, Omar was visited in a dream by a woman who told him that God would help him to bring peace. According to this narrative he then raised a group of fifty fighters from Afghan refugee camps in Pakistan and proceeded to fight against corrupt warlords who were terrorizing the countryside.[16] In 1996, the one-eyed Omar visited the Shrine of the Prophet Mohammed's cloak in Kandahar. Omar took the cloak, brought it to the roof of an old Mosque in Kandahar and raised it high before the crowd with his hands inside the sleeves. In the view of his followers, this action legitimized Mullah Omar as the amir-ul Momineen, the commander of the faithful.[17] Of Mullah Omar's origins, his exact whereabouts or even his age, little is known. His birth has been reported to be either in 1950, 1959, 1960 or 1962.[18] He lost one eye fighting against the Soviets in the 1980s and was now believed by some to be little more than a figurehead, issuing proclamations through his second in command, Mullah Abdul Ghani Baradar (a.k.a Brehadar).[19] In answer to a hand-delivered list of questions from *Newsweek* magazine, Mullah Baradar insisted that Mullah Omar still directed the Afghan Taliban and that their base of operations was inside Afghanistan and not in Quetta, Pakistan, as claimed by American intelligence sources. He also saw no benefit in negotiating with the Americans and insisted that his organization took neither advice nor support from Pakistan's Directorate for Inter-Services Intelligence.[20] But then, both Pakistani government and Taliban spokesmen routinely denied that the Taliban were supported by the Pakistani intelligence agency ISI.

Thomas E. Gouttierre is the director of the Center for Afghanistan Studies at the University of Nebraska.[21] He believes that by 2009 Mullah Omar was little more than a symbolic figure and certainly not the brains behind the Quetta Shura's success.[22] Jonathan S. Landay, senior national security correspondent for McClatchy Newspapers and a veteran embedded reporter with U.S. forces in Afghanistan, takes a less dismissive attitude to Mullah Omar's importance. Following a harrowing 2009 assignment in which his unit was caught in a firefight with Taliban fighters, he came to see Mullah Omar as the inspirational leader of an expanding Taliban movement with closer ties to Al Qaeda than before 9/11.[23] Landay maintains that Mullah Omar's influence on the spread of jihad in Pakistan and Afghanistan is actually underestimated by Western sources. He believes that Omar's Quetta Shura (council) has built its own high-level networks within the Middle East, that its religious mission overpowers its political one and that the group is drawing support from all over the Muslim world.[24] He and his colleagues also believe that the Obama administration continues to miss the big picture in Afghanistan and Pakistan by narrowing the argument to hunting Al Qaeda and then offering up solutions that will never work. He quotes Marvin Weinbaum, a former State Department intelligence analyst now with the Middle East Institute. "The White House, as well as Congress and the U.S. military, 'have got to level with the American people, and they are not doing it. . . . They are taking the easy way out by focusing on the narrow interests of protecting the homeland' from Al Qaida."[25]

The Haqqani Network

More notorious and widely known were the exploits of Jalaluddin Haqqani, his son Sirajuddin Haqqani and their Waziristan-based web of tribal and Al Qaeda affiliates known as the Haqqani Network. According to Matthew DuPee at the Naval Postgraduate School in Monterey, California, "The Haqqani network has proven itself to be the most capable [of the insurgent groups], able to conduct spectacular attacks inside Afghanistan."[26] According to Anand Gopal, the Haqqani network was responsible for a coordinated attack on government buildings in Khost in May 2009, which featured multiple suicide bombers as well as numerous high-profile attacks, "including a raid on a luxury hotel in Kabul in January 2008 and a massive bombing of the Indian Embassy in Kabul that left forty-one people dead in July 2008."[27] Haqqani is also blamed for the more recent December 30, 2009, attack on a U.S. base in eastern Afghanistan that killed seven CIA agents and contractors, and a January 2010 gun, grenade and suicide-bomb attack on a luxury hotel and government ministries in Kabul.[28]

Born of the U.S.-financed war against the Soviet Union, the Haqqani network represented the worst kind of blowback possible for the United States.[29] According to author Steve Coll, Haqqani's accomplishments against the Soviets had all been backed by the full support of the CIA.[30] Known to be the fiercest and most effective of the Mujahideen commanders, Jalaluddin Haqqani endowed his network of fighters battling the U.S. military with a close affiliation to Osama bin Laden and Al Qaeda,[31] as well as numerous personal relationships with wealthy Saudi sheikhs[32] and high-level operatives in Pakistani intelligence.[33] According to author Gerald Posner, the anti-Soviet Afghan war was as much a godsend for the Saudi royal family as it was for the Afghan Islamists. "Some prominent Saudi officials, like Prince Bandar, as well as his father, defense minister Prince Sultan, saw the Soviet aggression as a chance to form a closer bond with Washington. It was a rare chance, they argued to other Saudi ministers, to replace Israel as America's strategic partner in the Middle East. And as far as the Americans were concerned, the Saudis had suddenly become a cash cow."[34] Writes journalist Anand Gopal, "Haqqani was an early advocate of the 'Afghan Arabs,' who, in the 1980s, flocked to Pakistan to join the *jihad* against the Soviet Union. He ran training camps for them and later developed close ties to al-Qaeda, which developed out of Afghan-Arab networks towards the end of the anti-Soviet war."[35] Former Democratic Congressman Charlie Wilson referred to Haqqani as "goodness personified."[36] In describing Wilson's relationship to Haqqani in his book, *Charlie Wilson's War*, George Crile wrote that "He [Wilson] was moving with an army of technoguerrillas swaggering about the Hindu Kush looking for the opportunity to take on the biggest and baddest the Soviets had to offer."[37] Now, Haqqani's technoguerrillas had replaced bad Soviets with even badder Americans, and they were beating them too.

By 2009 Haqqani's network was aligned with the Taliban, Pakistan's ISI and Al Qaeda but operated independently. According to Anand Gopal, Haqqani joined the Taliban government during the 1990s but was never a part of their movement, nor did he agree with their objective of establishing an Islamic emirate. Instead, Haqqani supported the creation of an Islamic republic.[38]

Haqqani's terror campaign was known to express the wishes of Pakistan's ISI and its fixation on Pakistan's primary enemy—India. An October 8, 2009, car bomb that exploded outside the Indian embassy in Kabul, killing two police officers and fifteen civilians while wounding more than sixty people, was reported to be the work of the Haqqani network.[39]

According to Gopal, "The Haqqanis command the lion's share of foreign fighters operating in the country and tend to be even more extreme than their Taliban counterparts. Unlike most of the Taliban and Hizb-i-Islami, elements of the Haqqani network work closely with al-Qaeda. The network's leadership is most likely based in Waziristan, in the Pakistani tribal areas, where it enjoys ISI protection."[40]

In the areas under their control in Afghanistan's southeastern provinces of Paktia, Paktika, Khost, Logar and Ghazni, Haqqani's network functions as a parallel government, and even Afghan government officials need letters of transit from Haqqani to use the roads.[41]

Gulbuddin Hekmatyar and the Hesb-i-Islami

Much could be said about Gulbuddin Hekmatyar, going back to 1973 and the core of the original foreign-indoctrinated corps of Mujahideen fighters. Described as "brutal, capricious, and violently anti-American,"[42] Hekmatyar earned his earliest reputation not from fighting, but from throwing acid at women who did not share his preferences for clothing.[43]

In our book, *Invisible History: Afghanistan's Untold Story*, we relayed the story of an Afghan woman who witnessed Hekmatyar and his associate Ahmed Shah Massoud attack an unsuspecting young student at Kabul University during their student days. It wasn't until the war against the Soviet Union that the woman fully appreciated who the acid throwers were. She testified:

I learned from some of the professors that the assailants were Ahmadshah Panjshiri (from Panjshir provice) and Gulbudin Kunduzi (from Kunduz province). At that time people didn't know about the assailants' last names. Up to date, I do not remember if . . . any criminal investigation took place about the incident.

I had not seen the two assailants before nor [did I see] them after the incident. But I . . . vividly remembered the two pairs of eyes of those assailants after twelve years when they became famous for their fights against the invading army of the USSR. I saw their photos all over the world as mujahideen.[44]

Hekmatyar was also reported to have been imprisoned in Kabul for his part in the killing a Maoist fellow student at Kabul University in the early 1970s.[45] He received the bulk of CIA money during the 1980s, funneled through Pakistan's ISI. Although he was an ISI and CIA favorite, Hekmatyar's legitimacy as a fighter, his effectiveness, his loyalties and even his goals raised doubts in the Peshawar-based U.S. press corps. According to *CBS News* stringer Kurt Lohbeck, Hekmatyar's reputation had no basis in reality but was instead an elaborate ruse concocted by the CIA and Pakistan's ISI to elicit Congressional support for the Mujahideen.

Gulbaddin had no effective fighting organization. He had not a single commander with any military reputation for fighting the Soviets or the Afghan regime. He had made alliances with top regime military figures. And he had killed numerous other mujahaddin commanders. Yet the United States government and the covert agencies were doing their best to convert that lie into reality.[46]

Alfred McCoy, author of the *Politics of Heroin* explains how Hekmatyar got away with the charade.

During the decade-long covert war, the American press

published positive reports about Hekmatyar, the leading recipient of U.S. arms shipments, ignoring his heroin dealing and human rights abuses. A year after the Soviet withdrawal in 1989 stripped the Afghan war of its national security imperatives, the *New York Times* finally reported what it called "the sinister nature of Mr. Hekmatyar" and the *Washington Post* published a page 1 expose about his heroin syndicate.[47]

Hekmatyar's ambitions to seize Kabul during the final days of the war came with the full backing of the Pakistani military and with no regard for civilian casualties. Even the CIA became alarmed when, in 1990, 700 Pakistani trucks containing 40,000 long-range rockets rumbled from Peshawar towards the outskirts of Kabul for Hekmatyar's plan to rain death on the Afghan capital.[48] Following the collapse of the Afghan government, there was no one to stop him as he bombarded Kabul's heavily populated neighborhoods from the surrounding hills, killing and wounding untold numbers of people and reducing much of the city to rubble.[49]

Hekmatyar's Hesb-i-Islami party supported Hamid Karzai in the August 20, 2009, elections. In April 2009, special representative to Afghanistan and Pakistan Richard Holbrooke was reported to have met with a Hekmatyar emissary in the hope of luring him into a relationship with the Afghan government.[50] According to Peter Lee, a businessman with a background in Asian affairs, the campaign to rehabilitate Hekmatyar as an Afghan messiah was still alive and well despite his demonic reputation. "The unpredictable Hekmatyar, who has survived the Jihad, the civil war, defeat at the hands of the Taliban, exile in Iran, an assassination attempt by the CIA, and return to Afghanistan as an insurgent leader, is the great hope of all parties as the only Pashtun strongman untainted by al-Qaeda and possibly capable of taking on the Taliban."[51]

Crossing Zero: The Pakistani Taliban

In terms of their goals and whatever issues drove its members to fight, Pakistan's version of the Taliban was a more extreme variation of its cross-border namesake, the Afghan Taliban. The so-called Pakistani Taliban was a confusing and contradictory agglomeration of tribal and international foreign fighters. Each group was known to have its own web of Al Qaeda connections, its own tribal rivalries and its own agenda, some of which included bringing down the governments of Pakistan and Afghanistan and expelling foreign armies, while others included attacking India or undermining Central Asian states and aiding Pakistan.[52] Anand Gopal writes that from 2004 on, "small, tribal-based groups calling themselves 'the Taliban' began to emerge; by 2007, there were at least 27 such groups active in the Pakistani borderlands. The guerrillas soon won control of areas in such tribal districts as North and South Waziristan, and began to act like a version of the 1990s Taliban *redux*."[53]

Merged into one umbrella organization by the end of 2007 called the Tehrik-i-Taliban Pakistan or TTP (Student Movement of Pakistan) and led by Baitullah Mehsud (until Mehsud was assassinated in August 2009),[54] the Pakistani Taliban included a variety of local, Central Asian and Arab insurgent groups that controlled a vast and strategic corridor from the Punjab to Pakistan's North West Frontier Province and FATA. That same year, as a result of Mehsud's growing concentration of power another group, calling itself the Muqami Tehrik-i-Taliban (Local Taliban Movement), split from the TTP.[55] This Taliban, composed of numerous other groups trained by Pakistan's ISI to fight in Kashmir and led by Mehsud's former deputy, Hafiz Gul Bahadur, opposed fighting the Pakistani army while concentrating its attacks on supply lines servicing the U.S. and NATO forces in Afghanistan. Bahadur and his deputy Mullah Nazir's feud with the TTP's leadership also derived from the presence of non–Al Qaeda Uzbeks and Tajiks of the Islamic Movement of Uzbekistan (IMU) and the Islamic Jihad Union (IJU), because unlike Al Qaeda, the Central Asians had interfered in the local affairs of the region.[56]

According to the *New York Times*' Carlotta Gall, as recently as late 2008, the factional fighting between these groups was so intense that Mullah Mohammed Omar had to dispatch a six-member team to Waziristan to negotiate a truce in anticipation of the U.S. surge in Afghanistan.[57] In February 2009 an agreement was reached among the three leaders, who formed a new shura called the Shura Ittihad-ul-Mujihadeen (Council for United Holy Warriors) and declared that they had overcome all differences.[58] But upon the death of Baitullah Mehsud, the struggle for control resumed. On October 4, 2009, Hakimullah Mehsud, a distant relative of Baitullah Mehsud, met with reporters in Pakistan as the new leader of the Pakistani Taliban and described his group's relationship with Al Qaeda fighters as one of "love and affection."[59] But by the end of 2009 the issue of Al Qaeda's importance was only one of a growing list of problems for Washington as it struggled with policy options while a myriad of additional terror groups assembled in Waziristan on the Afghan border, intending to derail any and all of them.

Gopal writes, "The result of all this is a twisted skein of alliances and ceasefires in which Pakistan is fighting a war against al-Qaeda and one section of the Pakistani Taliban, while leaving another section, as well as other independent militant groups, free to go about their business."[60]

The business of Pakistani extremism was not limited to Waziristan-based tribal groups. In fact by late 2009 the entire extremist movement had taken on a regional character that incorporated elements from far beyond the imaginary border line between Afghanistan and Pakistan. According to Mukhtar A. Khan of *Terrorism Monitor*, Waziristan had become ground zero for multiple terror groups including the anti-Shia Sipah-e-Sahaba Pakistan (SSP), the Jaish-e-Muhammed (JEM, Army of Mohammed) and the anti-Shia Lashkar-e-Jhangvi (LJ, Army of Jhang) from South Punjab as well as Taliban militants from Swat, Bajaur, Mohmand, Kurram and Darra Adam Khel.[61]

Another influential group with free rein inside Pakistan was the Lashkar-e-Taiba (Army of the Pure), or LeT. Accused by the Indian government of responsibility for the 2008 Mumbai terrorist attack that killed nearly 200 people and wounded more than 300, the LeT has directed its main efforts against civilian targets in the disputed territories of Jammu and Kashmir since 1993.[62] Says a Federation of American Scientists report, "During the 1990s, experts say LeT received instructions and funding from Pakistan's intelligence agency, the Inter-Services Intelligence (ISI), in exchange for a pledge to target Hindus in Jammu and Kashmir and to train Muslim extremists on Indian soil."[63] According to Husain Haqqani, Pakistan's ambassador to the United States, Lashkar-e-Taiba is the most significant jihadi group of Wahhabi persuasion, also operating under the name Markaz al-Dawa wal-Irshad (Center for the Call to Righteousness).[64] According to the South Asia Terrorism Portal, the LeT's goals reach far beyond the issue of Jammu and Kashmir to include the restoration of Islamic rule over all of India.[65]

The South Waziristan Offensive

In mid-October 2009, the long-promised Waziristan offensive aimed at rooting out these insurgent groups finally began. Hitting out with some 28,000 troops against an estimated 10,000 Taliban and 1,500 foreign fighters,[66] the planned offensive, dubbed "Operation Rah-e-Nijat" (Path of Salvation), was considered (after the Swat offensive) to be Pakistan's only major military offensive since the beginning of the U.S.-initiated war on terror.[67] But questions loomed over whether Pakistan's military would actually allow the offensive to fundamentally alter its relationship with important Taliban figures.

Key to the success of the operation was the U.S.-trained Pakistani army chief and former head of Pakistan's intelligence service, General Ashfaq Parvez Kayani.[68] According to investigative reporter Gareth Porter, Chairman of the Joint Chiefs of Staff Admiral Mike Mullen had been arguing for some time that Kayani was committed to ending Pakistani military support to the Taliban.[69] But Kayani's track record said otherwise. "The historical evidence on Kiani's [sic] past relationship to the issue suggests that he has no intention of changing Pakistani policy toward the Taliban. Kiani himself served as head of ISI from late 2004 to late 2007 and presided over the development of a major logistical and training program for the Taliban forces operating out of Pakistan's Balochistan [sic] province."[70]

If anyone embodied the dual dealing of Pakistan's military and the undermining of the U.S. anti-terror ambitions in Pakistan, it was General Kayani. According to David E. Sanger of the *New York Times* in his book *The Inheritance*, Kayani was overheard by a U.S. intelligence intercept in 2008 describing Jalaluddin Haqqani as a "strategic asset."[71] No sooner had the Waziristan offensive begun than deals were being struck with some very familiar names friendly to the Pakistani military's longer-range objectives.[72]

U.S. military sources expressed confidence in Pakistan's move to drive a wedge between Taliban renegades Maulvi Nazir and Hafiz Gul Bahadur and Hakimullah Mehsud. Ishtiaq Mahsud of Associated Press writes, "U.S. officials said the strategy is not surprising or necessarily worrisome. Because the faction loyal to Taliban leader Hakimullah Mehsud poses the most direct threat to the Pakistani government and the army, it is the logical first target."[73] But within days it was clear that the new offensive was doing little more than angering local Mehsudi and Waziri tribesman already angry at both the U.S and the Pakistani military, as reports cited that up to 260,000 civilians had fled the fighting, trapped between Taliban fighters, General Kayani's forces and U.S. drone strikes.[74]

Most believed the operation was little more than an extravagant public relations campaign aimed at pleasing U.S. military brass and public opinion, only to leave the local population wounded, betrayed and even easier prey for the Taliban's revolutionary goals.

The *Telegraph*'s Saeed Shah writes:

Mehsud tribesmen told how they'd had to abandon their homes three, or sometimes four, times since 2004, to escape army operations against the Taliban, only to see authorities later cut peace deals with the extremists. The locals returned to their homes to find them in even tighter control of the jihadists. . . . "This fight [in South Waziristan] is for American dollars," said Zahidullah Mehsud, a 19-year-old student, at a registration center for those displaced by the operation in Dera Ismail Khan. 'The government always has some deal with the Taliban. It is ordinary people who suffer. This is all an ISI game."[75]

Pakistan's plans for military attacks on South Waziristan strongholds had not gone unnoticed. Before the assault had even begun, explosions rocked Pakistan's cities. On October 10, 2009, in the third attack by militants in a week, gunmen dressed in army uniforms seized forty-two hostages and killed six people, including a brigadier and a colonel, in a fierce attack on a Pakistani military headquarters in Rawalpindi. [76]

On October 12, 2009, forty-five people including six soldiers were killed and forty-five injured in a TTP suicide attack on a military convoy in the Alpuri area of Shangla District (which borders Swat District).[77] Three days later, eight civilians and three policemen were killed and twenty-two others injured in a truck bomb attack on the Saddar Police Station in Kohat NWFP.[78] On October 28, 2009, a car bombing in Peshawar's Meena Bazaar took the lives of 117 people and injured 147 just as U.S. Secretary of State Hillary Clinton arrived on a three-day visit.[79]

Instead of soothing relations between the United States and Pakistan, Clinton infuriated Pakistanis as she bluntly pressed for Pakistan's military officials to admit responsibility for allowing Al Qaeda to use the frontier territories as a safe haven, insisting that it was hard to believe the government didn't know where they were.[80]

Pakistanis expressed outrage at Clinton's statements. They challenged her to explain why the United States had abandoned Pakistan following the Soviet withdrawal from Afghanistan, why the Bush administration had supported the military government of General Pervez Musharraf, and how the United States could justify the use of aerial drones in what one woman described as "executions without trial."[81]

The issue of drone attacks raised questions about a highly classified assassination program that Clinton refused to answer, saying only that "there is a war going on."[82] But the issue of drones—targeted assassinations, extrajudicial abductions and interrogations—went beyond America's inexplicable tolerance for Pakistan's military. The issue went directly to the heart of why there was a war going on in Pakistan and Afghanistan at all.

9. **Death from Above**

For over sixty years the United States had played both Pakistan and Afghanistan against each other in a Manichean, dualist game of superpower politics with little regard for the consequences. But like the Soviet Union before it, the United States had carried with it into Afghanistan Cold War assumptions of military power that were rendered useless by the ethnic, political and military complexities it confronted in the Afghan-Pakistan region. "We f—ing missed the boat. We totally missed the boat, man,"[1] said Colonel John Agoglia in an interview with the *GlobalPost*'s Charles M. Sennott at the U.S. military's counterinsurgency training center just outside Kabul. "We were out there chasing Al Qaeda and Tommy Taliban, and their own government was becoming very corrupt and very problematic. The people are getting taken advantage of by those people who are supposed to be protecting them. We just haven't understood the place."[2]

Before the United States could hope to "win" anything in Afghanistan or Pakistan it had to decide on more than just whom it was fighting. It had to decide what it was fighting for. Was it democracy, oil, geostrategic positioning against Russia and China, for terror, against terror, or just to save face for taking direct hits on the Pentagon and the World Trade Center on September 11, 2001? As the decision-making dragged on, the search for a legitimate strategy seemed a confused mix, dominated by those wishing to withdraw troops and limit the U.S. commitment to containing Al Qaeda (Vice President Biden, Daniel Markey) and those favoring a robust counterinsurgency campaign (General McChrystal, Bruce Riedel) requiring a permanent political and military commitment that would last for decades.[3]

In a burst of nostalgia, Boston University professor and author Andrew Bacevich suggested a return to Cold War thinking as a way of containing an Al Qaeda threat.[4] Bacevich had criticized the first Bush and Clinton administrations for their failure to scale down America's militarist appetites following the Cold War.[5] His call for its return was a reflection of just how desperate U.S. defense intellectuals had become to dispense with the nightmare brewing in Central Asia.

General McChrystal was well aware that nothing could be accomplished in Afghanistan without a change in the psychology of the U.S. approach, stating in his August 30, 2009, report that the conflict in Afghanistan was a war of ideas.[6]

McChrystal realized that changing the ideas required a change in military culture.[7] But whether the very nature of the military/industrial/media/academic complex could be moved off its primary directive in order to accommodate McChrystal's request remained highly doubtful. The decentralized nature of the opposition in Afghanistan and Pakistan defied the very culture of the Pentagon's thinking. A decentralized, non-state enemy was anathema to the rigid, high-technology and high-cost "Command, Control and Communications approach" (C3),[8] developed throughout the Cold War to decapitate the centralized Soviet bureaucracy. But the Pentagon continued to insist on applying its expensive high-technology thinking, regardless of its persistent failure to eliminate—let alone define—the enemy.

In Afghanistan, the primary vehicle of the Pentagon's program was the MQ-1 Predator drone.[9] But the efficacy of assassinating Taliban and Al Qaeda leaders in Afghanistan and Pakistan with such weapons called into question at least two major assumptions. The first was that the weapons themselves were a technically suitable replacement for human counterinsurgency forces.

The second and perhaps more important, was that this kind of warfare—with all its "star wars" death-from-above implications—was not actually counterproductive, given the negative psychological impact as well as the political schism it created between the U.S. and the local population.

Robert A. Pape, Associate Professor of Political Science at the University of Chicago, warned of the negative consequences of an over-reliance on technology.

> Decapitating the enemy has a seductive logic. It exploits the United States' advantage in precision air power; it promises to win wars in just days, with few casualties among friendly forces and enemy civilians; and it delays committing large numbers of ground troops until they can be welcomed as liberators rather than conquerors. But decapitation strategies have never been effective, and the advent of precision weaponry has not made them any more so.[10]

According to counterinsurgency experts David Kilcullen and Andrew Exum, the strategy of Predator drone strikes in Pakistan failed on all counts by creating a siege mentality among Pakistan's civilian population, "exciting visceral opposition across a broad spectrum of Pakistani opinion," but was in fact merely a "tactic" masquerading as a "strategy," which only "encourages people in the tribal areas to see the drone attacks as a continuation of [British] colonial-era policies.[11]

Kilcullen and Exum attempted to simplify the logic.

> Imagine, for example, that burglars move into a neighbor-hood. If the police were to start blowing up people's houses from the air, would this convince homeowners to rise up against the burglars? Wouldn't it be more likely to turn the whole population against the police? And if their neighbors wanted to turn the burglars in, how would they do that exactly? Yet this is the same basic logic underlying the drone war.[12]

Drone attacks and targeted assassinations opened a Pandora's box of problems for the United States that moved the issue beyond the legality of making undeclared war without civilian control into a video game fantasy-land of privatized extrajudicial killing without even direct military oversight.

In late April 2010, Anthony D. Romero, executive director of the American Civil Liberties Union, wrote to President Barack Obama at the White House on behalf of the ACLU's 500,000 members declaring that the president's program of killing suspected terrorists "including U.S. citizens—located far away from the zones of actual armed conflict . . . violates international law and, at least insofar as it affects U.S. citizens, it is also unconstitutional."[13] Romero went on to warn the president that not only was the program of targeted killing patently illegal, but by violating the legal threshold of international law, he was actually making the United States wide open to attack.[14]

On June 2, 2010, Philip Alston, the United Nations special rapporteur on extrajudicial, summary or arbitrary executions, released a report calling for a halt to CIA drone strikes against Al Qaeda and Taliban suspects in Pakistan, charging that official secrecy violated the legal principle of international accountability and risked "developing a 'PlayStation' mentality to killing."[15] Rob Crilly of the *Telegraph* writes, "Under international law, targeted killings are permitted in armed conflicts when used against fighters or civilians who engage directly in combat-like activities, Mr. Alston said. 'But they are increasingly being used far from any battle zone.'"[16]

According to Gareth Porter of the *Asia Times*, even the CIA was growing concerned that the benefits of the drone war were increasingly outweighed by the danger of blowback. Porter cites Jeffrey Addicott, former legal advisor to U.S. Special Forces and director of the Center for Terrorism Law at St. Mary's University in San Antonio, Texas. "Addicott told IPS [Inter Press Service New Agency], 'The people at the top are not believers'. . . , referring to the CIA. 'They know that the objective is not going to be achieved.' The complaints by CIA operatives about the drone strikes' blowback effect reported by Addicott are identical to warnings by military and intelligence officials reported in April 2009."[17] Added to the growing backlash against Predator drones were the now infamous "snatch and grabs"—abductions of people the United States suspects of being linked to insurgents or terror networks. Citing anonymous sources because the program is classified, author Jeremy Scahill writes:

> At a covert operating base run by the U.S. Joint Special Operations Command (JSOC) in the Pakistani port city of Karachi, members of an elite division of Blackwater are at the center of a secret program in which they plan targeted assassinations of suspected Taliban and Al Qaeda operatives, 'snatch and grabs,' of high value targets and other sensitive action inside and outside Pakistan. . . . This arrangement, the former executive said, allows the Pakistani government to utilize former U.S. Special Operations forces who now work for Blackwater while denying an official U.S. military presence in the country.[18]

According to Scahill, one of the greatest concerns about the program—in addition to the lack of Congressional oversight—was the subversion of built-in safety measures that allowed the JSOC security manager to simply award high-level clearances and authorizations to anyone he pleased. It allows Blackwater personnel that "do not have the requisite security clearance or do not hold a security clearance whatsoever to participate in classified operations by virtue of trust. . . . Think of it as an ultra-exclusive level above top secret. That's exactly what it is: a circle of love."[19]

By late 2009 it was clearer than ever that both Congress and the State Department had come to rely on the American military to set the policy agenda. In fact, it appeared that it might even be impossible for Washington to return to a civilian-orchestrated strategy of nation-building anywhere, after thirty years of militarily enforced privatized foreign policy schemes. An entire industry now existed to lobby against any efforts to reverse the trend, change the status quo or even to make private contractors accountable for the taxpayer money they received. A book by Allison Stanger, *One Nation Under Contract*, outlined the dimensions of a problem where the private sector had become a "shadow government" operating outside the law with billions of federal dollars, but little to no accountability for how or where the money was spent.

Stanger writes, "For-profit foreign aid is now a booming business, with billions of U.S. government dollars flowing into sketchy projects. Afghanistan is a prime example. . . . A 2005 congressional study reported that, of 286 schools that were to be rebuilt with United States Agency for International Development (USAID) funds by the Louis Berger Group, only 8 had been completed and that only 15 of 253 planned health clinics were operational."[20]

The psychology at the root of the problem ran even deeper at the Pentagon. The national security state built up during the Cold War was designed to protect the United States and the West from a Soviet threat through high-tech weapons systems. The perceptions created to convey the illusions of strength and security became a substitute reality to which all others defaulted. Over time, "cold" war became a new normal, rarely challenged by that other normal called reality. But at its core, the new normal was an illusion, based on a phony war and supported by the shared belief that it was better than the cost and terror of a real war that would actually be fought and perhaps lost.

The post–Cold War national-security state on which the U.S. approach to Afghanistan was based had never returned to reality once the Cold War was over. In fact, the illusion had so enraptured those in power that they had neither foreseen the collapse of the Soviet Union nor accepted its demise. Washington's blind faith in the new normal disguised its flawed character, and as the Clinton and Bush administrations built upon its illusory strength during the 1990s, the stage was set for the collapse of U.S. strategic ambitions.

That collapse finally occurred in Afghanistan and the consequences were devastating, yet Washington continued along in a dream-like haze. Author Phillip Smucker writes for the *Asia Times*:

> The Pentagon's high-tech-centric approach to the fight
> in Afghanistan has produced—since 9/11—a half-dozen

gargantuan bases—with more on the way. These are little more than anachronistic monuments to the U.S. military's superior firepower. At Bagram and Jalalabad air bases, aerial drones, commanded by joystick pilots in the deserts of Nevada, circle and land. Invisible F-16's and F-15's lay figure-eight smoke trails in the blue skies above Tora Bora. At dusk, the snow line of the Hindu Kush is flush with Apache attack helicopters and larger Chinooks. None of them are the key to victory.[21]

By late 2009 it was clear that not only were the Taliban's presence, power and patience undefeated and undeterred, the group was gaining militarily and politically. What a U.S. "victory" might actually look like was still an open question. According to well-informed sources in Washington, the United States really had no new plan for Afghanistan—civilian or otherwise—except to enhance the military option.[22] The administration had pushed Hamid Karzai for the run-off election in the vain hope that it would "appear" to legitimize the political process enough to convince Washington's Beltway elite of the worthiness of giving General McChrystal more troops. But Karzai's skillful manipulation of the election process dropped the curtain on the ill-conceived plot.[23] Even U.S. military brass questioned the administration's mishandling of the delicate issue of Karzai's leadership. Rajiiv Chandrasekaran writes:

> Criticism of the Obama administration's manner of dealing with Karzai has been most pronounced among senior military officials, who question why the State Department has not dispatched more civilians to help the Afghan leader fix the government or worked more intensively with him to achieve U.S. goals. "We've been treating Karzai like [Slobodan] Milosevic," a senior Pentagon official said, referring to the former Bosnian Serb leader whom Holbrooke pressured into accepting a peace treaty in the 1990's. "That's not a model that will work in Afghanistan."[24]

AfPak planner Bruce Riedel expressed awe at Washington's failure to alter its disastrous course. "What we are seeing is that the people who were skeptical of the Afghanistan strategy in the winter are now reopening the argument. . . . Pretty much six months has gone by without a rigorous implementation of what was agreed to and that has only made a bad situation worse."[25]

Riedel supported General McChrystal's shift from the narrow counterterrorism approach to a broader-based counterinsurgency strategy, admitting, "We have a disaster. In order to address it quickly we need shock therapy."[26]

But the time for therapy was growing short.

At remote U.S. Combat Outpost (COP) Keating in Nuristan province on October 4, 2009, eight American troops were killed during a sophisticated and well-coordinated attack by hundreds of Taliban insurgents who nearly overran the base.[27] According to Bill Roggio of the *Long War Journal*, "The US military said the attack was 'complex,' meaning it was well organized and executed. The fighters used assault rifles, heavy machine guns, rocket-propelled grenades, and heavy weapons such as rockets and mortars."[28]

The daylong battle resulted in the near complete withdrawal from Nuristan province by U.S. forces and a huge strategic victory for the Taliban.[29] The idea behind the remote combat outposts in Nuristan had been to seal off key mountain passes along the border with Pakistan to Taliban insurgents. The withdrawal of U.S. forces gave the Taliban control of a vital corridor from the Chitral Valley in Pakistan, where Osama bin Laden was thought earlier in the year to be hiding,[30] to Afghanistan's Kunar province and all of Nuristan and Nangarhar provinces. Bill Roggio of the *Long War Journal* writes, "This is a major logistics route for the Taliban, Hezb-i-Islami, al Qaeda, and other groups that rely on support from across the border in Pakistan."[31]

In his "Commander's Initial Assessment"[32] (COMISAF), dated August 30, 2009, General McChrystal had thrown down the gauntlet. Without more troops the United States would face military defeat, but it was unclear whether more troops from either Washington or Pakistan would make much difference without a fundamental change of military, political and civil strategies.

By late November 2009 the much praised offensive in South Waziristan had wilted as the Tehrik-i-Taliban militants escaped across the imaginary Zero line into an abandoned Nuristan, just as they had been trained to do by Pakistani security forces.[33]

Both the Pakistani military and the Obama administration expressed satisfaction with the offensive. Major General Athar Abbas, a Pakistani army spokesman, argued that just dislodging Taliban militants from their hideouts was enough to disrupt their ability to organize attacks.[34] But the situation reeked of the same old game of deception, as insurgents quickly regrouped and reorganized outside the battle zone while continuing a string of deadly attacks inside Pakistan's major cities. Alex Rodriguez of the *Los Angeles Times* writes:

> Taliban and Al Qaeda militants were able to easily flee South Waziristan, experts say, because government and military leaders announced their intent to carry out a major offensive in the region weeks before troops moved in. That gave militants ample time to make their escape. "The strategy has been bad," said Imtiaz Gul, a security analyst based in Islamabad, the Pakistani capital. "You don't carry out operations after making such announcements. This area gives them huge space for mobility."[35]

As Washington's paralysis deepened and Afghanistan slipped further under Taliban control, the United States faced a crisis of credibility. On the eve of President Obama's much anticipated speech announcing an escalation in the war and an increase in the number of U.S. troops,[36] it was becoming clear that despite contradictory reports in the press, the situation had gone critical, with Pakistan at the epicenter of the vortex.

This Perfect Day

Only days before the Taliban's Nuristan attack, one major player on the world scene made its opinion known, but nobody in Washington appeared to be listening. On Monday, September 28, 2009, in the Chinese government–owned English-language newspaper *China Daily*, an article titled "Afghan peace needs a map,"[37] by Li Qinggong, deputy secretary-general of the China Council for National Security Policy Studies, stated flatly that the time had come for the United States to withdraw from Afghanistan.

> To promote much-needed reconciliation among the parties concerned, the U.S. should end its military action. The war has neither brought the Islamic nation peace and security as the Bush administration originally promised, nor brought any tangible benefits to the U.S. itself. On the contrary, the legitimacy of the U.S. military action has been under increasing doubt.[38]

A Chinese challenge to the war's legitimacy was of no minor consequence. The Chinese had their own well-established agenda for curbing the growth of Al Qaeda extremism on their southern border.[39] The Chinese viewed extremists and separatists as terrorists and employed harsh military force on Muslim Uyghur separatists in their own Xinjiang Province in July 2009.[40] What should have been a wakeup call to Washington was the willingness of an official Chinese newspaper to intervene in what would normally be viewed as an internal U.S. government debate, and at a decisive and vulnerable moment in its evolution.

Of shocking interest was Li Qinggong's willingness to separate the U.S. military from its own commander-in-chief, who "since taking office . . . has been under pressure from the Pentagon for military reinforcements in Afghanistan," advising him that "the calls of war opponents over that of supporters will give the young U.S. president the best chance to extricate himself from the Pentagon's pressure."[41] Coming at a critical moment when U.S. economic power was in unprecedented decline and China's on the rise, Li Qinggong's message should have been taken as a serious sign that if Washington was not willing to decide the limits of its empire, the Chinese were.

China's involvement in Afghanistan was nothing new, but until now it had kept its ambitions largely to itself. Although denied by Beijing, the Chinese had played a supporting role in pushing the Soviets to invade in December 1979 by arming and training Islamist extremists in Xinjiang Province.[42] According to a British Round Table of 1981, "earlier in 1979 China had already tried to set up a Muslim Republic of Pamir on the Afghanistan territory of Badakhshan and the Wakhan corridor. This republic would have adjoined Xinjiang (Sinkiang) and the Pakistani-held territory of Kashmir."[43]

Under a program of planned migration initiated in 1949 under Mao Zedong, Han Chinese (China's majority population) had increased their percentage of Xinjiang's population from 6 percent to more than 40 percent by 2009.[44] In Tibet, native Tibetans considered the flood of Han Chinese migrants to be nothing less than an "invasion."[45]

In the last few years China has emerged as a major player in the economies of both Afghanistan and Pakistan. In 2007, China's Metallurgical group won a controversial $3.5 billion bid to develop Afghanistan's Aynak copper field in Logar province from Afghanistan's government.[46] In Pakistan, China's development of the strategic port of Gwadar on the Makran coast along with the United Arab Emirates' state-run International Petroleum Investment Company (IPIC)[47] was described as Pakistan's flagship infrastructure project.[48] But Gwadar was a vivid example of the multinational political infighting, interlocking interests and conflicting geopolitical agendas facing the various players in the complex AfPak scenario. Pakistan's and Afghanistan's economies both desperately needed economic development to escape chronic poverty.[49] The Aynak mine represented enormous infrastructure improvements including a $500 million electric generating facility, a railroad, a coal mine, homes, roads, schools, hospitals and a ground-water system.[50] Tied into Gwadar, the combined projects would change the face of Central Asia by opening Afghanistan, Pakistan and China by direct rail-sea link to the Persian Gulf. But helping the economies of the

AfPak region was clearly not the only consideration for a United States already at war in two countries and an India that shared a long history of warfare with both China and Pakistan.[51] Strategically, Gwadar sits only forty-four miles from the Iranian border, astride the sea lanes to the Straits of Hormuz, through which 40 percent of the world's oil tankers pass.[52] Pakistani control of the world's energy jugular combined with a Chinese listening post or naval presence would mean a decisive shift in the balance of power in the Indian Ocean—away from the United States.

By January 2010, the international financial crisis, the war in Afghanistan, its spread to Baluchistan and the deteriorating security situation in the region had resulted in a temporary hold on both the port as well as a nearby refinery.[53] But Li Qinggong's late September 2009 announcement that American troops ought to be withdrawn from Afghanistan could not be ignored. China was in South Asia to stay. Its importance as a wealthy rival to a disintegrating Western dream for strategic dominance in Eurasia would soon have to be faced.

As the United States' largest creditor—owning more than $1 trillion of American debt[54]—China was intimately tied to whatever decisions Washington made and was growing increasingly uncomfortable about many of them. All through 2009, Chinese officials expressed growing concern about Washington's fiscal policies, while influencing decision-making at an unprecedented level.[55] Anthony Faiola of the *Washington Post* wrote: "Exerting new influence as the U.S. government's largest creditor, China yesterday demanded that the Obama administration 'guarantee the safety,' of its $1 trillion in American bonds. . . . 'We have lent a huge amount of money to the U.S. Of course we are concerned about the safety of our assets."[56]

Coming only days after a confrontation between a U.S. Navy surveillance ship (submarine hunter) and five Chinese military and fishing ships, Premier Wen Jinbao's stern warning to the world's leading capitalist nation about its own financial housekeeping should have been a wakeup call to America's financial and political leadership.[57] After sixty years of writing the economic rule book, the United States was no longer free to exercise its military muscle anywhere without incurring serious or even fatal economic consequences from its Chinese financiers.

What the shift in economic power from the United States to China meant to the current phase of the new great game for Central Asia, and especially AfPak, was staggering. As part of a geopolitical strategy, since the early 1970s the United States had cultivated China as a partner against Soviet and then Russian interests in the region. The anti-Russian tilt to the strategy was largely the doing of President Jimmy Carter's national security advisor, Zbigniew Brzezinski. For nearly twenty years following the Soviet invasion, Brzezinski and the CIA maintained the cover story that it was the Soviet invasion of Afghanistan that had provoked the arming of the so-called Mujahideen freedom fighters by the United States. Then, in a 1998 interview with the French newsmagazine *Le Nouvel Observateur*, Brzezinski admitted for the first time that a program to lure the Soviets into making a fatal blunder by invading Afghanistan had begun six months before the invasion, as part of a plan to "draw the Russians into the Afghan trap."[58] In a 2005 interview with filmmaker Samira Goetschel, Brzezinski further elaborated on his admission.

> The point very simply was this. We knew the Soviets were conducting operations in Afghanistan. We knew there was opposition in Afghanistan to the progressive effort which had been made by the Soviets to take over, and we felt therefore it made a lot of sense to support those who were resisting, and we decided to do that. This of course probably convinced the Soviets even more to do what they were planning to do, which was to try to make a general takeover of the country by force of arms, and got them embroiled in an adventure that proved disastrous for them.[59]

During the past four decades, little regard was paid to the ultimate political consequences of Brzezinski's Eurasian strategy as Russian influence receded and China's grew.

In January 2009, Brzezinski appealed directly to the Chinese to continue and expand the "complex interdependence" begun in 1978 by creating a special relationship with the United States outside the structure of the Group of Eight leading industrial nations, the G8. Brzezinski writes in the *Financial Times*, "We need to develop a shared view on how to cope with the global risks. . . . We should explore the possibility of creating a larger standby UN peacekeeping force. . . . We certainly need to collaborate closely in expanding the current Group of Eight. . . . But to promote all that we need an informal G2."[60]

Brzezinski's comments reflected traditional post–World War II, U.S.-centric opinions. But as the year progressed it became clear there was not much enthusiasm from Chinese officials for renewing what might be said to be the long-term goals of a bygone era, initiated by the British Empire centuries before.

Independent commentator Henry C.K. Liu had this to say:

> Chinese Premier Wen Jiabao took the opportunity to assuage European concerns by dismissing as "groundless," the view that China and the United States—through the framework of a G-2—will monopolize world affairs in the future. "Some say that world affairs will be managed solely by China and the United States. I think that view is baseless and wrong," Wen told the press. "It is impossible for a couple of countries or a group of big powers to resolve all global issues. Multipolarization and multilateralism represent the larger trend and the will of the people."[61]

But the "will of the people," was hardly the most important criterion for Brzezinski and his intellectual conception of Central Asia as a grand chessboard.[62] When questioned at a conference on Afghanistan at the RAND corporation on October 29, 2009, Brzezinski made short work of the influence of the 50 percent of the American public who opposed the war, saying, "I don't think the fact that there is a significant public view that we ought to disengage needs to be decisive in any decision. One has to look beyond the immediate reactions. The public fatigue with the war is understandable. . . . While this is a relevant consideration, it is not a decisive one in shaping what we ought to be doing."[63]

On the other hand, Brzezinski insisted that the U.S. had to be sensitive to Pakistani opinion saying:

> We ought to be more respectful and directly so and clearly so of Pakistani strategic interest in Afghanistan. . . . I think the evidence is quite clear that the vast majority of the Pakistani elite, of the upper classes, of most of the population, is against the Taliban taking over Pakistan. This same sensitivity, this same one-sided majority does not exist regarding Pakistan's effort in Afghanistan. . . . They are afraid that a non-Taliban Afghanistan could be a neutral Afghanistan in a generic sense, but a de facto, informal partner with India. And that obviously raises major security problems for the Pakistanis, and we have to be sensitive to that. That involves some difficult diplomatic choices.[64]

One of those difficult choices directly involved implementing a balancing act between China and India. It was no secret that the United States wanted a bigger slice of India's growing military budget as the country embarked "on a major military shopping spree."[65] Over the next ten years India was planning to spend $100 billion on acquiring new weapons systems. But India's move away from old Soviet suppliers and toward modern U.S. combat systems awakened some old ghosts. Emily Wax of the *Washington Post* writes:

> The U.S. role in selling this nuclear-armed nation more firepower is starting to worry its neighbors, especially perennial rival Pakistan. India also has ongoing border disputes with another Asian giant, China, which defeated it in a short 1962 war. "This increase in India's military spending is seen with rising anxiety here in Pakistan," said Hasan-Askari Rizvi, a leading defense analyst in Pakistan. . . . "As long as India builds pressure on Pakistan militarily, Pakistan won't move

troops to fight the Taliban, period. In the future, there could potentially be a situation like the 1965 war between India and Pakistan, where both used American weapons against each other."

A freewheeling policy of supplying weapons to both sides that worked in 1965 was bound to do the opposite in 2010. In Central Asia, the United States faced a growing list of mutually incompatible choices presented by India, China, Pakistan and Iran. And as Brzezinski remarked at the close of his RAND address, "I don't think it is exaggeration to express the concern that unless we are very clever about our policy in Afghanistan we could end up being bogged down [not only] in that country but the region as a whole in a self-destructive fashion for another decade or so."[66]

It was becoming increasingly obvious that the United States was pushing the boundaries of historical irony. The country had been building a strong relationship to India throughout the Clinton and Bush administrations. Washington relied on India as an ally. In December 2006, Bush had signed historic legislation permitting civilian nuclear cooperation, reversing three decades of nonproliferation policy.[67] In the midst of the worst recession since the Great Depression, the United States also desperately needed the jobs provided by those Indian contracts.[68]

But the United States was in no position to offend the People's Republic of China, whose closest ally, Pakistan, took American money borrowed from China and used it to prepare for another war with India, while hampering the American effort with India's ally, Afghanistan. In April 2009, the Treasury Department backed off criticism that China had been manipulating its currency to the disadvantage of U.S. exports. In July 2009, the president's budget director, Peter R. Orzag, had to answer detailed questions about American health care legislation by Chinese officials who were not particularly enthusiastic about the public option.[69] In a humiliating bow to China's colonization of Tibet, in October 2009 President Obama refused to welcome the Dalai Lama to the White House, the first such rejection since the Nobel Prize winner began visiting Washington in 1991.[70] The president finally relented and received the Dalai Lama on February 18, 2010. But instead of an Oval Office ceremony, the meeting was a modest affair held far away from photographers and reporters in the White House Map Room, after which the spiritual leader of the Tibetan people was unceremoniously escorted out the back door past a mound of White House trash.[71]

Not since the Carter administration did an American leadership team appear so internally conflicted over a strategy, and not since the Carter administration, had a Eurasian strategy been so central to American interests.[72]

In an article for *Foreign Affairs* in 1997, Brzezinski had laid out the underlying reasons for a Eurasian strategy and the blueprint on which the Obama administration would engage it through its AfPak policy, twelve years later.

> Eurasia is home to most of the world's politically assertive and dynamic states. All the historical pretenders to global power originated in Eurasia. The world's most populous aspirants to regional hegemony, China and India, are in Eurasia, as are all the potential political or economic challengers to American primacy. After the United States, the next six largest economies and military spenders are there, as are all but one of the world's overt nuclear powers. Eurasia accounts for 75 percent of the world's population, 60 percent of its GNP, and 75 percent of its energy resources.[73]

If anyone understood the historical significance of a Eurasian strategy it was Zbigniew Brzezinski, for whom the conquest of Eurasia had been a lifetime pursuit. His push towards a unilateral relationship with communist China during the Carter administration had ended détente, setting U.S.-Soviet relations back thirty years and the end of the Cold War by a decade. His efforts to maintain a Eurasian strategy that would contain post-Soviet Russia provided a rationale for widening NATO as well as the unilateral foreign policy pursued by the administration of George W. Bush.[74] Brzezinski had been consulted by the Bush administration at the outbreak of the 2001 war,[75] but his understanding of and concern for Afghanistan, its history and its people was focused strictly in terms of its reputed geopolitical advantage to the United States and nothing else.

The concept of Eurasia as the "World Island," or Heartland, was conceived by British geographer Sir Halford Mackinder in the early twentieth century. Its application as a strategy called "geopolitics" was used by numerous Western empire builders for the next hundred years. Mackinder foresaw Russia, as it emerged into the twentieth century, escaping its history and, with the advancement of railroads, expanding with ferocity toward India.[76]

But there were critics who felt that the entire concept of geostrategy was lacking in some basic reality that doomed it to failure as a conceptual framework for foreign policy. Gearóid Ó Tuathail writes:

> To understand the appeal of formal geopolitics to certain intellectuals, institutions, and would-be strategists, one has to appreciate the mythic qualities of geopolitics. Geopolitics is mythic because it promises uncanny clarity and insight in a complex world. It actively closes down an openness to the geographical diversity of the world and represses questioning and difference. The plurality of the world is reduced to certain "transcendent truths" about strategy. Geopolitics is a narrow instrumental form of reason that is also a form of faith, a belief that there is a secret substratum and/or a permanent set of conflicts and interests that accounts for the course of world politics. It is fetishistically concerned with "insight," and "prophecy." Formal geopolitics appeals to those who yearn for the apparent certitude of "timeless truths." Historically, it is produced by and appeals to right-wing countermoderns because it imposes a constructed certitude upon the unruly complexity of world politics, uncovering transcendent struggles between seemingly permanent opposites ("land power"

versus "sea power," "oceanic" versus "continental," "East" versus "West") and folding geographical difference into de-pluralized geopolitical categories like "heartland," "rimland," "shatterbelt," and the like. Foreign policy complexity becomes simple(minded) strategic gaming. Such formal geopolitical reasoning is . . . a flawed foundation upon which to construct a foreign policy that needs to be sensitive to the particularity and diversity of the world's states, and to global processes and challenges that transcend state-centric reasoning.[77]

Reminiscent of the bitter rivalry between Secretary of State Cyrus Vance and National Security Advisor Zbigniew Brzezinski during the Carter years, by the time of President Obama's visit to China in mid-November 2009, his administration was speaking with two voices. Obama's visit was intended to reassure Chinese lenders, mend frayed ties and demonstrate the new administration's capacity for leadership. Instead, his deferential approach met with apparent failure and strong criticism at home. The *New York Times* editorial-ized, "President Obama went into his meetings with President Hu Jintao with a weaker hand than most recent American leaders—and it showed."[78] Criticism from the *Financial Times* was blunt. "Mr. Obama, who visited China last week, sought but failed to secure ma-terial pledges of support from Beijing for the forthcoming increase in U.S. troops, trainers and civilian aid workers in Afghanistan."[79]

The storm and stress consuming the administration worsened the following week during the first official visit to the Obama White House by a state dignitary, India's prime minister, Manmohan Singh. Singh fully supported the Obama administration's foreign policy agenda in Afghanistan. His visit was intended to signal a new era in U.S.-India relations and a symbol of India's desire to assist its wounded American partner in the region "in the wake of last year's US-bred global meltdown."[80] But instead of breaking new ground, the administration's response signaled only confusion.[81]

The most revealing response to the Indian prime minister's vis-it came from AfPak chief Richard Holbrooke, who held a two-hour press conference to assuage Pakistani sympathies, saying, "And no one in Pakistan, and no one in any other country, should read this [Manmohan's state visit] as a diminution of the importance we attach to them. It's entirely appropriate that someone has to have the first trip. . . . [The visit] should in no way be read as a diminution."[82]

But a diminution it had to be. Holbrooke's efforts to hold the line on Pakistan while at the same time President Obama was extolling the special importance of giving the Indian prime minister the honor of the first state visit, was further evidence of the administration's diplomatic desperation. If anyone was the odd man out in Central Asia it was the United States. Since the end of the Cold War, the United States had de-emphasized diplomacy, placed all of its eggs in a military basket and then proceeded to drop the basket.

America's experiment in South Central Asia had run its course, but Washington was loath to admit it. The Eurasian strategy begun during the Nixon administration under Henry Kissinger was furthered during the Carter years. Its purpose was to defeat communist Russia by wooing communist China into the capitalist bloc, turn night to day and allow communism to destroy itself from within. But as U.S. prestige waned and its influence as a beacon of free-market capitalism dimmed following two disastrous wars and a long-term economic crisis, a different kind of China began to emerge.

In Beijing in October 2009, the communist party celebrated the sixtieth anniversary of the founding of the People's Republic of China with a massive military parade through Tiananmen Square. Featuring 200,000 servicemen and women, a 2,000-strong military band and the latest weapons developed by Chinese technology, the event was the clearest indication yet that communism and China were synonymous.[83] The assumptions behind Western support for China all along had been treated as dogma. Free markets and new communications technology and just plain old "freedom" would eventually break the Communist Party's ideological stranglehold and open the country to Western Style democracy as it had in Eastern Europe and Russia.[84] In an address at Johns Hopkins University on March 8, 2000, President Bill Clinton chided the Chinese government for trying to crack down on Internet traffic by saying, "Good luck. That's sort of like trying to nail Jello to the wall."[85] But the days of such hubristic optimism were gone. The global economic crisis changed the equation, but not in a way anyone in the United States had anticipated. According to Joshua Kurlantzick of the CFR, "One poll of Chinese citizens taken by the Pew Global Attitudes Project found that people in China have a higher degree of satisfaction with conditions in their nation than in almost any country."[86] Others saw China's authoritarian communist party as dynamic and flexible, which appealed to Chinese nationalism and a rising middle class, especially urban elites. "The 'middle class is the strongest supporter of the party,' notes John Lee, a fellow at the Hudson Institute in Washington. 'These elites comprise the fastest-growing groups wanting to become party members.'"[87]

Long thought to be a relic of China's past, even Chairman Mao and his philosophy found new meaning in these hard economic times. Wu Zhong, China editor at the *Asia Times* writes, "Although Mao Zedong died 33 years ago, the founding father of communist China seems to still be alive in the hearts of many Chinese. A new wave of nostalgia for the late chairman is sweeping the nation ahead of the 60th birthday of [the] People's Republic of China (PRC) and amid the global financial crisis."[88] According to Zhong, reprinted versions of Mao's *Little Red Book* have sold five times as many copies as before the global economic meltdown.

Throughout China, statues were being erected in government offices, universities and factories.[89] Willy Lam writes in the *Asia Times*:

> There are at least three dimensions to Maoism's resurgence in China. One is simply a celebration of national pride. . . . The other two dimensions of the Maoist revival portend struggles and changes within the CCP; it is emblematic of the CCP's shift to the left, as well as the intensification of political infighting among the party's disparate factions (in China, "leftism" denotes doctrinaire socialist values, emphasis on the

party's monopoly on power, and a move away from the free-market precepts).[90]

The return of Chairman Mao reached beyond the internal politics of China. In the eastern Indian state of Chattisgarh, Maoist rebels declared a "liberated zone." Maoist rebels, once "dismissed as a ragtag band of outdated ideologues"[91] but now described as "Red Taliban,"[92] were active in twenty Indian states where the government was preparing to send 70,000 paramilitary troops to wage a counter-insurgency campaign. In Nepal, Maoists gained political credibility with the population after a twelve-year insurgency and won power in free elections. It was a phenomenon that did not go unnoticed by U.S. military observers. According to Timothy R. Kreuttner, writing in *Small Wars Journal*:

> While the government of Nepal focused on a military solu-
> tion, the Maoists grew in strength by out-governing the
> state and building a solid popular base. . . . A key Maoist suc-
> cess was its ability to mobilize dissatisfied classes and ethnic
> groups. . . . U.S. and other foreign training and material sup-
> port to Nepal were helpful militarily, but insufficient because
> they did little to address the core political, social, and eco-
> nomic problems unique to Nepal.[93]

In the face of growing global disenchantment with free-market capitalism,[94] the rise of China as an economic superpower and the surprise return of Mao as a revolutionary inspiration, the Obama administration's decision to plow ahead with a troop surge in Afghanistan looked like the wrong move at the wrong time and in the wrong place.

By the thirtieth anniversary of the Soviet invasion of Afghanistan, President's Obama's speech announcing an increase in 30,000 troops was history.[95] Hunting Al Qaeda terrorism and plots against the United States was still the cover story. But in a country the size of Afghanistan, even ten times that number of boots on the ground wouldn't matter. What did matter was that little had changed in

Washington, and it appeared that Washington could not change. Obama's speech had narrowed the parameters of America's interests in Afghanistan once again while ignoring the fact that it was the social, political and economic interests of the Afghan and Pakistani people that were key to victory.

Inklings that Washington was beginning to get the authentic message on Afghanistan had filtered out in the media prior to President Obama's speech. On October 16, 2009, Steve Coll of the New America Foundation wrote in *Foreign Policy*:

> The international effort to stabilize Afghanistan and protect it from coercive revolution by the Taliban still enjoys broad support from a pragmatic and resilient Afghan population. Nor does the project of an adequately intact, if weak and decentralized, Afghan state, require the imposition of Western imagination. Between the late eighteenth century and World War I, Afghanistan was a troubled but coherent and often peaceful independent state.[96]

Two days later in the *New York Times*, Elizabeth Bumiller wrote, "American and Afghan scholars and diplomats say it is worth recalling four decades in the country's recent history, from the 1930s to the 1970s, when there was a semblance of a national government and Kabul was known as 'the Paris of Central Asia.'"[97]

Before the Cold War settled over Central Asia, the Afghans had come to the United States asking for help. But the United States made it clear to the Afghans, often in insulting and demeaning ways, that Pakistan would be America's ally and that Afghanistan would have to fend for itself. Washington liked Pakistan's plucky military brass. They liked their style, their uniforms and their British accents. Kabul finally got the message and turned to Moscow. It was only then that Washington got interested, but even then, not very interested.

Washington's Beltway lived in perpetual fear of repeating Vietnam. It had to be romanced into escalating a conflict, and President Obama was the man to do it. The speech was the same old song and dance, but coming from this new president's lips, the old song that "We did not ask for this fight"[98] sounded particularly off key. If the United States had asked for a fight anywhere in the world it was Afghanistan. It had stoked a bonfire under Kabul throughout the 1980s and into the 1990s and then walked away as the country melted down. The United States had wanted a Russian Vietnam in Afghanistan (Secretary of Defense Robert Gates had written about it in his book)[99] but instead lit the fuse on Armageddon by helping to atomize Afghan civil society and empowering Pakistan's Islamists.[100]

President Obama's speech skirted the enormous tasks facing Washington in the months ahead. It reframed them so as to elicit public support for the military's surge while belaboring a narrow threat from Al Qaeda that paled in comparison to what was really happening in the region. In announcing his decision to send an additional 30,000 troops the president said, "These additional American and international troops will allow us to accelerate handing over responsibility to Afghan forces, and allow us to begin the transfer of our forces out of Afghanistan in July of 2011."[101] But neither the Afghan National Army nor the proposed "transfer" date of July 2011 was close to being the truth.

Retired British army officer Bob Churcher, who had helped establish the Afghan National Security Council, provided a reality check on the plan's chances for success.

> Obama wants Karzai to fight corruption and he wants to side-step Karzai to effectively deliver aid. Good luck with that. But what about the heart of the strategy, the Afghan National Army? This force is supposed to "stand up as we stand down." Sadly this is a phantom Army. Made up from the recombined remnants of Northern Alliance militias, held together by British and American money and training, it has nowhere near the numbers needed nor claimed. Drug addiction and demoralization are rampant among its soldiers. Most importantly, the ANA is a largely Tajik army.[102]

It was a Richard Nixon moment, telling the American people

he was building an exit strategy on the phantom army of an ethnic minority when in fact he was opening the door for escalation and a permanent U.S. military presence. Within days of the speech, Secretary of Defense Robert Gates and Secretary of State Hillary Clinton were backing away from the July 2011 withdrawal date.[103] On CNN's *State of the Union*, Obama's national security advisor, General James L. Jones, put it bluntly. "We have strategic interests in South Asia that should not be measured in terms of finite times. We're going to be in the region for a long time."[104] Worse still were America's Pakistani allies, who knew exactly how to keep the United States paying for their covert war against India by selectively servicing the Pentagon's fantasies. Bob Churcher writes, "Sometimes it looks different, because the Pakistanis do just enough by way of arresting Arabs and other Islamic extremists to keep the U.S. happy. . . . So it can look like the Pakistanis really are allies. But that is an illusion. Whilst the Pakistani Taliban maintain strong connections with the Afghan Taliban and other Islamic rebels and extremists, the Pakistani military regards the two forces as entirely separate."[105]

Whichever way the administration spun the plan, it didn't work. On Tuesday, December 8, 2009, General Stanley McChrystal was questioned by representative John Kline, Republican of Minnesota, at a hearing before the U.S. House of Representatives armed services committee on the veracity of the July, 2011 troop withdrawal date.

> **McChrystal**: I did not recommend that date but I did identify to my leadership that I felt 18 months, that in about 18 months, about the summer of 2011that we felt that we could make significant progress against this insurgency.

> **Kline**: I understand. Excuse me. But you didn't recommend that such a date be put out there and announced. I just want to be clear about that.

> **McChrystal**: No Congressman I did not.[106]

The administration found itself spinning in circles as the vortex drew it in deeper. In August 2009, the *Los Angeles Times* reported that the chairman of the Joint Chiefs of Staff, Navy Admiral Michael Mullen, had created what he referred to as the Pakistan-Afghanistan Coordinating Cell (PACC). Operated by General McChrystal from the basement of the Pentagon in the National Command Center, PACC was intended to bring a dose of reality to the Pentagon's detached culture, draw in the best experts on Afghanistan, cut through the Washington bureaucracy, and wrench the Afghan-Pakistan war back from the jaws of defeat. "'Adm. Mullen understands the Pentagon has to change from planning wars to fighting them,' said Army Maj. Gen. Michael T. Flynn, who served as Mullen's intelligence officer, then joined the command in Afghanistan."[107]

But how could an institution that had been at war since September 11, 2001, and had a military budget that was nearly equal to every other nation on the globe combined[108] still not have shifted from planning a war to fighting one? By December 2009 the operation, headed by General Stanley McChrystal, was in full swing. But though the PACC structure did cut through some of Washington's lingering Cold War bureaucracy and straighten out the chain of command, it did so by cutting America's civilian government out of the picture, while ensuring that general McChrystal would have an exclusive monopoly on decision-making.

Mark Perry of the *Asia Times* writes, "The PACC bypassed the normal command structure—and the State Department. It reported to McChrystal." Perry quoted a senior Pentagon official, saying "The PACC is a 'stovepipe operation . . . it's beautiful. It's headed by McChrystal acolytes, former special operations officers who view him [McChrystal] as their patron. So they follow his lead and there is no requirement for them to share any of the information they get from Kabul with the State Department or anyone else—let alone with [U.S. Ambassador Karl] Eikenberry. This is McChrystal's game.'"[109]

Perry went on to cite a former Pentagon deputy assistant James Clad who "sees the president's announcement as an unworkable compromise between contending Washington factions, each of which has a strongly militarized face. . . . 'By militarizing the response to 9/11,' Clad continues, 'we took the view that America "owns" Afghanistan in perpetuity, a foolish unilateral approach that the president's policy seems to endorse.'"[110]

An even harsher critic of the President Obama's surge was Boston University's Andrew Bacevich who saw Obama's efforts to clean up "Bush's mess"[111] as merely an excuse to continue fundamentally flawed, Bush administration policy. Bacevich writes:

> What Afghanistan tells us is that rather than changing Washington, Obama has become its captive. The president has succumbed to the twin illusions that have taken the political class by storm in recent months. The first illusion, reflecting a self-serving interpretation of the origins of 9/11, is that events in Afghanistan are crucial to the safety and well-being of the American people. The second illusion, the product of a self-serving interpretation of the Iraq War, is that the U.S. possesses the wisdom and wherewithal to guide Afghanistan out of the darkness and into the light.[112]

As Bacevich strongly implied, if the United States was doing anything by expanding the Afghan war into Pakistan, by crossing the Durand Line it was moving the United States deeper into a mythic Central Asian darkness and not the other way around. Despite an understanding that a Eurasian strategy was a myth-based philosophy and not a rational one, there was no other way to explain how the United States now found itself in the same moment as its Cold War "other," the Soviet Union had thirty years before—facing the same enemy in the same place and for the same reasons.

In Pakistan, the CIA's covert war got blacker and blacker as it merged forces with the security firm Blackwater (now renamed as Xe) to form a top secret hybridized killing unit that was both private security and government operated. It was a unit that went beyond the law, beyond Congressional or even State Department efforts at control and beyond its own classified Blackwater contract.[113] The CIA's use of off-the-books private contractors after 9/11, like Xe's founder Erik Prince, was a huge international time bomb waiting to explode. Following a January 2010 profile on Prince in *Vanity Fair*,[114] German prosecutors opened an investigation, alleging that Blackwater employees had plotted to murder terror suspect Mamoun Darkazanli inside Germany without ever informing either the German government or even their own CIA station.[115] Then in March 2010 the lid blew off a secret operation run by Defense Department official Michael D. Furlong after the CIA reportedly filed a complaint, alleging that Furlong and friends had used government funds illegally to hire a network of private Iran-Contra-era contractors as spies to track down and kill suspected insurgents.[116] One could trace the current involvement of the private sector in the U.S. war effort back to World War II, when business and government merged in unprecedented ways to combat and defeat Germany and Japan and then gear up for the Cold War against the Soviet Union. Since then, and especially since the Carter administration, as the corporation assumed more and more of the state's authority, the privatization of public wealth became the raison d'être of American capitalism, until today it is impossible to see where the state ends and the corporation begins. As Allison Stanger points out in her book *One Nation Under Contract*, "After decades of privatization, the U.S. federal government is today but a shadow of its former self."[117] But if Afghanistan and Pakistan represented the ultimate end product of the U.S.-corporate partnership in the affairs of foreign states, it could also be said that in Afghanistan and Pakistan this partnership went much deeper. In fact, the marriage of corporate/state interests that we know today was invented in the AfPak region over 400 years ago, where a government-chartered company known as the East India Company came to rule an empire and began the evolution of capitalism, from its cradle to its grave.

In the last weeks of the first decade of the twenty-first century, the Obama administration was demanding that Islamabad take action against Sirajuddin Haqqani's network and his Al Qaeda associates in North Waziristan, or the United States would cross Zero line to capture or kill them, whether Pakistan liked it or not. Declan Walsh of the *Guardian* writes, "'This is crunch time,' said a senior Pakistani official. 'The tone of the Obama administration is growing more ominous. The message is 'you do it, or we will.'"[118]

As if to answer Washington's threat, on December 30, 2009. the CIA's Forward Operating Base Chapman in Khost was infiltrated by Jordanian double agent Humam Khalil Abu-Mulal al-Balawi, who detonated a bomb killing seven CIA agents and contractors and wounding six others.[119]

Considered by the CIA to be a trusted informant, al-Balawi's easy access to an intelligence hub raised serious doubts about the agency's blindness to its long-standing relationship with Islamic extremists.

> Details about the suicide bomber's identity provided jarring insight into how a vital intelligence post in eastern Afghanistan was penetrated in the deadliest attack on the CIA in more than 25 years. Initial reports suggested that the bomber was an Afghan soldier or perhaps a local informant who had been brought onto the base for debriefing. Instead, the new evidence points to a carefully planned act of deception by a trusted operative from a country closely allied with the United States in the fight against al-Qaeda.[120]

If General McChrystal needed any more of a mandate to intensify his campaign of targeted assassination against the Taliban and Al Qaeda in Pakistan, the Chapman incident was it. Rumors that the Haqqani network engineered the attack as an act of revenge only served to heighten the drama.[121] America's war in Afghanistan was quickly devolving from being a sales brochure for sanitized, futuristic high-tech assassination to being an old-world blood feud. Pakistani journalist Rahimullah Yusufzai writes:

> The U.S. army, or the CIA to be specific, and the Haqqanis were already involved in a deadly war of revenge against each other and their blood feud has now become deadlier and

personal. In the 80s, the elder Haqqani and the CIA cooperated with each other fighting the Soviet occupying forces in Afghanistan. Today, they are rivals. The U.S. Special Forces and the CIA have killed scores of Haqqani's men, women and children in secret operations and drone strikes in Afghanistan and North Waziristan, where the family migrated from Khost after the Soviet invasion in December 1979.[122]

McChrystal wasted no time retaliating for the Khost suicide bombing. Beginning the day after, the United States launched the largest strike of Predator drone attacks since the war began. By mid-January 2010 missiles were raining down on Pakistan, killing thirteen people in two attacks on January 6, 2010, alone, in an area suspected to have been involved in staging the attack by al-Balawi.[123] According to reporter Rasool Dawar of the Associated Press, the killings involved four foreigners and two Arabs, but as was the case in many instances, intelligence officials were uncertain whether the victims were militants or civilians.[124]

On January 24, 2010, Dawar reported the deaths of six Pakistani men allegedly killed for allegedly spying for the United States, as an alleged retaliation for the alleged retaliation to the attack on the CIA base. "In the roughly three weeks following the attack, suspected U.S. drones carried out 12 missile strikes in North Waziristan and neighboring South Waziristan, an unprecedented volley since the CIA-led program began in earnest in Pakistan two years ago. . . . The militants have responded by carrying out a wave of killings targeting people they suspect of helping facilitate the drone strikes."[125] But the looming questions remained, was an escalating campaign of mutual revenge any way to win the AfPak war, and how could such a primitive blood-letting do anything but sow long-lasting seeds of anger, bitterness and determination to fight against the United States?

The techniques employed in AfPak and the wider war in general were exposing the American government to profound questions about its global military operations that led to horrific moral, legal and ethical issues both at home and abroad. On February 14, the *Washington Post* reported on the gory details of how the Obama administration had come to deal with the inflammatory legal issue of interning suspected terrorists. "On the morning of Sept. 14, helicopters flying from a U.S. ship off the Somali coast blew up a car carrying Saleh Ali Nabhan. While several hovered overhead, one set down long enough for the troops to scoop up enough of the remains for DNA verification. . . . The Nabhan decision was one of a number of similar choices the administration has faced over the past year as President Obama has escalated U.S. attacks on the leadership of al-Qaeda and its allies around the globe."[126] The article maintained that the new administration was choosing to kill, rather than capture, those it deemed terrorists. But the issue of scooping up DNA to verify an identity indicated that there was more to the story than just confirming a kill. Matching DNA required that an extensive U.S. military DNA database already existed to confirm the match. And if a DNA database existed for terrorists like Saleh Ali Nabhan, who else did it exist for? One hint of where the U.S. military was going with its high-tech biological tracking system came in a February 22, 2010 article in the Austin, Texas, *American-Statesman*. Mary Ann Roser writes, "An Austin lawyer threatened to pursue a new federal lawsuit Monday after learning that some newborn blood samples in Texas went to the U.S. military for potential use in a database for law enforcement purposes."[127] A health department spokeswoman, Carrie Williams was quoted in the article, maintaining that Texas agreed to take part in the Armed forces DNA Identification Laboratory database project because it would help in missing person's cases. According to Roser, Jim Harrington, the director of the Texas Civil Rights Project was lied to by the state's Department of State Health Services about the national database despite an earlier lawsuit brought by him over the indefinite storage of newborn blood. Roser quoted Harrington saying, "I can't tell you how many times we sat there, and they said no law enforcement. . . . They said, 'It's only about medical research, it's only about medical research.'"[128]

The McChrystal Ship

By February 2010, McChrystal's Jedi starship was being filled and the catch was grabbing headlines. On January 16, 2010, the Associated Press reported the January 9 execution by Predator drone of Palestinian Al Qaeda member Jamal Saeed Abdul Rahim in the tribal region of North Waziristan. Rahim was wanted by the FBI for his "alleged role" in the September 5, 1986, hijacking of Pan American World Airways Flight 73.[129] On January 18, 2010, the Associated Press reported the execution of twenty people in the Shaktoi area of South Waziristan—the eleventh Predator attack since the suicide bombing against the CIA in Afghanistan.[130] Despite the much heralded switch from counterterrorism to counterinsurgency, General David H. Petraeus testified to the Senate Foreign Relations Committee in December that attacks against hard-core Islamic militants would be a key part of the offensive. "We actually will be increasing our counterterrorist component of the overall strategy. . . . There's no question you've got to kill or capture those bad guys that are not reconcilable."[131]

But after the incident at Forward Base Chapman, the more the United States struck out at "the bad guys," the more it looked like a straightforward case of revenge. According to published reports in Pakistan's *The News*, "Afghanistan-based U.S. predators carried out a record number of 12 deadly missile strikes in the tribal areas of Pakistan in January 2010, of which 10 went wrong and failed to hit their targets, killing 123 innocent Pakistanis. The remaining two successful drone strikes killed three al-Qaeda leaders, wanted by the Americans."[132] According to the report, the highest number of previous drone attacks in one month was six in December 2009. By late January 2010 rumors circulated that even Hakimullah Mehsud had been successfully executed in a Predator strike.[133] Although the Pakistani Taliban denied it, within two weeks Mehsud's death was confirmed by Pakistan's interior minister, Rehman Malik who simply wrote, "Yes, he is dead."[134] According to the Associated Press report, Mehsud was targeted specifically in the stepped-up Predator campaign after he appeared in a video alongside December's CIA bomber Humam Khalil Abu-Mulal al-Balawi.[135] Then in May 2010 Mehsud appeared in an Internet video alive and well,[136] raising further doubts about the quality of the intelligence being gathered in the region.[137]

And so it went. As the technical data poured in and the killings mounted, the more the U.S. effort seemed to spiral uncontrollably over the Zero line, with the United States struggling to separate fact from fiction. Even as the confusion mounted and the purpose blurred, Washington's fixation on technological solutions barreled along at record speed. The *Boston Globe* editorialized on January 11, 2010, "Government agencies are still having trouble making sense of the flood of data they collect for intelligence purposes, a point that was underscored by the 9/11 Commission and, more recently, by President Obama after the attempted bombing of a Detroit-bound passenger flight on Christmas Day."[138]

Following the latest terror scare, opinion polls immediately reflected the American public's willingness to further sacrifice both their privacy and their civil liberties in exchange for the perception of added security.[139] The attending hysteria would provide the rationale for spending much-needed stimulus dollars on full-body scanners for U.S. airports.[140] Former Homeland Security Secretary Michael Chertoff, who was subsequently revealed to have an overt conflict of interest with a scanner manufacturer, shamelessly exploited the scare for his own financial gain.[141] But once again, the campaign for added security measures only further masked the real problem. *New York Times* correspondents Eric Lipton, Eric Schmitt and Mark Mazzetti write:

> Worried about possible terrorist attacks over the Christmas holiday, President Obama met Dec. 22 [2009] with top officials of the CIA, FBI, and Department of Homeland Security. . . . Yet in those sessions, government officials never considered or connected links that, with the benefit of hindsight, now seem so evident. . . . Just as lower-level counterterrorism analysts failed to stitch together the pieces

of information that would have alerted them to the possibility of a suicide bomber aboard a Detroit-bound jetliner on Christmas.[142]

Current and ongoing failures of America's massive intelligence directorate did not derive from a lack of data, technology, funding, personnel or talent but from the chronic dysfunction of a sclerotic Cold War national security bureaucracy that had lost track of where the game ended and reality began.[143] As applied to the AfPak war zone, the dysfunction was causing a virtual paralysis of the war effort. A scathing report compiled by NATO's top intelligence officer, U.S. Major General Michael Flynn, and released by the Center for a New American Security think tank on January 4, 2010, painted a surreal picture of U.S. intelligence.[144] "The problem is that these analysts—the core of them bright, enthusiastic, and hungry—are starved for information from the field—so starved, in fact, that many say their jobs feel more like fortune telling than serious detective work. . . . It is little wonder, then, that many decision-makers rely more upon newspapers than military intelligence to obtain 'ground truth.'"[145] Yet even there, the problem had worsened during the Bush years as reporters were not only encouraged to "embed" with U.S. military units in both Iraq and Afghanistan rather than roam free, but were graded as to their cooperativeness.[146] A story, broken by Charlie Reed of the military's own *Stars and Stripes* newspaper, revealed in August 2009 that any reporter seeking to embed with U.S. forces was subject to a background profile by the Rendon Group which branded them as either "positive," "negative" or "neutral."[147] The Rendon Group had gained notoriety in the 2003 run-up to the Iraq invasion for its role in helping the Iraqi National Congress build a case for war on false information.[148] Now they were busy padding the truth on Afghanistan. The decade-long process of neutering journalists had ensured a military-friendly and subservient media, but it had also cut off the military's only functioning mechanism for digging out the truth. In Major General Michael Flynn's final analysis, "The U.S. intelligence community is only marginally relevant to the overall strategy. . . . I don't want to say we're clueless, but we are."[149]

Published reports[150] indicated that General McChrystal was combining his intensified campaign of Predator drone strikes and expanded commando missions with a major offensive into the Taliban stronghold of Marja[151] in a bid to force the Taliban to the negotiating table.[152] According to the *Financial Times*, "By using the reinforcements to create an arc of secure territory stretching from the Taliban's southern heartlands to Kabul, Gen. McChrystal aims to weaken the insurgency to the point where its leaders would accept some form of settlement with Afghanistan's government."[153]

In London, a major conference hosted by British Prime Minister Gordon Brown, President Hamid Karzai and UN General Secretary General Ban Ki-moon was planned for January 28, 2010, to establish exactly what that settlement would look like.[154] In reality, the conference more resembled a last-minute bid to secure the lifeboats before the coalition broke apart and sank beneath the waves. *Der Spiegel*'s Gerhard Spörl writes, "There are as many objections as there are proposals. There are even differing degrees of pessimism and many secretly wish they could leave the 'Graveyard of Empires,' as Afghanistan has been called, as soon as possible."[155]

The highlight of the conference came when Afghan President Hamid Karzai invited members of the Taliban to a spring peace meeting, fueling speculation that talk of a Taliban reconciliation was more than just part of the ongoing psychological warfare campaign.[156]

Karzai had been openly inviting Mullah Omar and even Gulbuddin Hekmatyar to join his government for years.[157] According to Ahmed Rashid, secret talks were held in Saudi Arabia in the spring of 2009 at the request of Hamid Karzai with former (or now retired) Taliban, former Arab members of al-Qaeda, and Karzai's representatives.[158] Prior to the formal announcement of a U.S. military escalation in July 2009, Karzai insisted that additional troops would not be enough and called for negotiations with Mullah Omar.[159] His November 2009 call for unconditional talks with the Taliban and a national "Loya Jirga" (Grand Council) met with criticism from

Secretary of State Hillary Clinton. Gareth Porter writes, "Hillary Clinton responded by pressing Karzai to demand far-reaching concessions from the Taliban in advance of the meeting. Clinton's conditions on Taliban participation included renunciation of al Qaeda and of violence and acceptance of the Afghan constitution."[160]

Despite the various shades of political agreement on Taliban participation, a host of economic, ideological, ethnic and security issues plagued the peace-making process.

In a lengthy piece in the *New York Review of Books*, Ahmed Rashid writes, "The prevailing view in Washington is that many Taliban fighters in the field can eventually be won over, but that the present U.S. troop surge has to roll them back first, reversing Taliban successes and gaining control over the population centers and major roads. According to the current American strategy, the U.S. military has to weaken the Taliban before negotiating with them."[161] Rashid believed that the Taliban should be negotiated with, and set out a series of points under which that might become possible. Some of Rashid's suggestion were to convince Afghanistan's neighbors to agree to reconciliation; withdraw Taliban leaders' names from a UN terrorist list; have the UN Security Council give the Afghan government a mandate to negotiate; guarantee Taliban members and their families a safe return along with compensation, housing and job training, and encouraging Pakistan and Saudi Arabia to help the Taliban set up a legal political party like Gulbuddin Hekmatyar's Hesb-i-Islami.

But even if Rashid's suggestions could be implemented, the program would require a multibillion-dollar aid program that would guarantee the same safeguards to every Afghan regardless of their political views. It would face the resistance of millions of ethnic Tajik, Hazara, Uzbek and Turkmen peoples whose families suffered ethnic cleansing under Taliban rule and would require a viable Afghan government that could coexist with an influx of thousands of Taliban fighters whose very reason for existence was the destruction of anything resembling a secular Afghan nation-state. Joshua Partlow of the *Washington Post* writes, "Across the political spectrum in Afghanistan, groups have raised concerns about pushing ahead with both low-level reintegration and talks with the Taliban leadership. Ethnic minorities worry that international money intended to woo Taliban fighters will favor mainly Pashtun areas where the insurgency is most virulent."[162]

Ahmed Rashid based his assumption on what could be done in the Afghanistan of 2010 on what could have been done in the Afghanistan of 1989, when Soviet Foreign Minister Eduard Shevardnadze attempted to forge a desperate, last-minute three-way deal between Afghanistan's communist regime, the CIA and Pakistan's ISI.[163] Rashid argued that what was possible then was possible now. But 1989 was a different world. According to Mathew Rosenberg of the *Wall Street Journal*, today's Afghan warlords like Sirajuddin Haqqani were light-years apart from their forefathers. They were ruthless, savvy, well connected to foreign financial support and with no need to negotiate. "The rise of Mr. Haqqani, who is in his late 30s or early 40s, is part of a broader changing of the guard in the Afghan militant movement. A younger generation of commanders have helped transform the Taliban from a peasant army that harbored al Qaeda and was routed by the U.S.-led invasion in 2001 into a formidable guerrilla force that killed a record 520 Western troops last year."[164]

What was hardest to factor into any theorem of conflict resolution for the pro-Pakistani, Western-educated intelligentsia (among whom Rashid could be counted), was how bad the situation had become. Rosenberg writes:

> After three decades of almost continuous conflict in Afghanistan and more than a decade of upheaval in Pakistan's tribal areas, all these young men have little memory of life without war, said Rustam Shah Mohmand, a former Pakistani official. . . . "Peace talks are about bringing people into the political power structure. . . . I don't think this younger generation has any idea of politics or any desire to take part in them. . . . All they've grown up around is war and fighting."[165]

What Washington's "talk-to-the-Taliban" movement was also missing was what a return of the Taliban to power would mean to Afghanistan's women. Congressman Stephen F. Lynch (D-MA), editorialized in the February 17, 2010, *Boston Globe*, "I recently met with female members of the Afghan parliament who were very angry Karzai had proposed the Taliban appeasement plan in London[166] without getting the input of women in parliament. They said they fear for the women of Afghanistan, their basic rights of free speech, freedom of travel, freedom of association and voting rights."[167]

Lynch ridiculed the campaign to give the Taliban and Mullah Omar a more acceptable face for public consumption. "Women who violate the Taliban rules have been publicly whipped with car antennas and ferociously beaten. And if there is any lingering doubt about 'outlawing' the Taliban, consider this: in an absurd attempt to gain the support of the local Afghan population the Taliban's leader, Mullah Omar, recently announced that its members will, for now, 'cease the practice of cutting off the lips, noses and ears of detainees.'"[168]

Sima Samar, a former Afghan Minister of Women's Affairs and currently the chair of the Afghanistan Independent Human Rights Commission, expressed outrage at the prospect of Karzai forgiving Taliban atrocities and granting insurgent leaders high-level positions in the government. "I think it's just legalizing impunity. . . . Nobody is accountable, not for the past crimes and not for future ones. Anybody can come and join the government and they will be protected."[169] Karen DeYoung and Joshua Partlow of the *Washington Post* reported that it was Britain that had pushed Karzai to move further and faster than many coalition members thought advisable. Although denying it "categorically," a British official did admit that it was easier for Britain to play the midwife to a Taliban reconciliation because "The British public is more eager to leave Afghanistan and is less concerned about 'things like women's rights.'"[170]

In an interview with Ahmed Rashid by National Public Radio's Terri Gross,[171] the scenario surrounding a Taliban return began to take on surreal qualities. Rashid admitted that the Taliban were tired and were not popular, citing a recent BBC poll revealing that only 6 percent of the Afghan population would accept their return. Yet he insisted that their ability to spread fear and terror was widespread and should be the deciding factor in their reintegration, and not their lack of popularity. Gross seemed confounded at the apparent contradiction: "Now, a couple of minutes ago, you said that the Taliban are really tired, and now you're saying that they can't be defeated militarily. But if they're really tired, and they're having trouble recruiting suicide bombers, why can't they be defeated militarily?" Rashid's response—that they had penetrated a broad swath of Afghan territory beyond their own indigenous Pashtun boundaries and moved into "the west and the north. . ."[172] and that conducting a permanent war against the Pashtun Taliban was politically unsustainable for both the United States and Afghanistan—raised more questions than it answered.

Afghan human rights expert Sima Wali had taken issue with talk-to-the-Taliban advocates since their emergence in the early 1990s. It was the Taliban's horrific treatment of women that finally brought on the world's condemnation of their regime. She supported the disarming and return of Afghan Taliban to normal life after the 2001 war ended, but she consistently protested bringing Afghan Taliban into the government. Since 9/11 she expressed concern over what she referred to as the "Taliban-Lite"[173] mentality that reigned in certain inner circles of Washington and she saw the recent negotiations as simply the continuation of a policy of betrayal. She expressed her revulsion of the current efforts in a telephone interview.

> Show me a moderate Talib and I'll show you a moderate Nazi. The Taliban are a creation of ISI, and that makes them a foreign political movement regardless of whether they happen to be Afghan. They will be run by the ISI. Afghan civil society should not be expected to absorb their poison, represented by war crimes and torture perpetrated by trickery and orchestrated by the ISI. Rather than negotiating with them, women should continue to expose the truth and explode the

myths created to perpetuate their agenda through the actions of Hamid Karzai. It is clear to me now that he was installed to sell out the Afghan people. The Taliban's record of their treatment of Afghanistan's women should be the only guide to this process.[174]

By intent or incompetence, the Bush administration's "war on terror" had virtually forced the marriage of the ultraconservative Taliban to the long-smoldering issue of the Durand line and the creation of an independent Pashtunistan.[175] But the importance of the issue as a core problem facing the U.S. effort continued to elude president Obama's advisors. Scott Shane writes in the *New York Times*:

> In his address Tuesday night [December 2009], the president mentioned Pakistan and Pakistanis some 25 times, and called Pakistan and Afghanistan collectively "the epicenter of the violent extremism practiced by Al Qaeda." But he might have had an easier time explaining what he was really proposing had he set the national boundaries aside and told Americans that the additional soldiers and marines were being sent to another land altogether: Pashtunistan. . . . Today, the enemies of the United States are nearly all in Pashtunistan, an aspirational name coined long ago by advocates of an independent Pashtun homeland.[176]

Instead of addressing the core issue of Pashtun nationalism, the Obama administration was continuing to fight Pashtuns on both sides of the Zero line exactly the way the British had nearly two centuries before. The Pashtun Taliban were linking up with other terror groups in Central Asia and, according to Ahmed Rashid, infiltrating weapons, ammunition and men back into Central Asia and "preparing the ground for a long, sustained military campaign."[177] But if the U.S. didn't want Islamic extremism expanding throughout Central Asia, was legitimizing it by giving extremists a political base in the Afghan government really a genuine solution?

M.K. Bhadrakumar suggested a possible motivation for the strange course of American diplomacy. "There is an ominous overtone to Western reports. Al-Qaeda was used after all as justification for the overthrow of Saddam Hussein in Iraq in 2003. This is where the US's idea of reconciliation with the Taliban merits scrutiny. The idea is eminently sensible, at a time when Muslim anger is rising, there is growing disillusionment with Obama, and when the U.S. is dangerously close to confronting Iran and a need arises to 'split' Muslim opinion. At the same time, the Taliban's reconciliation also makes realpolitik."[178]

The U.S. had used many of these same Islamic militants as a "realpolitik" tool for destabilizing the Soviet Union during the 1980s. Was Obama's AfPak strategy really a break with the past, or was it just the next phase of Zbigniew Brzezinski's Eurasian conquest? "The ascendancy of malleable Islamist forces also has its uses for the U.S.'s containment strategy towards China (and Russia). Islamists lend themselves as a foreign policy instrument. The rise of Islamism in Afghanistan cannot but radicalize hot spots such as the North Caucasus, Kashmir and the Xinjiang Uighur Autonomous Region in China. China has the maximum to lose if a Taliban regime re-emerges."[179]

Dealing with the Taliban in some form or other had been part of a master plan for resolving Afghanistan since the early days of the Clinton administration. For a handful of Washington insiders like Richard Holbrooke, now regrouped inside the Obama administration, it looked like the old plan was being resumed. "Holbrooke thumb-sketched a futuristic scenario for the region. . . . On the one hand, Holbrooke gently eased Central Asian concerns regarding the U.S.'s expected reconciliation with the Taliban. At the same time he calmed the Central Asian mind regarding the Taliban's extremist ideology. This is not the first time that Central Asian leaders have heard from a visiting U.S. official a projection of the Taliban as a benign movement. Holbrooke echoed what U.S. diplomats almost routinely propagated in the 1996–1997 period as the Taliban came to power in Kabul."[180]

As the weeks rolled on, the inconsistencies that came with juggling the numerous conflicting interests began to show through the rhetoric. McChrystal's campaign to free the village of Marja of Taliban insurgents was presented as a key military component of the new AfPak strategy.[181] Code named Moshtarak, meaning "together" in the Afghan language of Dari, Marja was conceived as an example of the United States military working with the Afghan government on a major offensive for the very first time. More than just a battle to defeat entrenched Taliban fighters and to win Afghan hearts and minds, Marja was a crucial test in a desperate battle to win back lost credibility, reassure America's NATO allies and prove that the new intellectual doctrine of COIN could succeed where eight years of counterterrorism had failed.[182] As seen from McChrystal's viewpoint, Marja was a battle for the American public's imagination and the very future of the American military. *Washington Post* reporters Greg Jaffe and Craig Whitlock write:

> Military officials in Afghanistan hope a large and loud victory in Marja will convince the American public that they deserve more time to demonstrate that extra troops and new tactics can yield better results on the battlefield. . . . The other group McChrystal wants to influence is the Afghan people and the Taliban, who saw the July 2011 withdrawal deadline as a sign of wavering U.S. will. "This is all a war of perceptions," McChrystal said on the eve of the Marja offensive. "This is all in the minds of the participants."[183]

The battle for perceptions featured what General McChrystal described as "government in a box," a kind of franchisable, political "happy meal" for Afghanistan with a pre-selected government administration, mayor and police force, ready to go the minute the shooting stopped.[184] But whether the "perception" of something new and different was enough remained an open question. On the day an Afghan government flag was raised over the village of Marja[185] suicide bombers struck Kabul, killing sixteen people.[186] According to reports, at least six of the dead were Indian citizens working in

Kabul, including government officials. The attack was the worst since October 8, 2009, when seventeen people were killed outside the Indian embassy by a car bomber.

Authors Thomas H. Johnson and M. Chris Mason likened General McChrystal's operation at Marja to nothing less than British literature's most famous pipe dream. "The release of Tim Burton's new blockbuster movie, *Alice in Wonderland*, is days away. The timing could not be more appropriate. Lewis Carroll's ironically opium-inspired tale of a rational person caught up inside a mad world with its own bizarre but consistent internal (il)logic has now surpassed Vietnam as the best paradigm to understand the war in Afghanistan."[187]

Johnson and Mason described Marja as nothing more than a massive exercise in public relations, with one intention only; "to shore up dwindling domestic support for the war by creating the illusion of progress," while the media gulped down the bottle labeled "drink me," and shrank into insignificance.

> So here we are in the AfPak Wonderland, complete with a Mad Hatter (the clueless and complacent media), Tweedledee and Tweedledum (the military, endlessly repeating itself and history), the White Rabbit (the State Department, scurrying to meetings and utterly irrelevant), the stoned Caterpillar (the CIA, obtuse, arrogant, and asking the wrong questions), the Dormouse (U.S. Embassy Kabul, who wakes up once in a while only to have his head stuffed in a teapot), the Cheshire Cat (President Obama, fading in and out of the picture, eloquent but puzzling), the Pack of Cards army (the Afghan National Army, self-explanatory), and their commander, the inane Queen of Hearts (Afghan President Hamid Karzai).[188]

End Game

General McChrystal had promised a different, more effective kind of war that would deliver results by the summer of 2011. Key to its success was the United States' relationship to Pakistan and Pakistan's relationship to the Taliban. The late-January 2010 capture of the Taliban's top commander and second in command to Mullah Omar, Mullah Abdul Ghani Baradar, was at first thought to represent the long-awaited pivotal shift necessary to cripple the Taliban leadership. Touted as the product of a joint operation between Pakistani and U.S. intelligence, Bruce Riedel referred to the raid as a "sea change in Pakistani behavior."[189] Within days, further arrests were made, leading Dexter Filkins of the *New York Times* to write, "The arrests—all three in Pakistan—demonstrate a greater level of cooperation by Pakistan in hunting leaders of the Afghan Taliban than in the entire eight years of war."[190] A late-February 2010 report suggested that Baradar would be turned over to the Afghan government as soon as judicial authorities had a chance to consult on the matter. But no sooner had the roundup of additional members of the Taliban's leadership begun[191] than it was realized the game had taken on a whole new level of deception. Lyse Doucet of the BBC writes, "Reports are now emerging that Mullah Baradar may have been detained earlier than the dates cited in the original story in the *New York Times*. It's also still not clear how much involvement U.S. intelligence had in the raid and how much access they have to this valuable source, who has an enormous store of knowledge about the movement, including their contacts with the ISI."[192] According to later reports, Baradar's capture had not been part of a targeted action at all but was an "accident."[193] Pakistan had subsequently denied the CIA access to Baradar after his arrest and kept them away from him for two critical weeks. Instead of throwing open the door to a wealth of the Taliban's most important secrets, Pakistan's courts slammed it shut on February 25, 2010, when a close aide to Osama bin Laden—retired ISI squadron leader Khalid Khawaja—filed a constitutional petition to block any transfer of prisoners.[194] By the first week of March, Baradar and a slew of the highest-level Taliban leadership were safely under the protective custody of Pakistan's military, and the United States was left holding the bag. Gareth Porter writes, "The refusal of Pakistani intelligence to turn over Taliban leader Mullah Abdul Ghani Baradar and as many as six other top

Taliban figures to the United States or the Afghan government has dealt a serious blow to the Barack Obama administration's hopes for Pakistani cooperation in weakening the Taliban."[195]

In their March 2010 *Foreign Policy* Article, Johnson and Mason unwound the Baradar speculation to reveal the fiasco beneath:

> The military and political madness of the AfPak Wonderland has entered a new chapter of folly with the detention of a few Taliban mullahs in Pakistan, most notably, Mullah Baradar. . . . Instant Afghanistan experts at the White House and pundits at august Beltway institutions like the Brookings Institution are absurdly calling the detentions a "sea change" in Pakistani behavior. In fact, it is no such thing. Pakistan has not abandoned overnight its 50-year worship of the totem of "strategic depth" its cornerstone belief that it must control Afghanistan, or its marriage to the Taliban, and anyone who believes that is indulging in magical thinking.[196]

In Johnson and Mason's opinion, the current U.S. AfPak agenda and the mainstream media's reporting on it was no longer just misinformed or misguided, it has crossed the line into being completely out of touch with reality. "This is not cooperation against the Taliban by an allied state; it is collusion with the Taliban by an enemy state. Pakistan is in fact following its own perceived strategic interests, which do not coincide with those of the United States."[197]

Johnson and Mason's assessment of Pakistani intentions and Beltway fecklessness would be confirmed when, in late August 2010, Dexter Filkins of the *New York Times* offered an alternative telling of the Baradar capture:

> Both American and Pakistani officials claimed that Baradar's capture had been a lucky break. It was only days later, the officials said, that they finally figured out who they had. Now, seven months later, Pakistani officials are telling a very different story. They say they set out to capture Mr. Baradar, and used the CIA to help them do it, because they wanted to shut

down secret talks that Mr. Baradar had been conducting with the Afghan government that excluded Pakistan, the Taliban's longtime backer.[198]

Although U.S. authorities denied some of the details, the account remained consistent with Pakistan's long-established animosity towards India and its goals for Afghanistan, citing an anonymous Pakistani security official as saying, "We protect the Taliban. They are dependent on us. We are not going to allow them to make a deal with Karzai and the Indians."[199]

As spring 2010 approached it was clearer than ever that Pakistan continued to control events, and the United States appeared either helpless or unwilling to stop it. Pakistani General Ashfaq Parvez Kayani and the ISI would continue to covertly support elements of the Taliban and would use Baradar and his ruling circle as bargaining chips against India, Afghanistan and its ally and benefactor, the United States.[200] If anything had changed it was Kayani's boldness in openly claiming Pakistan's right to control the destiny of Afghanistan as part of its "strategic paradigm"[201] and sphere of influence.[202] It also provided Kayani with the opportunity to establish his authority over Pakistan's sickly civilian government. On March 16, 2010 Kayani took the unprecedented step of presiding over a meeting of Pakistan's key federal secretaries at the military's General Headquarters. According to a secretary, it was the first time ever that a military chief had presided over what had traditionally been considered a "civilian set-up."[203]

Obama's AfPak strategy appeared to have been quickly overwhelmed by the realities of the new Great Game for Central Asia. As brazenly summed up by retired Pakistani general and former head of the ISI Hamid Gul, "America is history, Karzai is history, the Taliban are the future."[204] But even more damaging to the United States was the further loss of faith in American leadership. The London conference on Afghanistan provided a critical opportunity for the Obama administration to rebuild America's image and reputation on the world stage. Instead, the chaotic aftermath provided even further proof that the United States could barely negotiate in its own interests, let alone control the interests of the other parties.

By March 2010 it was clear that Richard Holbrooke's AfPak strategy was viewed as a failure. M.K. Bhadrakumar writes, "The US's AfPak special representative Richard Holbrooke has run into headwinds almost simultaneously in four key capitals in and around the Hindu Kush—Islamabad, Kabul, Tehran, and New Delhi. . . . No sooner had the crowd dispersed from London, than AfPak diplomacy began unraveling."[205]

Pakistan's sudden "capture" of Taliban deputy head Mullah Abdul Ghani Baradar set off a chain of events prompting Hamid Karzai to issue a decree removing Afghanistan's Electoral Complaints Commission (ECC) from United Nations control and place it under his authority, thereby denying the NATO countries key leverage over the future of the Afghan parliament.[206] Holbrooke's subsequent trip to the capital of Bishkek in Kyrgystan was seen by the Iranians as a thinly disguised plot to meet with the notorious leader of the Baluch-Iranian Jundullah terrorist organization Abdul Malik Rigi at the U.S. airbase at Manas.[207] Rigi was subsequently snatched out from under the Americans by Iranian security forces, leading to accusations by Iranian opposition groups that either U. S. intelligence had reached new levels of incompetence or the United States had somehow engineered his capture in a "backroom deal" with the Iranian government.[208] According to Iranian news reports, Rigi was executed on June 20, 2010, after confessing that a U.S. operative in Pakistan had contacted him after clashes in the Iranian city of Zahedan. Rigi claimed the U.S. promised "military equipment, arms and machine guns," as well as a base along the Iranian border with Afghanistan. "The Americans said Iran was going its own way and they said our problem at present is Iran . . . not al-Qaeda and not the Taliban."[209]

In India, Holbrooke shocked authorities by denying that the recent terrorist attack in Kabul, which claimed sixteen lives including those of six Indian citizens, was a "targeted" attack on Indians,[210] despite an Afghan intelligence service claim that evidence pointed to Pakistan's involvement.[211]

Holbrooke's efforts were reminiscent of his earlier attempts to play down the state visit of Indian Prime Minister Manmohan Singh to Washington in order to soothe Pakistani sensitivities.[212] But whatever the reason for Holbrooke's actions, combined with the previous events, the incident was viewed internationally as just another indication that the Obama administration was in out of its depth. M.K. Bhadrakumar writes, "The *Washington Post* reported that the AfPak diplomacy has confused all protagonists, including the Afghans. . . . The worst thing that can happen to a diplomat is to be expected to stay in the limelight and yet not do anything. Second, unlike the 1990's, the US's influence is much diminished today, but its diplomats work as if they operate in a unipolar world."[213]

On February 20, 2010, Washington's unipolar world got a little smaller as the Dutch government collapsed in a dispute over its involvement in Afghanistan, forcing the withdrawal of 2,000 Dutch NATO forces from service in Uruzgan Province.[214] Added to rising public opposition in Germany and Britain, the cracks in the NATO commitment were shaking the foundation of Washington's national security establishment. Days later Defense Secretary Robert Gates crossed his own personal zero line in an address to the National Defense University when he criticized Europe's growing anti-war sentiment as a threat to peace.[215]

By the spring of 2010, Afghanistan had become emblematic of the growing crisis between Washington and Europe's capitals, with Cold War hawks like Zbigniew Brzezinski and former U.S. Secretary of State Madeleine Albright trying desperately to breath new life into what the U.S. military's own thinkers were describing as "a discredited Cold War rule set."[216]

According to its latest mission statement, written by a team headed by Albright, NATO had to win in Afghanistan, expand ties with Russia and China, counter the threat of Iran's missiles, and assure the security of its twenty-eight members.[217] But not everyone saw NATO's demand for a European rededication to a cold-war-global-security-order ruled over by a diminished United States as a desirable policy for the future. Foreign policy commentator William Pfaff wrote from Paris on May 18, 2010:

> At the NATO experts' meeting Monday, which considered proposals for what NATO should become by 2020, former U.S. Secretary of State Madeleine Albright asked why the Europeans should pay twice for their defense. I can think of one unspeakable but not unthinkable reason why European countries might wish to defend themselves. What if it should prove one day that the threat the Europeans need to defend themselves against is of American and Israeli origin?[218]

Pfaff admitted that his speculation of a future Europe vs. U.S.-Israel conflict was an "hysterical geopolitical fantasy." Yet the very idea that a veteran policy observer like Pfaff should find such a development thinkable was indicative of the fundamental geopolitical shifts at work as America's defense intellectuals staggered into the second decade of the twenty-first century.

In apparent disregard for Afghan public opinion,[219] in March 2010 the British government dispatched its special representative for Afghanistan, Sir Sherard Cowper-Coles, to Kabul as a caretaker ambassador to supervise the endgame of negotiating the Taliban into the Afghan government. According to Julian Borger of the *Guardian*, Cowper-Coles was now being sent to Kabul because "British officials believe that significant Taliban leaders are ready to start talking about a political settlement in which they would sever ties with al-Qaida and put down weapons in return for a role in politics."[220] The report stated that Cowper-Coles' primary mission was to "inject more substance" into the gathering by ensuring that the Loya Jirga planned for April 29, 2010, was more than just a political stunt by Hamid Karzai. In the fall of 2008 the *Times* of London reported that Cowper-Coles, then the British ambassador to Afghanistan, had "reportedly" expressed no confidence in the American plan to expand the war and claimed that the best hope for U.S. "would be the installation of 'an acceptable dictator' within five or ten years and that public opinion should be primed for this."[221]

On March 28, 2010, President Obama made a highly secretive surprise visit to Kabul that featured a personal confrontation with Afghan president Hamid Karzai. Staying in Afghanistan only three hours after a thirteen-hour nonstop flight, the U.S. president was reported to have expressed his "growing vexation" with the Afghan president on a range of issues, including "promises that Mr. Karzai has made on governance and even reintegration with certain reconcilable members of the Taliban insurgency."[222] But instead of reviving international confidence in his AfPak leadership, the visit betrayed the growing impression that time was running out on the administration's ability to influence Karzai and the direction of events. Alissa J. Rubin and Helene Cooper write:

> "He's slipping away from the West," said a senior European diplomat in Kabul. Mr. Karzai warmly received one of America's most vocal adversaries, President Mahmoud Ahmadinejad of Iran, on an official visit to Kabul in early March. Mr. Karzai met with him again this past weekend in Tehran, when the two celebrated the Afghan and Iranian New Year together. Last week Mr. Karzai made a three-day trip to China, a country that is making economic investments in Afghanistan, notably in its copper reserves, taking advantage of the hard-won and expensive security efforts of the United States and other Western Nations.[223]

As with his failed attempt to boost Massachusetts Attorney General Martha Coakley's flagging campaign for Ted Kennedy's vacant Senate seat with a last minute visit to Boston, Obama's secret dash to Kabul smelled of desperation. Only days before the visit, China's government-owned *China Daily*, criticized the United States for running a "protection" racket for its contractors in Afghanistan, threatening China's security, putting extra pressure on China's defense plans and consolidating its military presence in Central and

South Asia. In short, "The U.S. has an offensive counterterrorism strategy, in which Afghanistan is being used as a pawn to help maintain its global dominance and contain its competitors."[224]

But if, as the Chinese claimed, the U.S. mission was really all about containing global competition while running a protection racket for an unpopular Hamid Karzai, by early June 2010 it was obvious that even Karzai was getting tired of it. By then, Cowper-Coles' role in "injecting more substance" into the Afghan peace process had itself succumbed to the serpentine meanderings of the London-Washington foreign policy aristocracy. Simon Tisdall of the *Guardian* mourned the loss of Cowper-Coles' experienced hand. "The sudden departure of Sir Sherard Cowper-Coles, Britain's special envoy to Afghanistan, represents another body blow for a US-led policy that is already shredding at the edges. . . . With Obama's deadlines for a December policy review looming and a start to the withdrawal scheduled for July next year [2011], the west's Afghan policy, as directed from Washington, is in deep trouble. Losing a talented and savvy operator like Cowper-Coles can only make matters worse."[225]

Capitulation

In May 2010 Ahmed Rashid summed up the "Three Continuing Crises" facing the United States that the Obama administration had been unable to address. "The first is the lack of a consistent Afghan partner. A new Pentagon report to the U.S. Congress states that only 29 out of 121 key districts support President Hamid Karzai. . . . The second problem is that even if the U.S. maintains a troop presence in Afghanistan for another five years, as it is likely to do, the Europeans will certainly decline to do so. . . . The third problem is that the Afghan Taliban and other extremists groups are still able to find sanctuary in Pakistan."[226] Rashid went on to cite recent polls suggesting that 72 percent of Britons, 62 percent of Germans and over 50 percent of Europeans from Spain to Sweden wanted their troops withdrawn immediately.

No matter how badly things had gone in Obama's first year,

by June 2010 it was clear that the combined stresses of a spreading Taliban insurgency, a duplicitous Pakistan, an increasingly disgruntled China and a profoundly corrupted Afghan government were rapidly pushing both Afghanistan and Pakistan towards a collision. The storm broke on the opening day of the Kabul peace conference on June 2, 2010, when a multipronged attack began within moments of Karzai's opening address to the 1,600 hand-picked delegates invited to the conference.[227] Bending to Karzai's wishes, over the next three days, delegates agreed to a number of proposals to declare an immediate ceasefire and to establish a high commission that would open dialogue with the Taliban. But whether this was an actual step towards peace or just another public relations stunt wasn't immediately clear. A Reuters report noted after the event, "But there were few signs that the Taliban, who have dismissed the jirga as a phony American-inspired show to perpetuate their involvement in the country, were ready to respond to the peace offer."[228]

Following the conference, Karzai made his move by accepting the resignations of his two top security officials, Amrullah Saleh, head of the National Directorate of Security, and Interior Minister Hanif Atmar. Reportedly spawned by the security breach, the real reason for the resignations went to the core of the ongoing U.S.-Karzai feud. As a major figure in the Northern Alliance, Saleh (an ethnic Tajik) had helped the United States to overcome the Taliban in 2001, while Atmar as a young man served in the communist-era intelligence agency of the People's Democratic Party of Afghanistan, fighting against the U.S.-backed Mujahideen holy warriors.[229] American officials expressed concern that Karzai's action against people they admired and trusted in their fight against the Taliban was "very bad news." "'Atmar really disagreed with the reintegration of the Taliban into the police and the army,' the official said. 'He had some problems with it, and, frankly, we agreed with him.'"[230]

Within days the Saleh-Atmar conflict erupted into a new round of accusations, with Karzai proclaiming he had lost faith in the Americans' ability to defeat the Taliban. Jon Boone of the *Guardian* writes, "Privately Saleh has told aides he believes Karzai's approach is dangerously out of step with the strategy of his western backers. . . . According to the source, Saleh is deeply concerned by Karzai's noticeably softer attitude towards Pakistan."[231] But the heart of the American concern wasn't Karzai's newfound eagerness to sell out his country to his longtime Pakistani enemies. It was Karzai's apparent willingness to suddenly deal his American backers out of the game at the very moment of their greatest strategic weakness.

10. Decrypting the Afghan-U.S. Agenda

Our government complains that the Karzai administration is corrupt, but the greater problem—never mentioned—is that it is fundamentalist. The cabinet, courts and the Parliament are all largely controlled by men who differ from the Taliban chiefly in their choice of turbans.[1] —Ann Jones

Karzai's move was the latest in a long series of enigmatic events surrounding the U.S. involvement in Afghanistan. But it was impossible to know whether his actions and those of his profoundly corrupted government were the intended or unintended consequence of the neoconservative philosophy of the George W. Bush administration. If anyone was the hand-picked choice of the Bush administration neoconservatives it was Hamid Karzai, and if anyone could be said to be the hand doing the picking it was Bush's Afghan specialist Zalmay Khalilzad. According to Thomas Ruttig, a United Nations official present at the mid-2002 Kabul Loya Jirga that installed him:

> Khalilzad was the driving force behind THE mistake committed in the post-Taleban period that basically and fundamentally undermined the—possible!—emergence of a stable Afghanistan by bringing in the warlords again and allowing them unrestricted access to the new institutions. . . . Re-empowered militarily and politically, the warlords expanded the realms of their power into the economy. With their [U.S. Special Forces] Alpha Team seed capital they took over that part of the economy that matters in Afghanistan, the poppy- and heroin business. With the profits from this they expanded

into what remains of the licit economy: import of luxury goods, cars, spare parts, fuel and cooking gas [and] real estate, often by occupying government-owned land."[2]

When asked in the spring of 2010 whether Khalilzad should be invited back to assist the Obama administration, former Special Assistant to President Reagan, Reagan-Doctrine Architect and honorary Afghan "Freedom Fighter"[3] California Congressman Dana Rohrabacher told interviewer Michael Hughes:

[Khalilzad] oversaw the establishment of a government that was unable to function in Afghan society. And on top of that he browbeat people into accepting Karzai. He even browbeat the ex-King of Afghanistan Zahir Shah into accepting him. Khalilzad was not in the anti-Taliban camp in the 1990s, so why the hell would we bring him in now? By forcing Karzai into office, Khalilzad snatched defeat out of the jaws of victory because the Taliban were beaten at that point.[4]

To both Ruttig and Rohrabacher, Khalilzad's ultimate crime— like the U.S. manipulation of the Ngo Dinh Diem regime in Vietnam—was his corruption of the Karzai regime. Yet the idea that chaos, as a form of extreme social engineering, may have actually been the plan cannot be ignored.

If anyone represented the core philosophy of the neoconservative defense intellectual class that came to dominate U.S. foreign and military policy from the Reagan era to that of George W. Bush era, it was Zalmay Khalilzad. Born in the northern Afghan city of Mazari Sharif in 1951, Khalilzad first came to the United States as a high school exchange student sponsored by the American Field Service program.[5]

He received his bachelor's and master's degrees from American University in Beirut and his doctorate degree from the University of Chicago. There he met and studied along with Paul Wolfowitz under the RAND nuclear warfare theorist, former Trotskyite and father of neoconservatism Albert J. Wohlstetter.[6] It was Wohlstetter's early 1970s series of articles in the *Wall Street Journal* and *Strategic Review* that had prompted the politicized corruption of CIA analysis known as the Team B experiment.[7] It was the Team B's adherents both inside and outside the Carter administration who set the stage for luring the Soviets into the Afghan trap.[8] And it was the same Team B brain trust of Wohlstetter acolytes that brought on the strategic military disasters of Iraq and Afghanistan by corrupting and politicizing the intelligence process.[9]

In her 1972 book about Vietnam, *Fire in the Lake*, author Frances FitzGerald wrote of the perverse illogic of another of Wohlstetter's onetime RAND protégés, Herman Kahn.[10]

> Just before his departure for a two-week tour of Vietnam in 1967, the defense analyst, Herman Kahn, listened to an American businessman give a detailed account of the economic situation in South Vietnam. At the end of the talk—an argument for reducing the war—Kahn said, "I see what you mean. We have corrupted the cities. Now, perhaps we can corrupt the countryside as well." It was not a joke. Kahn was thinking in terms of a counterinsurgency program: the United States would win the war by making all Vietnamese economically dependent upon it. In 1967 his program was already becoming a reality, for the corruption reached even to the lowest levels of Vietnamese society.[11]

After three decades of war it took little time and less effort to corrupt every level of Afghan society, but in Afghanistan, official corruption, both American and Afghan, seemed to have been the objective from the outset. By June of 2010 it appeared that even the Taliban had gotten in on the take. Dexter Filkins of the *New York Times* writes, "For months, reports have abounded here that the Afghan mercenaries who escort American and other NATO convoys through the badlands have been bribing Taliban insurgents to let them pass. . . . The officials suspect that the security companies may also engage in fake fighting to increase the sense of risk on the roads and that they may sometimes stage attacks against competitors."[12] Filkins went on to write, "The investigation is complicated by the fact that some of the private security companies are owned by relatives of President Karzai and other senior Afghan officials."[13]

Charges that Hamid Karzai and his family engaged in corrupt practices were nothing new.[14] But the bizarre marriage of America's pro-business, neoconservative Washington to Afghanistan's pro-business and often pro-Taliban right wing, was a hidden political dynamic dishing up a perpetual "war on terror" gravy train for the Pentagon and an amoral and hungry new breed of Washington insiders. A 2007 report by Canadian journalist Arthur Kent described the DNA that ordered the Bush administration's Afghan agenda.

> In the 1990s, a new generation of displaced Afghans, the sons and daughters of diplomats and businessmen—and former guerrilla commanders—took root in their parent's adopted homeland. It was within that diaspora that Hamed Wardak came of age. . . . Hamed wrote his senior thesis under the mentorship of Jeane Kirkpatrick, formerly Ronald Reagan's ambassador to the UN, and the godmother of the neoconservative movement.[15]

According to Kent, after graduating from Georgetown University in 1997, Wardak won a Rhodes scholarship to Oxford and flirted with Taliban sympathies after feeling pressure from other young, D.C.-area extremists. "Gradually, however, Hamed came under the influence of Kirkpatrick's philosophical soulmates, notably Marin Strmecki, a Republican essayist and political facilitator with the Smith Richardson foundation. Strmecki worked at the Pentagon under Dick Cheney in the first Bush administration, along with Lewis 'Scooter' Libby—and Zalmay Khalilzad."[16]

Hamed Wardak's rise to fame and fortune was just one example of a neoconservative Afghan-American establishment represented by Zalmay Khalilzad with no philosophical or political aim other than the transfer of hundreds of billions of American tax dollars directly into private hands under the banner and covert protection of the "war on terror."

When Khalilzad was appointed ambassador to Afghanistan in December 2004 and Strmecki was appointed "Afghanistan policy coordinator," the same month, the program went into high gear. Arthur Kent writes, "Within Khalilzad's makeshift provisional authority in Kabul, he championed a creation called the Afghanistan Reconstruction Group. ARG achieved two cherished goals for the administration: putting a select group of loyal American and Afghan-American business hawks in charge of US-funded development projects; and doing so while completely bypassing the State Department."[17]

Outside the boundaries of normal oversight procedures while under the auspices of Donald Rumsfeld's office at the Pentagon, ARG became a watering hole of high priced contracts for well placed friends of the Bush administration with Marin Strmecki joining the board of directors and Louis Hughes, a former president of Lockheed Martin, at the helm. In 2005, when Khalilzad's successor, career diplomat Ronald Neuman, tried to break up ARG and return contracting to the State Department, Khalilzad arranged for Rumsfeld to send Marin Strmecki to Kabul. The result of Strmecki's "political audit" was Neuman's replacement by the White House.[18]

By June 2010, Congress was just beginning to catch up on the systemic corruption and culture of failure built into the American aid program when more relatives of Hamid Karzai showed up on the radar in the form of a private security company known as Watan Risk Management. Controlled by Karzai cousins Ahmed Rateb Popal and his brother Rashid Popal, the huge Watan Group consortium engaged in telecommunications, logistics and security, specifically, the protection of trucking convoys under contract to the U.S. government.[19] According to Dexter Filkins of the *New York Times*, "The source of the taxpayer money is a $2.1 billion contract called Host Nation Trucking,[20] which pays for the movement of food and supplies to some 200 American bases across this arid, mountainous country, which in many places has no paved roads."[21]

Watan Risk Management was no ordinary security firm, and the Popals no ordinary Afghan businessmen. According to Aram

Roston of *The Nation*, in addition to Ahmed Rateb Popal having once served as interpreter for the Taliban regime's ambassador to Islamabad, both he and his brother Rashid had been charged and convicted in the United States of trafficking in heroin.[22]

Another company featured in the investigation was NCL Holdings, controlled by Zalmay Khalilzad's neoconservative Afghan-American poster boy, Hamed Wardak. Listed in a Congressional report by the Subcommittee on National Security and Foreign Affairs titled "Warlord, Inc.,"[23] Hamed and his company it seemed were privileged players in a U.S.-invented cult of "mafia networks"[24] that transferred vast sums of U.S. dollars through a handful of favored front companies directly to Afghan gangsters, warlords and the Taliban as well. Aram Roston writes, "In this grotesque carnival, the U.S. military's contractors are forced to pay suspected insurgents to protect American supply routes. It is an accepted fact of the military logistics operation in Afghanistan that the U.S. government funds the very forces American troops are fighting."[25] According to the Congressional report, Wardak's NCL Holdings wasn't even in the trucking business. It subcontracted out all of its trucking operations under its Host Nation Trucking (HNT) contract and had no direct experience with managing trucking before this contract.[26]

Congressman Tierney's "Warlord, Inc." painted a sordid picture of chaos, deception and destruction in Afghanistan that was the hallmark of America's neoconservative brain trust. However it appeared on the surface, President Obama's AfPak war had been built upon chaos from its inception. By the summer of 2010, there was little left for him to do but to face up to it.

Collapse

It wasn't just the sharp increase in violence that finally brought the message home to Washington,[27] or that civilian casualties were up 31 percent in the first six months of 2010,[28] or that the United States had passed the sad milestone of reaching 1,000 Americans killed,[29] or that Army suicides had reached a record number not seen since the Vietnam era,[30] or that reports indicated Pakistan's ISI continued to control the Taliban and plan attacks,[31] or even that Afghanistan had become America's longest war.[32] It was the realization that General McChrystal's counterinsurgency campaign in Marja did not work and that the United States faced the real possibility of defeat in Afghanistan.

If anything stood as a metaphor for the U.S. military's mental exhaustion it was the collapse of America's top commander, General David Petraeus, before a Senate armed service committee hearing on June 15, 2010.[33] Author James Carroll wrote of the myth-like resonance of the event. "An inch below the open skepticism that greeted the general at the Senate hearing is the mounting fear that American troops will be removed from both countries, if ever, not in withdrawals but evacuations. Given Petraeus's status as the embodiment of contemporary martial hope, it was impossible not to take his momentary fainting spell as an omen. A national breaking point approaches. At issue is nothing less than the inbred sense of American goodness."[34] Coincident with House committee hearings on the corporate/regulatory incompetence behind the BP Gulf oil spill, Petraeus's momentary ill health painted the stark picture of a punch-drunk American leadership on the verge of collapse.

The accepted wisdom of the Obama administration's AfPak policy rested on the fact that the Bush administration had undercut the U.S. effort early on by diverting troops and money away to Iraq while leaving Afghanistan to drift back under Taliban control. General McChrystal's troop surge and counterinsurgency campaign was intended to address that "mistake," and the battle for the rural town of Marja was intended to show how. But after months of playing hide and seek with the Taliban and failing to finish even the first stages of the operation as defined by Anthony Cordesman's The New Metrics of Afghanistan, support for Marja as well as the counterinsurgency program itself faced a major reassessment.[35]

Portrayed stoically in early June 2010 by the *New York Times* as "too soon to call,"[36] and the *Washington Post* as "Still a long way to go,"[37] by the end of the month support for the surge and the follow-up campaign for Kandahar, was evaporating.[38]

Compounding the high anxiety was the Michael Hastings interview in *Rolling Stone* magazine[39] in which an intemperate General Stanley McChrystal savaged Obama administration official Richard Holbrooke and referred to Vice President Joseph Biden as "Bite Me." McChrystal paid for his comments when President Obama called him to the White House and personally fired him from his job within days of the interview's public release. But the issue of counterinsurgency and whether it could ever be made to work anywhere remained the more serious issue looming behind McChrystal's firing. Retired colonel Douglas Macgregor, who attended West Point with McChrystal, was cited by Hastings in the article as saying, "The entire COIN strategy is a fraud perpetrated on the American people. . . . The idea that we are going to spend a trillion dollars to reshape the culture of the Islamic world is utter nonsense."[40] William R. Polk, a veteran U.S. government official, foreign policy consultant and author, wrote, "We were sold a phony policy in counterinsurgency—one that essentially tried to substitute technique for politics, enthusiasm for wisdom, money for knowledge. There is no record that counterinsurgency ever worked anywhere, and it is certainly not working now in Afghanistan."[41]

Polk zeroed in on a fundamental flaw in the Marja campaign. "General McChrystal decided to employ overwhelming force. So, what is particularly stunning about the failure in Marja is that the force applied was not the counterinsurgency model of 1 soldier for each 50 inhabitants but nearly 1 soldier for each 2 inhabitants. If these numbers were projected to the planned offensive in the much larger city of Kandahar, which has a population of nearly 500,000 they become impossibly large."[42] Polk's argument not only undercut the thinking behind the planned Helmand offensive but the entire movement for counterinsurgency. If a ratio of 1 soldier to every two civilians didn't work, there weren't enough soldiers in the Western world to make COIN a viable option and without COIN, the U.S. had no viable working strategy at all.

The U.S. Senate's unanimous confirmation of General David

Petraeus as McChrystal's successor was an immediately attempt to cap Washington's leaking support for the spreading Afghan war. "We are in this to win," Petraeus said as he took command.[43] But if William R. Polk's arguments against COIN were anywhere near to being right, there was nothing that Petraeus could do to avoid a Vietnam-style disaster. Nor would it prevent Pakistani General Ashfaq Parvez Kayani and a host of Middle East backers of Al Qaeda from believing that the moment they had been waiting for had finally arrived.

If any further evidence was needed of Pakistan's true ambitions in Afghanistan and of their loyalty as a U.S. ally, it was the front-page story in the June 24, 2010, *New York Times*[44] revealing that Kayani was "exploiting the troubled United States military effort in Afghanistan" in order to negotiate the Al Qaeda–linked Haqqani network into the Afghan government of Hamid Karzai. But it didn't stop there. Only the week before, a report by Harvard researcher Matt Waldman claimed that the ISI, the Haqqani network and the Taliban all maintained an extensive collaboration.[45] Waldman also claimed President Asif Ali Zardari had made a secret visit to Taliban prisoners in a Pakistani prison to arrange for their release earlier in the year, consoling them with promises of future support.[46]

Since the end of the Cold War, the United States had been looking for an enemy to match the Soviet Union and had come up empty-handed until 9/11. Refocusing the efforts of the world's largest and most expensive military empire on Al Qaeda would provide the incentive for a massive rearmament, just the way the Soviet "invasion" of Afghanistan had done two decades before.

Following the American invasion of Afghanistan, hunting Al Qaeda had become the raison d'être of the American national security bureaucracy employing 854,000 military personnel, civil servants and private contractors with more than 263 organizations transformed or created including the Office of Homeland Security.[47] The sheer scope of the growth and the extensive privatization of intelligence and security was so profound that, according to the *Washington Post*'s Dana Priest and William M. Arkin, it represented "an alternative geography of the United States, a Top Secret America hidden from public view and lacking in oversight."[48]

The report admitted that after nine years of unprecedented spending and growth, the labyrinth of secret bureaucracy put in place after 9/11 was so massive and convoluted that its ability to keep Americans safe was impossible to determine. Even worse than that, by the summer of 2010 the bureaucratic monster had taken on a life of its own. The logic train of the war on terror and its fundamental rooting in Afghanistan had finally become clear. The perpetual Taliban/Al Qaeda threat fueled a perpetual war that could never be won, justifying an endless string of military expenditures, which required restrictions on civil liberties and governmental transparency, which then prevented Americans from seeing how their money was spent.[49] Locked out of this "alternative geography of the United States," Americans were thereby helpless to stop their democracy and their economy from being pirated right out from under them.

Thanks to General Kayani, Hamid Karzai and the revelations by the *New York Times*,[50] by the summer of 2010 the word was finally out that whatever impact the "war on terror" had made on Islamic worldwide extremism (which many claimed it made only worse)[51] it was above all a spectacular boondoggle.

The shocking Sunday, July 25, 2010, WikiLeaks release of 92,000 documents[52] by the *New York Times*, *Der Spiegel* and the *Guardian* was the opportunity for Washington's experts to square themselves with the fatal collapse confronting them and who was to blame for it. According to the *New York Times*, "Some of the reports describe Pakistani intelligence working alongside Al Qaeda to plan attacks."[53] The documents also revealed numerous embarrassing specifics that had been either downplayed or avoided entirely by the U.S. military in the nine-year-old war, including that the Taliban used portable heat-seeking missiles against NATO aircraft; that the United States employed secret commando units to "capture/kill" insurgent commanders that claimed notable successes but at times had also gone tragically wrong, killing civilians and stoking Afghan resentment; that the military's success with its Predator drones was highly overdramatized—some crashed or collided, forcing American soldiers to undertake risky retrieval missions to prevent the Taliban from claiming the drone's weaponry.[54] In addition, the reports revealed that retired ISI chief Lieutenant General Hamid Gul "has worked tirelessly to reactivate old networks, employing familiar allies like Jalaluddin Haqqani and Gulbuddin Hekmatyar, whose networks of thousands of fighters are responsible for waves of violence in Afghanistan."[55]

If anything was a guide to who'd been drinking the Kool-Aid being dished out on Washington's K Street it could be measured by the degree of acceptance to the new information. According to the *Boston Globe*, Congressman James McGovern (a Worcester, Mass. Democrat) maintained, "that the documents show a far grimmer situation than members of Congress have been told about in classified briefings."[56]

Massachusetts Senator John Kerry initially declared that the documents raised "serious questions," about policy.[57] By Monday, July 26, 2010, Kerry was echoing the official line, defending Obama administration policy while insisting there was little new in the documents. The reasons for Kerry's second thoughts were obvious. Matt Viser of the *Boston Globe* writes, "Kerry has what is seen as a special relationship with Pakistan; he has welcomed the country's army chief to his house for dinner and accepted flowers from the country's president. 'There's no question that senator Kerry was instrumental in leading the initiative to triple our economic assistance to Pakistan,' said Molly Kinder, a senior policy analyst at the Center for Global Development, which tracks U.S. aid to Pakistan."[58]

Kept out of the document release by WikiLeaks, the *Washington Post* hissed and fumed, editorializing dismissively that the 92,000 documents contained little of interest,[59] while citing counterterrorism expert Andrew Exum as comparing the importance of the documents to the discovery that "Liberace was gay."[60]

Had the documents amassed an equal amount of evidence that Iran or Syria were working with Al Qaeda to carry out attacks on American troops, U.S. bombers would have been warming up on the flight decks by sundown. But when it came to Pakistan, there was only restraint. James Ridgeway writes for *Mother Jones*:

> The documents are dark reading indeed. They describe Pakistani agents meeting directly with the Taliban, supporting commanders of the insurgency, and even training suicide bombers. But for anyone versed in the contemporary history of Afghanistan, they are hardly news. The Wikileaks data dump is just the tip of the iceberg; ISI black ops and double-crosses date back at least three decades. Pakistan's Directorate for Inter-Services Intelligence, or ISI, is merely feeding a monster it helped create back in the 1990s—with the full knowledge of the United States.[61]

Darker still were the revelations about the CIA's suggested use of the Afghan women's issue as a propaganda tool to enliven public support for the NATO-led International Security and Assistance Force among European women.[62] Written up in a Red Cell Special Memorandum[63] dated March 11, 2010, under the heading "Appeals by President Obama and Afghan Women Might Gain Traction," the memo suggested that "Afghan women could serve as ideal messengers in humanizing the ISAF role in combating the Taliban because of women's ability to speak personally and credibly about their experiences under the Taliban, their aspirations for the future, and their fears of a Taliban victory."[64] To accomplish this the memo recommended that media opportunities should be created "to share their stories with French, German, and other European women" with the express objective of overcoming a "pervasive skepticism among women in Western Europe toward the ISAF mission."[65]

Coincidentally or not, one prominent media opportunity arrived with the August 9, 2010, *Time* magazine cover story featuring an Afghan woman named Aisha who had run away from her husband and was punished by the Taliban by having her nose and ears cut off.[66] The cover story, under the heading "What Happens If We Leave Afghanistan," painted a compelling picture for staying the course. But to author Ann Jones, who had interviewed the woman weeks before the story broke, the sensational cover article only diverted attention away from the double bind the United States found itself in. Jones wrote in *The Nation*. "If we leave, the Taliban may seize power or allow themselves to be bought in exchange for a substantial share of the government, to the detriment of women. But if we stay, the Taliban may simply continue to creep into power, or they may allow themselves to be bought (or 'reconciled') in exchange for bribes and a substantial share of the government, all to the detriment of women, while we go on fighting to preserve that same government."[67]

The women's issue had been a central theme of the Afghan conflict for generations, yet was consistently passed over by a U.S. government and major media obsessed with ridding Afghanistan of any vestiges of modernity or Soviet-backed socialism at any cost. In our own first trip to Afghanistan in 1981, we documented the vital role played by women and their male supporters in advancing Afghan society through education and modernization. We discovered in the countryside that women and their schools were the frequent targets of Mujahideen "freedom fighters." But we also found absolutely no interest from our mainstream media sponsor, *CBS News*, in making the complexity of Afghanistan's internal struggle a part of the story about the anti-Soviet war in Afghanistan. Nor do we find the issue clearly defined even today, as Washington's efforts rest more on public relations than genuine attempts to help both Afghan men and women forge a moderate Afghan society. To quote Ann Jones:

> Every Afghan woman or girl who still goes to work or school does so with the support of a progressive husband or father. Several husbands of prominent working women have been killed for not keeping their wives at home, and many are threatened. What's taking place in Afghanistan is commonly depicted, as it is on the *Time* cover, as a battle of the forces of freedom, democracy and women's rights (that is, the United States and the Karzai government) against the demon Taliban. But the real struggle is between progressive Afghan women

and men, many of them young, and a phalanx of regressive forces. For the United States the problem is this: the regressive forces militating against women's rights and a democratic future for Afghanistan are headed by the demon Taliban, to be sure, but they also include the fundamentalist (and fundamentally misogynist) Karzai government, and us.[68]

To the Washington insiders the actual revelations disclosed by the leaked documents circulated by WikiLeaks were less important than the exposure of systemic failure they represented. The disclosures had taken the floor out from under the assumptions of the war on terror, the invasion of Afghanistan and the U.S. mission there imposed following 9/11. America's ally Pakistan collaborated with the Taliban against American interests, and U.S. contractors paid protection money to Taliban insurgents.[69] While billions poured in from the United States to support a hopelessly corrupted Afghan government, suitcases filled with over a billion dollars in banknotes left Kabul airport every year for safe havens in the Middle East.[70] As months turned into years it was becoming obvious that the "war on terror" produced more terrorists than it could ever defeat.

Yet Washington seemed aloof—a city of isolated mandarins, completely detached from the world they governed and dismissive of any effort to bring them down to earth. Little wonder that the U.S.-led enterprise in Afghanistan had lost the public's support. Even the Afghan people themselves had come to believe the United States wasn't really there to fight the Taliban, but pretended to fight as an excuse for remaining in the region.[71]

Daniella Peled writes for the *Guardian*, "It is common belief among Afghans that the west has no intention of ending the conflict in Afghanistan. It's near impossible to find anyone in Afghanistan who doesn't believe the U.S. are funding the Taliban: and it's highly educated Afghan professionals, those employed by ISAF, USAID, international media organizations—and even U.S. diplomats—who seem the most convinced."[72] Peled cited a general belief among Afghans that both the United States and Britain had an interest in prolonging the war in order to remain for the long term, and that the continuing violence was proof.[73]

Despite the WikiLeaks revelations, the firing of General Stanley McChrystal, the failure of the Marja "surge" and the growing disapproval of the American public at the longest war in American history, on Tuesday, July 27, 2010, the United States Congress voted to pay for President Barack Obama's Afghan troop increase. The bill, which had already been passed by the Senate, provided $33 billion to fund U.S. troops in Afghanistan and Iraq but only $4 billion in foreign aid.[74] But aside from the increase in troop strength, exactly where the Obama administration differed significantly from the Bush administration remained a mystery. Even the cornerstone of the Obama plan—the July 2011 timetable—seemed less and less politically feasible as the war ground on into the late summer of 2010.

In response to criticism by Pakistani president Asif Ali Zardari in early August 2010 that the international community was "losing the war against the Taliban,"[75] U.S. Undersecretary of Defense Michele Flournoy countered, "Neither are we losing nor is July 2011 set for the forces to pack their bags. We are not going anywhere."[76] On August 11, 2010, the *New York Times* appeared to affirm Flournoy's statement, strongly implying that however many troops were to be withdrawn in the summer of 2011, it would "be of fairly limited numbers."[77] The article went on to say that administration officials were holding to their plan for a "conditions-based" withdrawal in July 2011. But whether those conditions could ever be met remained highly improbable.

On August 12, 2010, in a lengthy editorial citing the WikiLeaks disclosures, the *New York Times* raised mortal doubts about the Obama administration's handling of the war. The list of fundamental concerns included the persistent weakness of the Afghan Army, the ongoing corruption of the Afghan government, the relentless double game being played by Pakistan and whether the United States could rely on Hamid Karzai and General Ashfaq Parvez Kayani.[78] The *New York Times* also pointed out the consistent ambiguity of the president's message, citing the conflicting signals about the deadline, the strategy and its commitment to the war.[79] Adding to the ambiguity were the facts on the ground. On August 23, 2010, the *Washington Post* reported on the ongoing expansion of three $100 million air bases in northern and southern Afghanistan, none of which were expected to be completed before late 2011 and all of which were intended for U.S. and not Afghan forces. Walter Pincus writes, "Despite growing public unhappiness with the Afghan war— and President Obama's pledge that he will begin withdrawing troops in July 2011—many of the installations being built in Afghanistan have extended time horizons."[80]

By autumn 2010 it was clear that whatever objective the administration claimed for its AfPak agenda, little had changed. In fact it could be said that when it came to the Durand/Zero line,the underlying strategic objective remained the same as it had with the first British invasion of 1839.

Selig Harrison cut through the president's rhetoric and homed in on the Pentagon's ulterior motives as the key to American thinking.

> The biggest obstacle . . . is not likely to come from Pakistan, but from a Pentagon mindset in which the projection of U.S. power is viewed as a desirable end in of itself. Some of the 74 U.S. bases in Afghanistan, including airfields, are designed solely for counterinsurgency operations. . . . But the mammoth airfields at Bagram and Kandahar are projected to grow in the years ahead. . . . Congress is considering funding requests, totaling $300 million, to establish new bases at Camp Dwyer and Shindand, close to the Iranian border, and Mazare-Sharif, near Central Asia and Russia. . . . The underlying issue that the President has yet to address is the future of the air bases, and the larger question of whether the Pentagon will still be using Afghanistan to further its global power projection goals long after the Taliban and Al Qaeda are a distant memory. Until he faces up to this issue, no diplomatic cover for U.S. disengagement will be possible.[81]

11. Closing Zero

Looking back at active U.S. involvement in Afghanistan since the 1970s, it appeared that the world's self-proclaimed defender of freedom and democracy had become lost in a distorted vision of itself as it pursued and then became its own opposite. From the end of the Vietnam war in 1975 to the Marxist coup of 1978, to the Soviet invasion of 1979, to the privatization of the Central Asian conflict through the notorious Bank of Credit and Commerce International (BCCI),[1] to the financing and training of Mujahideen "holy warriors," to the emergence of Al Qaeda and the Taliban, Afghanistan set new limits for greed, corruption and reckless policy. It is only when you remembered that it was the British East India Company that charted this kind of chaos, that the whole picture of corporate-state corruption became as clear as an azure sky of deepest summer.

Beginning in the year 1600, the East India Company became the model for a whole new kind of cooperative business venture that combined private enterprise with state backing. Its agents and directors ran opium to China; its mercenary soldiers murdered indiscriminately and invented secret wars with private armies, which drew in governments and created self-fulfilling prophecies within self-fulfilling prophecies.

Centered around the vast wealth of Eurasia, the quest for treasure was always a toxic mix of Christian zeal and high finance, which built a British empire under which all the conquered peoples were subsumed.

The United States owed its current policy framework to that empire, much as it owed its current failures in Central Asia to Britain's failed nineteenth-century policy objectives. Pakistan's Directorate for Inter-Services Intelligence (ISI) was created by

British Major General R. Cawthorne,[2] who stayed on after partition in 1947 in order to help Pakistan wage a more effective terrorist war against India. The CIA itself was modeled after British India's Political and Secret Service from the days of the empire (the Raj). In the 1980s Britain's foremost military historian, Sir John Keegan, would compare it in nineteenth-century Kiplingesque-terms as having "assumed the mantle once worn by Kim's masters, as if it were a seamless garment."[3] In addition to the mantle, the CIA would adapt a century-old British political strategy for putting pressure on the Russian empire's southern flank. Applied to Afghanistan, that strategy soon found the United States aligning itself with Pakistan's British-trained military establishment, which was by 1948 emulating Britain's aggressive "Forward Policy" of Afghan destabilization in the North West Frontier Province.

America's British bias towards Pakistan was reflected by U.S. Secretary of State John Foster Dulles, who in 1953 delivered Afghanistan's Prime Minister Mohammed Daoud into Soviet arms by denying Daoud the military modernization necessary for maintaining order in the tribal areas bordering Pakistan.[4] That unstable border would eventually provide Pakistan, China, Saudi Arabia and the United States with the resources needed to conduct a secret war against the Afghan government and lure the Soviet Union into its own Vietnam.

The Circle of Love

Today, the United States continues in the tradition established by the East India Company as it fights another taxpayer-financed, privatized and largely secret war in a region controlled by the British Empire not so long ago. But claiming to defend democracy by breaking all its rules, and then concealing the illegality of its deeds under a cloak of secrecy, didn't wash for Britain 200 years ago and it won't wash for the United States now.

The blurring of lines between the highly profitable business of killing people and the legitimate defense of U.S. security has repercussions in the United States that are already being felt. In

Lancaster, California, aerial surveillance platforms billed as "crime-fighting" planes are on the agenda, where the community debates whether the daily, aggressive use of a high-flying surveillance plane is a preemptive crime-fighting tool or a serious threat to privacy.[5]

In October 2009, Boston's World Trade Center hosted Milcom 2009, the largest conference on military communications in the world.[6] On view at Milcom were the latest battle-tested devices, including wearable computers, onboard technologies for military vehicles, battle-ready portable communications systems, a scale model of Mitre's unmanned aerial "Predator" vehicle and General Dynamics' "Land Warrior" C4 battlefield communications system. D.C. Denison of the *Boston Globe* writes, "The system, which includes a camouflaged vest stuffed with computer and networking technology, connects 'the soldier at the pointy end of the spear with higher operations and all the way back to strategic,' said company chief executive Chris Marzilli." According to Marzilli, the market for this technology has expanded in recent years, "because it is being adopted 'closer to home.'" [7]

In a war where the privatized secret killing of terrorist suspects by Predator drone is accepted by official Washington as a viable replacement for establishing civil authority and political justice, can the use of such devices for extrajudicial executions "closer to home" be far off?

On Wednesday, September 1, 2010, the United States Customs and Border Protection agency began flying a Predator drone out of Corpus Christie Texas for aerial surveillance. Homeland Security Secretary Janet Napolitano described the move as "yet another critical step we have taken in ensuring the safety of the border and is an important tool in our security toolbox."[8] With the U.S. economy sagging, investment firms saw advanced drone technology like the Northrop Grumman RQ-4 Global Hawk as one of the few growth areas. W.J. Hennigan of the *Los Angeles Times* writes, "The new sensors enable flying drones to 'listen' in on cellphone conversations and pinpoint the location of the caller on the ground. Some can even 'smell' the air and sniff out chemical plumes."[9]

The use of Predator drones was just another in a growing list of high-tech military weapons and practices that included street-roaming full-body scanners,[10] a CIA-Google Web monitoring collaboration,[11] the application of "crime prediction software,"[12] and an aggressively expanded DNA-arrest database[13] that had crept from the battlefield to the streets of the U.S. "homeland." But was the safety and security of the American public the primary intention behind such draconian practices, or is America's increasingly privatized national security state just a dangerous anachronism, a modern-day, high-technology East India Company whose unsupervised, out-of-control behavior is as dangerous to itself and the country it serves as it is to those whom it makes its enemy? In the United Kingdom, citizens won't have long to find out, as police will use security for the 2012 Olympics as the reason to launch a fleet of "unmanned spy drones, controversially deployed in Afghanistan, for 'routine' monitoring of antisocial motorists, protesters, agricultural thieves and fly-tippers [illegal waste dumpers], in a significant expansion of covert state surveillance."[14] Developed by arms manufacturer BAE Systems "as a national strategy with [a] consortium of government agencies," Britain's latest surveillance tool breaks new ground in the privatization of state security. A Freedom of Information Act request by the *Guardian* indicated that its use "could span a range of police activity—and that officers have talked about selling surveillance data to private companies."[15] Combined with a new police program that rebrands anyone in Britain who lawfully protests virtually anything as "domestic extremism,"[16] the strategy has opened the door for the wholesale abrogation of human rights and the end of justice and individual freedom as we have come to know it in the West for the last 1,000 years.

In the United States, that door led to the Federal Communications Commission, where AT&T and Verizon Communications argued in a fourteen-page letter to the FCC that FCC Chairman Julius Genachowski was "extremist"[17] in his efforts to reclassify Internet service providers as common carriers in order to guarantee affordable, universal access to America's broadband networks. It seemed that by 2010, the beginning of the seventh decade of U.S. involvement in Central Asia, the language and the roles had somehow become reversed, with a corporatized state increasingly labeling anyone who opposed its interests at home as "extremist," while the real extremists that it helped to create (with guns and bombs) in Afghanistan and Pakistan got offered government jobs, financial incentives and guarantees of a safe return for themselves and their families. It was a bad omen for the future, but perhaps not a surprising one, given that the East India Company and the United States share a legacy that dates to the birth of the American republic.

As the United States expanded its fight in Afghanistan and Pakistan into Taliban-controlled territory under the stars and stripes, it was worth noting that the first commander in chief of the United States, George Washington, originally fought under a different flag. Known as the Grand Union Flag, it differed from today's American flag only in that the upper left hand quadrant contained the Union Jack of Great Britain and not the white stars of America's new states. It was this flag, authorized by the Second Continental Congress in May of 1775, that was raised by General George Washington's troops at his headquarters on Prospect Hill in Cambridge, Massachusetts, on January 1, 1776, and it was this flag, and not the stars and stripes, under which Britain's North American colonies officially took the name "United States" on September 9, 1776.[18] Whatever the reasons for this choice, at the time of the American revolution, the Grand Union flag was also the flag of the British East India Company and had been since 1707. The East India Company flag dotted the forts of India at least until 1824, and was flown by ships of the Indian Navy until 1863.[19] In 2001 it returned in a slightly modified form and dotted the forts of Afghanistan for a further decade as British and American flags flew jointly over territory once denied to the Company.

In its violent and reckless response to 9/11, the United States completed a quest begun by the British East India Company in the seventeenth century and found its "other" in a war in Afghanistan. In crossing Zero, the United States challenges the authority of the sovereign state of Pakistan, the national security interests of China, India, Russia and Iran, a regional independence movement that has been fighting outside invaders for centuries and an insurgent army called the Taliban that views itself as an army of God. In crossing Zero, the United States has finally found itself. The sooner it realizes the circle of its global conquest is complete, the sooner it can face itself and come home.

12. Issues, Answers and Recommendations

The Bush administration's counterterrorism-heavy and diplomacy-light approach doomed the post-9/11 U.S. effort in Afghanistan from the start. The short, sharp blitzkrieg of "shock and awe" that temporarily drove the Taliban from power was replaced by no organized form of government recognizable to Afghans. The reintroduction of U.S-friendly warlords who had been driven from the scene by the Taliban during the 1990s and then "reconciled" into the powerless government of Hamid Karzai only institutionalized corruption and alienated a desperate and fractured population. An anti-narcotics program that targeted poor poppy farmers, not the opium traffickers or the drug labs, opened the population in the countryside to Taliban recruitment.[1] Billions of reconstruction dollars sent to rebuild the country never got to where they were needed or aided anyone outside a favored short list of U.S. corporations and a circle of well-connected Afghan-Americans. Civilian casualties, night raids, the use of torture,[2] internments and extrajudicial executions[3] of suspected extremists by America's military progressively transformed popular resentment at foreign occupation into outrage.

With the advent of the Obama administration's AfPak policy and the escalation of U.S. combat forces to somewhere around 100,000 soldiers on the ground, attempts were made by General Stanley McChrystal and General David Petraeus to focus on more "population centric" military tactics that spared civilian casualties.[4] But by the late autumn 2010, even the military itself had come to accept that the strategy was not working.[5] General Petraeus's return to a mix of counterterrorism and counterinsurgency (which had failed the first time) and backing "reconciliation" talks with Taliban leaders while pounding them with overwhelming firepower, confused everyone.

Veteran observers saw the reconciliation talks as nothing more than an elaborate U.S. disinformation campaign known as "information strategy," designed to sow distrust within the insurgency. On October 22, 2010, Jonathan S. Landay and Warren P. Strobel reported for McClatchy Newspapers, "Despite reports of high-level talks between the Taliban and the Afghan government, no significant peace negotiations are under way in Afghanistan, U.S. officials and Afghanistan experts said Thursday. . . . 'This is a psychological operation, plain and simple,' said a U.S. official with firsthand knowledge of Afghan President Hamid Karzai's outreach effort."[6]

Never mind that the same policy of bomb-and-talk had proved useless in Vietnam or that General Petraeus's strategy of making back-channel deals with fundamentalist insurgents, as he had in Iraq, disintegrated in favor of Al Qaeda and fractured tribal politics once the pressure of U.S. firepower was withdrawn.[7] Reconciliation itself wasn't the problem. Giving a legitimate place in the Afghan government—to reconciled criminals who were trained and paid by foreign interests, directed by Pakistan's Inter-Services Intelligence Directorate and never held to account for their crimes against the Afghan people—*was* the problem. The West's practice of favoring former Northern Alliance Uzbek, Tajik and Hazara warlords at the expense of Pashtuns on both sides of the border had also set the stage for transforming the insurgency into a protracted civil war.[8] After ten years, just the mention of accelerated peace talks triggered panic among Afghanistan's ethnic minorities and generated anger toward Karzai for even contemplating power sharing with the Taliban. Ben Farmer writes for the *Telegraph*, "Anger is growing in the north of Afghanistan at the prospect of a deal with President Hamid Karzai after emissaries from the rebel group were escorted to Kabul for talks last week. . . . 'If people are not actually digging up their old guns, they are at least locating them and putting a little marker on them,' one diplomat told the *Sunday Telegraph*."[9]

In an October 2010 email exchange with McClatchy Newspapers' veteran reporter Jonathan Landay, he expressed serious concern with the misconceptions plaguing Washington's Afghan debate.

> It is the minorities who are feeling politically marginal-ized—dangerously so—because of Karzai's purges of most of the Northern Alliance leaders from the cabinet and the idea of power-sharing with the Taliban under national reconciliation. [General Mohammed Qasim] Fahim is considered a traitor and part of the ruling mafia and the only other senior former NA leader, Interior Minister Bismullah Khan is busy stacking the Interior Ministry with Panjshiris in anticipation of a power-sharing agreement that he opposes.[10]

In July 2010 a delegation of U.S. congressmembers including California Republican Dana Rohrabacher, met in Berlin with Tajik, Uzbek and Hazara leaders and former warlords to discuss remodel-ing Afghanistan's government into a "federalized" system. A federal-ized Afghanistan would theoretically guarantee each separate ethnic group a voice in the government while preventing the Pashtuns from monopolizing government functions. But federalization came with a legion of its own obstacles, most of which would overwhelm the already weak and divided country before it got off the ground. S. Frederick Starr, chairman of the Central Asia Caucus Institute at Johns Hopkins University–SAIS, rejected the idea of federalizing Afghanistan when it was first proposed as U.S. bombs still pounded Taliban-controlled Kabul in November 2001.

> The United States endured a bloody civil war before it achieved a sustainable balance between federal and state au-thority; Germany did not adopt a federal system until it lost World War II; Switzerland's was hundreds of years in the making; and Quebec is still testing the limits of Canadian fed-eralism. . . . In Afghanistan it is a dangerous and irresponsible proposal. . . . Afghanistan needs a unitary system, but one that accords a substantial role to local initiative . . . grounded not

in an army of local bureaucrats but in the existing institutions of self-government at the village, tribal, and district levels.[11]

In an increasingly desperate effort to find a solution, George W. Bush's former deputy national security advisor for strategic planning, Robert D. Blackwill, proposed partitioning Afghanistan. In a major foreign policy statement posted on the Web site *Politico* on July 7, 2010, he attempted to explain how breaking up Afghanistan would (sort of) benefit everyone:

> Announcing that we will retain an active combat role in Afghanistan for years to come," writes Blackwill, "and that we do not accept permanent Taliban control of the south, the United States and its allies could withdraw combat forces from most of Pashtun Afghanistan (about half the country), including Kandahar, over several months. . . . We would then focus on defending the northern and western regions—containing roughly 60 percent of the population. . . . We would offer the Afghan Taliban an agreement in which neither side seeks to enlarge its territory. . . . We would then make it clear that we would rely heavily on U.S. air power and special forces to target any Al Qaeda base in Afghanistan, as well as Afghan Taliban leaders who aided them.[12]

According to Blackwill, all that was needed to make his plan work would be "a longtime residual U.S. military force in Afghanistan of about 40,000 to 50,000 troops," as well as the enlistment of thousands of regional forces and transformation of the Pashtun south into a vision from hell. Blackwill writes:

> In the context of de facto partition, the sky over Pashtun Afghanistan would be dark with manned and unmanned coalition aircraft—targeting not only terrorists but, as necessary, the new Taliban government in all its dimensions. Taliban civil officials—like governors, mayors, judges and tax collectors—would wake up every morning not knowing if they

would survive the day in their offices, while involved in daily activities or at home at night.[13]

Thomas Ruttig, co-director of the Afghanistan Analysts Network and a former United Nations official, commented on the plan.

> His [Blackwill's] illusions about the Northern Alliance leaders show that Blackwill still lives in the Cold War. He obscures the fact that their inability to govern Afghanistan after the withdrawal of Soviet occupation forces and the downfall of Dr. Najibullah's regime was a major source for the emergence and success of the Taliban. Does it occur to Blackwill that the recycling of these same warlords and political mujahedin leaders is a source and not a remedy for the current mess in Afghanistan? Meanwhile, Blackwill even hopes to "enlist" the UN Security Council for his crazy scenario. . . . To me, the whole thing sounds like a wet dream of the military-industrial complex.[14]

Major legacy issues weighed in on the Obama administration's success in Afghanistan. Each was interrelated and nothing could be resolved without addressing the others in whole or in part.

As described by Karen DeYoung of the *Washington Post*:

> Saudi Arabia, which has served as a venue for talks between the Afghan President Hamid Karzai's government and the Taliban, remains concerned about Iranian influence. Turkey, which sees itself as a bridge between the West and the Islamic world, is anxious to play a role. India worries that integrating the Taliban will come at the expense of New Delhi's Afghan proxy, the former Northern Alliance of ethnic Uzbeks and Tajiks. India's concern on this issue, shared by Iran and others in the region, is largely directed toward Pakistan. . . . Iran also found common cause with Russia. . . . China, in competition with India and Russia, has tightened its ties with Pakistan . . .

Added to the regional pressures to modify the AfPak agenda were the interests of the oil lobby, which unabashedly pushed for a reversal of AfPak and the "Pakistanization" of the war. According to George Friedman of the Texas-based geopolitical intelligence company STRATFOR, Pakistanization didn't mean, "extending the war into Pakistan but rather extending Pakistan into Afghanistan. . . . The Pakistani relationship to the Taliban, which was a liability for the United States in the past, now becomes an advantage for Washington because it creates a trusted channel for meaningful communication with the Taliban. . . . The United States isn't going to defeat the Taliban. The original goal of the war is irrelevant, and the current goal is rather difficult to take seriously."[15]

In this version of crossing back through Zero (clouded by a toxic haze of South Asian oil and gas), *bad* Taliban were now magically *good* again. The time had come for the Obama administration to welcome them back, get behind Pakistan and build some pipelines as if nothing had changed between 1997 and the present.

The AfPak scenario has been confounded by a number of pipeline schemes, some of which have been on the drawing board for nearly two decades, but which require a stable Afghanistan to build and secure. Texas-based Unocal supported the Taliban in its bid to build a gas pipeline from Turkmenistan through Afghanistan to Pakistan starting in 1995 with the backing of the Clinton administration.[16]

On October 28, 2010, Pakistan voted to green-light[17] the latest version of the project known as TAPI—the Turkmenistan, Afghanistan, Pakistan, India pipeline. The *Asia Times'* M.K. Bhadrakumar saw the deal as a coup for the United States. "The most important geopolitical factor, is that the U.S. is the 'ideologue' of the project and its Great Central Asia strategy—aiming at rolling back Russian and Chinese influence in the region and forging the region's links with South Asia—is set to take a big step forward."[18] Bhadrakumar saw the TAPI pipeline scheme as dovetailing neatly into the administration's Afghan endgame, with the U.S. picking up where it left off with the Taliban in 2001, before those "militant

'Arab fighters,' began influencing the Taliban leadership and spoiled everything."[19]

Setting the stage for a return to the Taliban was no small undertaking, especially given its members' reputation as religious thugs who have stoned women to death, destroyed ancient artifacts of other religions and ethnically cleansed non-Pashtun areas under their control. Over the last ten years, Afghan public opinion polls regularly indicated that a large majority of Afghans expressed little support for their return. Yet on November 10, 2010, a survey released by the San Francisco–based Asia Foundation maintained that 83 percent of Afghans backed negotiations with insurgent forces.[20]

According to Katharine Houreld of the Associated Press, the report was the strongest sign yet of the population's growing frustration with the military solution. "Analysts said the survey reflected the growing doubt that the government and its NATO allies can defeat the insurgency with military means and that after thirty years of war, some Afghans are willing to sacrifice some freedoms for the sake of peace."[21] But was the Asia Foundation the best source for this kind of information, considering its long history of association with the U.S. Central Intelligence Agency and the CIA's long history of advancing an oil industry agenda?

As of mid-November 2010, how any of this might fit into General David Petraeus's plan to "win" in Afghanistan[22] remained a mystery. In October 2010, portraits of General Petraeus's "success" in Iraq were further redrawn with new revelations by Wikileaks from official reports that "hundreds of the well-disciplined fighters—many of whom have gained extensive knowledge about the American military—appear to have rejoined Al-Qaeda-in-Mesopotamia. Beyond that, officials say that even many of the Awakening fighters still on the Iraqi government payroll, possibly thousands of them, covertly aid the insurgency."[23]

These defections came as no surprise to Matthew Hoh who heads the Afghanistan Study Group, a joint project of the New America Foundation and the Center for International Policy. Hoh is a former U.S. Marine officer and State Department official who worked with regional tribal leaders in the campaign to win over the Sunni insurgency of Anbar province in 2006–2007. When we spoke with Hoh on November 5, 2010, he said he thought the defections were "foreseeable."

> You have to go back. We invade in '03. We remove these Sunnis from power. We disband the Iraqi army. Now that we've usurped these Sunnis, we exclude them from the government. Then we stood up this Iraqi national army again, but we fill it with Shia troops . . . and we put them in Sunni areas. So we just pushed. We pushed the Sunnis toward the insurgency. I think if the Sunnis are excluded from a Baghdad government and security forces dominated by the Shia, as we may now be starting to see, then a return to supporting the insurgency as a means of protecting or defending themselves, or resisting oppression or exclusion, even though it may lead back into the terrible cycle of violence we saw for most of the last decade, will be the likely result.[24]

Hoh came to see that U.S. ineffectiveness derived not so much from the complexity of tribalism or Sunni-Shiite conflict but from the way in which hubristic and aloof American planners had mismanaged the problem. "What I saw was this fundamental belief in our system, that we were doing good and that delivering a modern state to the Iraqis would take care of everything. . . . Just the lack of knowledge, the lack of intellectual honesty, the lack of courage and the bureaucratic inefficiencies and the ideological nature of what we were doing and the fact that we were on the side of right. President Bush even said that God was pushing him to do this, and that all filtered down."[25]

The complete deterioration of Iraq following the U.S. invasion had its parallel in Afghanistan. With Iraq once again descending into violence, Hoh believed that the only chance General Petraeus had for any form of "success" in Afghanistan depended on whether the United States could take off the "white hat" and have the intellectual honesty to question a process that, up to now, relied on opportunists or collaborators at the expense of the Afghan people. By November 2010, the military campaign to bring down the Taliban was failing on all counts,[26] but the November election in which Republicans gained control of the U.S. House of Representatives, guaranteed that a military solution would continue to stay at the top of the agenda.

And then there was the vital issue of U.S.-Pakistan relations. Pakistan's continued support for the very Taliban "enemy" that the United States had been trying to defeat lent an air of absurdity to the entire AfPak enterprise and the "war on terror." The illogic of this relationship was spotlighted in late September 2010 when Pakistan abruptly closed its vital Torkham border crossing north of Peshawar to NATO supply convoys after a U.S. helicopter returned fire and accidentally killed three Frontier Corps troops 200 yards inside Pakistan.[27] Tensions were further heightened days later when a White House assessment criticized Pakistan and its President Asif Ali Zardari for their unwillingness to take action against Al Qaeda and other extremist groups.[28]

In a visit to India on November 7, 2010, President Obama attempted to placate India's concerns over U.S.-Pakistani relations, citing the need to cooperate with Pakistan on numerous issues.[29] But the dysfunction and skewed reasoning that plagued the Obama administration's efforts at maintaining close ties to both Pakistan and India could no longer be disguised by rhetoric. In a *Los Angeles Times* op-ed, Selig Harrison cut to the core of the growing crisis in U.S.-India relations in which the United States indirectly supported the sponsoring of terrorists dedicated to India's destruction. "Since 9/11, the U.S. has showered $13.5 billion in military hardware on Islamabad, and pledged another $2 billion last month. The Pentagon justifies this buildup in the name of combating terrorism. But the big-ticket items have all strengthened Pakistani air and naval capabilities needed for potential combat with India, not for counterinsurgency mountain warfare against the Taliban."[30]

Throughout its history, Pakistan's obsession with India has governed its political thinking, and its political thinking has been governed exclusively by Pakistan's Punjabi military establishment.

This arrangement has justified its abhorrence of modern demo-cratic reforms, its neglect in developing a sound structure for its economy, its development of nuclear weapons, its participation in the illicit global narcotics trade and its direct support for ultra-or-thodox Islamic groups that the United States describes as terror or-ganizations. This support was most recently demonstrated in the testimony of convicted terrorist David Headley in the ongoing in-vestigation into the 2008 Mumbai hotel attack, which killed 166 people and injured hundreds more.[31]

Ravi Nessman and Ashok Sharma of the *Washington Post* write, "According to the report, Headley said the Pakistani spy agency provided individual handlers—many of them senior officers—for all the top members of Lashkar [-e-Taiba] and gave them directions and money to carry out their reconnaissance of prospective targets. The group's chief military commander, Zakir-ur-Rahman Lakhvi, was close to the director general of the spy agency, Lt. Gen. Ahmed Shuja Pasha, the report said."[32]

The revelation that David Headley worked with Pakistani in-telligence was also a reminder that Islamic terrorists were intimately tied to the U.S. intelligence community as well. Headley, a U.S. citizen, had been recruited by the United States Drug Enforcement Agency while serving probation on a drug-related conviction.[33] According to published reports, Headley was granted an early re-lease so that he could travel to Pakistan, and once there, he immedi-ately began training with terrorists and played a key role in the 2008 Mumbai attacks.[34]

Headley's story is a disturbing and increasingly recurrent theme emerging from the darkness of the U.S. war on terror. Not only have trusted U.S.-trained agents frequently turned against the United States and its allies, but efforts to convince U.S. authorities of their duplicity go unheeded. On October 17, 2010, the Associated Press reported that two of Headley's ex-wives had warned U.S. authorities years before the violent assaults in 2008.[35] According to the report, one wife informed the FBI's Joint Terrorism Task Force in 2005 that Headley had trained extensively in the Lashkar-i-Taiba's Pakistani camps and had shopped for night-vision goggles and other equipment, yet no action was taken.[36] A second wife alerted officials at the U.S. Embassy in Islamabad in 2007 that her ex-husband was actively involved with a terrorist group, but officials declined to act.

On October 19, the *Washington Post* reported that the CIA had ignored a warning that it was being lured into an ambush by the Jordanian double agent Humam al-Balawi. Balawi's December 30, 2009, suicide bombing at the U.S. Forward Operating Base Chapman in Khost, Afghanistan, was the deadliest incident for the CIA in twenty-five years.[37] CIA director Leon Panetta admitted that the killing of seven CIA agents and contractors and the wounding of six others represented "a systemic breakdown with regard to the kind of judgment and scrutiny that should have been applied here."[38]

But as the outrage exploded at the implementation of naked full-body scans and aggressive "groin checks," of small children and adults at U.S. airports,[39] it was becoming increasing obvious that the time had come for the serious judgment and scrutiny to be applied to an out-of-control U.S. national security establishment.

Saudi Arabia played another spoiler to the U.S. AfPak endgame with its existential anti-Shiite, anti-Iranian posture. Its dual agenda of expanding its influence into oil-rich Central Asian markets while extending its ultraconservative religious mandate played well to Pakistan but foiled U.S. efforts to undermine the insurgency. Saudi Arabia played the perfect dysfunctional partner to a dysfunctional American foreign policy in which the Saudi royal family bought off its extreme Wahhabi clerics to leave it alone while it continued to maintain a military alliance that rewarded the United States with massive arms contracts. The latest arms deal worth $60 billion[40] and apparently headed for Congressional approval, was the largest yet in a long series of deals forged between the United States and Saudi Arabia begun at the end of World War II.

Author Stephen Kinzer writes, "The al-Saud family's balancing act—preaching austere Islam while embracing the United States and allowing princes to live notoriously un-Islamic lives—requires a special arrangement. This arrangement is a bargain between the family and the Wahhabi clerics. It brought the regime to power and has sustained rule ever since."[41]

Kinzer believed that the U.S.-Saudi relationship had failed to keep up with the times and had in fact become a dangerous inhibitor to much-needed change on everyone's part. Could the United States finally negotiate its way out of an architecture that proved so beneficial during the Cold War, or would Washington continue to ignore the lessons of America's devastating crises in Afghanistan and Iraq until it was too late?

Following the Democratic Party's defeat at the hands of Republicans in the 2010 mid-term elections, President Obama will now struggle for the next two years just to get himself reelected. After ten years of combat in Iraq and Afghanistan, the U.S. military was psychologically and materially depleted and the economy billions more in debt with nothing to show for it. The "shock and awe," victory delivered to the Taliban and Al Qaeda forces in 2001 had devolved into a slow death by a thousand cuts as the United States succumbed to the same inexorable forces that swallowed the armies of Alexander the Great, Britain and the Soviet Union. Whether the Obama administration could somehow alter its strategy, prop up its reluctant ally Pakistan, and strengthen Afghanistan's economy and National Army to defend itself while avoiding the ultimate catastrophe of having Pakistan's nuclear weapons fall into the hands of terrorists remained a real and terrifying mystery.[42]

A June 2010 audit by the U.S. government raised serious doubts about the $25 billion effort to build up the Afghan National Army and police, indicating that the standards used to appraise Afghan forces since 2005 were "woefully inadequate, inflating their abilities."[43] In August 2010 an elaborate operation designed to prove the Afghan army's effectiveness turned to a debacle when a battalion of Afghan soldiers had to be rescued by NATO troops after a battering by Taliban fighters.[44] On November 1, 2010, an entire garrison of police burned down the police station and defected to the Taliban along with their guns, trucks, uniforms and food in a contested area southwest of Kabul known as Khogeyani.[45]

Also a mystery was exactly how the Obama administration expected to meet its timetable for withdrawal and accomplish its transition strategy.[46] On November 10, 2010 the *New York Times* reported that the administration was backing away from the July 2011 deadline in favor of 2014, given that "it undermined its mission by making Afghans reluctant to work with troops perceived to be leaving shortly."[47] The *Times* saw the move as a victory for the military. On November 17, 2010 David S. Cloud of the *Los Angeles Times* wrote "Mark Sedwell, NATO's senior civilian representative to Afghanistan, said this week that the transition to Afghan control could go into '2015 and beyond.' The year 2014 is a 'goal' that is 'realistic but not guaranteed,' he said."[48] In an interview with the *Washington Post*, Hamid Karzai challenged Petraeus to reduce military operations immediately, claiming the time had come to "reduce the presence of, you know, boots in Afghanistan."[49] By November 2010, raids by U.S. Special Operations troops had increased six times to some 200 a month and were considered by U.S. commanders to be a crucial weapon in weakening the insurgency and disrupting bomb-making networks.[50] But Karzai insisted that the stepped-up campaign of night raids had to be stopped because they violated the sanctity of Afghan homes and incited more people to join the insurgency.

General Petraeus responded immediately to Karzai's complaint, reportedly expressing "astonishment and disappointment" while warning that Karzai's statements were making his own position "untenable."[51] But if anything made General Petraeus's job untenable it was the even more astonishing revelation on November 23, 2010, that his peace talks with Mullah Akhtar Muhammad Mansour, the Taliban's second-highest commander, were being conducted with an imposter.[52] The revelation confirmed what critics of the talks as well as the Taliban leaders themselves had been saying from the beginning: there was no peace to be made short of acquiescing to the Taliban's demands and a complete withdrawal of foreign forces. Talking to the Taliban was a deluded fantasy that had sucked in the Pentagon, the administration and a host of Beltway pundits. To some, like *The Nation*'s Robert Dreyfuss, it was a cause for outrage.

Dreyfuss admitted that he'd been fooled by Petraeus and demanded that "Obama has to fire everyone involved in the charade."[53] To others, like Max Fisher at the *Atlantic Magazine*, it was the acceptance of a darker reality that if the high-level Taliban leader was a fake, then so was the administration's peace plan.[54]

If after nine full years of war, U.S. and NATO intelligence couldn't identify something as simple as the authenticity of one of the Taliban's highest-ranking members, how could it possibly hope to negotiate an end to what had to be the most complex foreign policy problem in America's history?

The years 2011 and 2012 promised to be the most dangerous years for the United States since the period beginning with the political and economic instability preceding World War II and culminating in the Cuban Missile Crisis. They could even prove more dangerous, given America's political, economic and social dislocations. Like the Soviet Union in 1989, the United States faces profound systemic problems that the system created but is incapable of addressing. This paradoxical situation sees a detached elite trying to govern a country more divided now than at any time since before the American Civil War. The Republicans' return to power in the U.S. House in the November 2010 elections has made certain that the Obama administration will be pressured back into a unilateral foreign policy. This approach will lead Washington to turn to its remaining military strength, which will in turn lead to a larger and more devastating crisis.

What Can Be Done?

The issues that fester at the root of the Afghan's dissatisfaction must be redressed. Without this, none of the other interconnected issues relating to militant Islamic groups, ethnicity or civil war can be resolved.

I. The Durand/Zero Line

As cited earlier, the original AfPak issue began when the British usurped Afghan tribal land and authority in the nineteenth century and imposed the artificial border known as the Durand line in 1893. Conflicts created by the border were given new life and further complicated in 1947 with the partition of Britain's Empire in India and the creation of the state of Pakistan. Pakistan resumed Britain's "Forward Policy" towards Afghanistan during the 1970s in part because Afghan territory offered Pakistan the potential for security known as "strategic depth" where its forces could theoretically retreat, rearm and mount a counterattack against an Indian invasion.[55] According to the well-known U.S. anthropologist Louis Dupree, there exists strong evidence that this boundary separating Afghanistan from Pakistan was never intended to be permanent. Dupree writes, "In his illuminating biography (1900), [Amir] Abdur Rahman repeatedly states he never considered any Pushtun areas as permanently ceded to the British. . . . He insisted the 'boundary' delineated zones of responsibility, and did not draw an international boundary. In addition [there is] convincing evidence that the Amir did not actually write the 'I renounce my claims' sentence."[56] Convinced by his own and numerous others' research that the Durand line was not, is not and was never intended by either party to be a permanent national boundary, Dupree cites the evidence. "The last paragraph in the final agreement of November 12, 1893, is vague and inconclusive. . . . At what point does coercion cease to be legal? . . . Other British administrators, however, contend the Durand Line was never meant to be an international boundary: 'The Durand Agreement was an agreement to define the respective spheres of influence of the British Government and the Amir.'"[57] Members of the Afghan diaspora currently have a motion in the works to take the Durand line issue to the World Court in order to decide once and for all whether the ninety-nine-year "lease" that the British applied to their control of Hong Kong (which expired in 1997) applies to the border separating Afghanistan and Pakistan. As U.S. and NATO troops fight and die over an issue that remains at the heart of the Afghan-Pakistan conflict, this is a motion that desperately deserves the world's attention. Removed from the framework of a brutal Islamic insurgency and placed into the historical legal context whence it originated, it could begin the long road back to establishing Western respect for an international system based on just laws and regional sovereignty. It would also allow the indigenous ethnicities the opportunity to articulate their grievances publicly for the first time and remove the issue from the narrow sectarian framework in which it is now trapped.

II. Women's Rights

A declaration of the rights of women in an Islamic society should be established once and for all, made universal and not subjected to the whims, misconceptions and outright falsehoods of various radical Islamists as well as anti-Islamic elements within the Western intelligentsia. The root of this issue lies not in Afghanistan—which, prior to the advent of the 1980s Mujahideen era, experienced a slow but steady progress towards women's equality. Today's problem with Afghan women's rights derives directly from the influence of Saudi Arabia and Sunni Muslim clerics who wish to impose a questionable interpretation of ultra-orthodox Sharia law throughout Central Asia. The issue of Afghan women's rights has become a political football, used originally as a propaganda tool by the Bush administration to help justify the invasion. Ten years later it is being used as a justification for remaining in Afghanistan and for legitimizing a military solution. In the meantime women's rights are being bargained away by outside forces in NATO and the United States to escape their obligation to help the Afghans form a just society. The time has come for progressive Muslims to demand an accounting of their arch-conservative brethren, insist that a standardized interpretation of this issue be accepted by the highest Koranic authorities and move on. This will remove the pressure from Afghanistan's fragile democracy and place the burden where it belongs, on the sponsors of radicalism.

III. A Regional Solution

Says longtime South Asian regional expert Selig Harrison:

Iran, Russia, India, and Tajikistan all played a key role in help-ing U.S. forces dislodge the Taliban in 2001 . . . all of them, together with China and Uzbekistan, fear that a resurrected Taliban regime would foment Islamist insurgencies within their own borders. Russia faces nascent Islamist forces in its Muslim south. India worries that Taliban control in Kabul would lead to an upsurge in Pakistan-based terrorism. The Shiite theocracy in Iran fears that a Taliban regime would help the Sunni Jundullah separatist movement in Iranian Baluchistan and Salafi extremists in other regions. Tajikistan faces Sunni extremist groups led by Hizb ut-Tahrir and is increasingly unsettled by an influx of Afghan refugees, which could grow if the Taliban were to return to power. China is beset by Islamist Uighur separatists in Xinjiang.[58]

Central Asia's regional powers have a strong vested interest in cauterizing Afghanistan's wounds, neutralizing the Taliban and insuring Afghanistan's sovereignty. Some Afghan-American voices like Jawied Nawabi, adjunct professor of Economics and Sociology at the City University of New York, believe the United States and NATO have failed because they insist on backing the wrong horse.

If there were a sincere international effort for a negotiated withdrawal of US/NATO forces, some form of regional military presence (like Turkey, Indonesia, Malaysia, India, etc.) could take over for a limited transitional period. First it must be understood that there are three political groups in Afghanistan:

1. The Islamic fundamentalists from Karzai to the Taliban who differ only in their length of beards. 2. A mix of moderate and secular Muslims whose economic policies are Neoliberal. 3. A mix of moderate and secular Muslims, prag-matic nationalists and former PDPA members. This group is mostly trained professionals and former bureaucrats during Zahir Shah, Daoud Khan and PDPA governments. They

have Keynesian, liberal and a third world perspective in their economic, social and political policies but have never been appointed to important government positions.[59]

Nawabi believes that if these 100,000 or so Afghan moderates, combined with roughly 15,000 diaspora Afghans, can be given the chance they deserve, together they can maintain the stability necessary to partner with regional powers.

IV. Squaring Pakistan

If anything stands in the way of resolving Washington's Afghan conundrum it is Pakistan. Pakistan is the monster in the Afghanistan nightmare, and the time has come to deal with it. Of all the regional interests invested in creating a peaceful and prosperous Afghanistan, only Pakistan reserves the right to undermine any and all initiatives that don't serve its own interests. Pakistan has numerous well-heeled partners helping to push this agenda, but all remain safely remote from the consequences of their actions by operating far from the front lines in places like London, Boston, Houston, Dubai and Jeddah. Corporate-sponsored think tanks connected to friendly intelligence services that recommend favoring the "Pakistanization" of the war, governing Afghanistan through "acceptable dictators," or reconciling unrepentant terrorists represent a bankrupt solution from a bankrupted era with no more claim to credibility in 2010 than NINJA loans,[60] credit default swaps[61] or Lehman Brothers stock.[62] Paralleling a host of U.S.-supported military dictatorships from Latin America to the Philippines, Vietnam and Iran, the Pakistani military's control of the country's agenda has led its country's population into a dark hole. President Obama knows the problem centers around Pakistan. According to the *Washington Post*'s Bob Woodward, in an Oval Office meeting on November 25, 2009, Obama declared, "We need to make clear to people that the cancer is in Pakistan."[63] According Woodward, following the failed Times Square bombing attempt on May 1, 2010, National Security Advisor James Jones informed Pakistan's President Asif Ali Zardari, that if SUV had blown up in Times Square. "No one [would] be able to stop the response and consequences." Jones was referring to an American "retribution" plan to bomb "150 identified terrorist camps in a brutal, punishing attack inside Pakistan."[64] Bombing Pakistan in this manner would not only further destablize South Asia, it could detonate a hemispheric war. Washington must straighten out its priorities regarding Pakistan before it's too late.

V. Reconciliation

Reconciling warlords and Taliban may appear to be a workable solution for Washington's powerful lobbies and international oil conglomerates, but reintegrating the leaders of brutal, ultraconservative crime syndicates into the Afghan government will create problems that make current difficulties of corruption and malfeasance experienced with Hamid Karzai seem mild in comparison. This raises the question, how do Afghans gain sovereignty when prominent Western intellectual, corporate and military centers refuse to accept the rights of Afghans to make this decision for themselves? U.S. neoconservatives, Saudi financiers and Pakistan's leadership class have controlled Afghanistan's narrative, leaving its people voiceless in their own affairs. In a speech at the neoconservative Washington Institute for Near East Policy in New York on October 5, 2010, Tony Blair warned about the dangers of failing to heed the Muslim reaction to Western provocation by admitting it was impossible to defeat extremism "without defeating the narrative that nurtures it."[65] If Tony Blair can openly say it, then the time has finally come for a new narrative. Breaking this chain of institutional thinking is essential to solving the Afghan problem. But most suggestions to "think outside the box" aren't really intended to create new thinking as much as to try to maintain the same old thinking with a different approach. What is needed now is a wholly different way of thinking and a whole new group to do it. To accomplish this, the issue of Islam needs to be moved off center stage where the current acrimony has been intentionally focused and replaced with another model that incorporates ideas, histories and enduring beliefs that link humanity together in a common struggle and a better life for all.

VI. Afghan Solutions for the Afghan People

Solutions that have been proposed involving federalizing the Afghan government or partitioning the country into ethnic enclaves won't work, because these decisions are being made without the sovereign participation of the Afghan people. Existing efforts to governmentalize Afghanistan by infusing a bureaucratic structure from Kabul are failing miserably. Neither can reconciliation succeed in establishing a legitimate government that will be acceptable to the Afghan people. As Khalil Nouri of the New World Strategies Coalition (an Afghan-American organization seeking to implement a demilitarized tribal solution to the conflict) puts it, "Can reconciliation work? The Answer is 'NO' it will never work in the long term; first the country has not healed from its past 35 years of war, the ethnic divide has widened and has complicated the path to nationalism, and there is not a unifier figurehead to calm the country down."[66] Nouri believes that the only solution that will work before NATO withdraws its troops is a traditional Afghan tribal council (Jirga) free of the kind of outside interference that brought Hamid Karzai and the warlords to power in 2002. The irony remains that today's crisis occurred not because the Jirga failed, but because the will of the Jirga was overridden by the political desires of the Bush administration. Nouri foresees that if this "All Afghan Jirga" is assembled by Afghans for Afghans it can return Afghanistan to a stable state by creating a traditional government that is acceptable to all Afghans regardless of their tribal or ethnic affiliations. According to Nouri, "The Taliban will succeed in ruling neither the country—proven by their reign from 1996 to 2001—nor the puppet government of Hamid Karzai. Nor will the Northern Alliance's endeavor bear any fruit. Afghans who brainstorm together on how to coexist in an 'All Afghan Jirga' can neutralize the warlords' grip on power by restoring memories of a time when Afghanistan's own political process enabled the people to live in harmony and peace."[67]

VII. Throwing the Box Away

Parallels have been drawn by numerous experts between the complexities of Afghanistan's sectarian-tribal dynamic and the ongoing conflict in Northern Ireland. Various tactics employed by peacekeepers in Northern Ireland have been tried in Afghanistan with limited success, but the two countries' circumstances are not dissimilar, and for very good reasons. Aside from sharing a long colonial heritage with Britain, and in Pakistan the Frontier Crimes Regulations (which were adapted from the medieval Irish penal codes), Ireland and Afghanistan share an ancient legacy of tribal law and secular codes of moral conduct that long precede the Christian and Islamic eras. Ireland's pre-Christian Brehon Laws provided a sophisticated set of rules for every aspect of Irish society, from the quality of poets to the "ordering of discipline" to the worthiness of kings. Prior to hostile European invasions, Pashtunwali was a guide for a peaceful and hospitable Afghanistan that was known to accommodate Jews and Christians, considering them both to be religions of "the book." The first British explorers wrote of their warm reception in Afghanistan's cities and marveled at the striking contrast between Afghan Muslims and the rest of the Muslim world.

A new and shocking departure from the existing narrative is needed to change the tone of the Afghan crisis and reorient people's thinking. We therefore propose that as part of the indigenous solution to restore the tribal balance to Afghanistan, Afghans allow Europeans to remove themselves from the existing extremist narrative by reconnecting to their own ancient past. This can be achieved by hosting the first meeting of the New World Strategies Coalition tribal Loya Jirga at an ancient, 5,000-year-old UNESCO World Heritage Site north of Dublin known today as New Grange,[68] but traditionally by its mythological Celtic name, *Bru na Boinne*, the mansion on the Boyne river.

VIII. Resetting America's Broken Clock: Some Practical Ideas

Time is running out on America's ability to sustain endless wars by finding or creating endless strings of enemies. Whatever the current danger of Islamic terrorism, it has been worsened by a U.S. approach that favors military over political solutions. The U.S. military-political-corporate leader must take responsibility for their own actions in an international setting, and accept that they are not Jedi knights but mere mortals. They must learn to accept that their behavior shows all the signs of the hubris, miscalculation and decline exhibited by the failed empires drawn into the region before them. The only way to change course is to reorganize the way the U.S. government deals with South Asia. Ashley J. Tellis of the Carnegie Endowment for International Peace writes in *Change the Rules of the Game Plan in Pakistan*:

> The most important problem is that suddenly challenging Pakistan after a decade of acquiescence to its mendacity is tantamount to abruptly changing the rules of a game that Washington and Islamabad have gotten used to: It could result in even greater Pakistani obduracy and further support for its jihadi proxies. Although that is certainly an unpalatable possibility, the bitter truth is that the current state of affairs—in which Washington indefinitely subsidizes Islamabad's sustenance of U.S. enemies—poses far greater dangers to the United States.[69]

And Christopher Preble of the Cato Institute writes in *Cut (Really Cut) Military Spending*:

> Despite all the hype about Defense Secretary Robert Gates and his cuts of big-ticket military projects, the Pentagon's $680 billion budget is actually slated to increase in coming years. This is unconscionable at a time when taxpayers are under enormous stress and when the U.S. government must reduce spending across the board. . . . If Obama is serious about reducing the deficit and keeping U.S. troops out of "dumb wars," as he famously dubbed them, he should put his money where his mouth is. Cutting defense spending is the only reliable way to stifle Washington's impulse to send U.S. troops

on ill-considered missions around the globe. The hawks will scream, but America will be just fine.[70]

America will be fine. Afghanistan will remain the graveyard of empires, and the world will go on. But where will the United States be in that world without the values that established it? Only time will tell.

EPILOGUE

I think it's a mistake people make to think in terms of different administrations as being a sharp break from prior administrations. If you read American history carefully, you begin to see continuity and you begin to understand that there's very little that comes afresh, that really there's a kind of permanent approach to things. Maybe there's a different face on it from time to time, but the approach is absolutely the same approach.[1]

—Jack A. Blum, Former Special Counsel to the United States Senate Foreign Relations Subcommittee on Terrorism, Narcotics and International Operations.

It was assumed by many in the run-up to the 2008 election that if anyone would represent a break with the past and a return to normalcy it would be Barack Obama.

In 2008, the Obama campaign *streaked* along on the slogan "Change We Can Believe In" and was rewarded with the presidency as a result. Two years later it was clear that if anything had changed it was merely the pace with which his administration had accelerated Bush's post-9/11 agenda and not the agenda itself. Karen DeYoung and Greg Jaffe write in the *Washington Post*, "Beneath its commitment to soft-spoken diplomacy and beyond the combat zones of Afghanistan and Iraq, the Obama administration has significantly expanded a largely secret U.S. war against al-Qaeda and other radical groups, according to senior military and administration officials. Special Operations forces have grown both in number and budget, and are deployed in 75 countries, compared with about 60 at the beginning of last year [2009]."[2] Jeremy Scahill at *The Nation* made clear that, instead of cutting back on highly controversial and questionably legal operations, President Obama had embraced the covert program established by Bush neoconservatives Deputy Defense Secretary Paul Wolfowitz and Undersecretary of Defense for Intelligence Stephen Cambone, and aggressively accelerated it. Scahill writes, "'The Obama administration took the 2003 order and went above and beyond,' says the special forces source. 'The world is the battlefield, we've returned to that,' he adds, referring to the Obama administration strategy. 'We were moving away from it for a little bit, but Cambone's "preparing the battlefield" is still alive and well. It's embraced by this administration.'"[3]

After the failure of counterinsurgency (COIN) and the firing of General McChrystal, there was nothing left for the U.S. military to do than to return to its counterterrorism program (a.k.a. targeted killing). But according to the *New York Times*' Helene Cooper and Mark Landler, as of July 2010, targeted killing was suddenly the "new U.S. focus in Afghanistan."[4] How could this backward thinking suddenly "change the nature of the war and potentially . . . hasten a political settlement with the Taliban,"[5] when it had done nothing but alienate the population, encourage a Taliban resurgence and sow the seeds of defeat for nine years?

Bush's exploitation of the "war on terror" to fundamentally alter the relationship between the United States and the world had been the cause of universal concern. In February of 2009, a panel of sixty eminent judges and lawyers from around the world, organized by the International Commission of Jurists in Geneva, issued a call to the new president to "immediately and publicly renounce" the "immense damage" done to international law by the war on terror.[6] In an announcement, a member of the committee, the former chief Justice of South Africa Arthur Chaskalson, stated, "We have been shocked by the damage done over the past seven years by excessive or abusive counterterrorism measures in a wide range of countries around the world."[7] In the report, the panel determined that "conflation of acts of terrorism with acts of war was legally and conceptually flawed" and had done immense damage to a shared international "legal framework underlying both human rights and humanitarian law."[8]

In a commentary on the report, Stella Rimington, former head of MI5, Britain's equivalent to the U.S. FBI, indicated that the prosecution of suspects through the military system was counter-productive, insisting that it "has achieved the opposite effect—there are more and more suicide terrorists finding a greater justification."[9] Yet months after Obama assumed office, his administration's approach to terror suspects had changed in name only, as targeted assassinations and "snatch and grabs" accelerated to unprecedented levels.[10] Stuart Gottlieb, the director of the Policy Studies Program at Yale University's MacMillan Center for International and Area Studies, writes:

> If you were under the impression that the U.S. President Barack Obama's promise to craft new counterterrorism policies "in a manner that is consistent with our values and our ideals" could be accomplished without exposing dangerous contradictions, consider this: Since Obama's swearing-in, the United States has executed dozens of suspected al Qaeda leaders and operatives without court hearings, the presentation of evidence, or the involvement of defense lawyers. These executions, typically carried out by missile strikes from unmanned CIA drone aircraft, have taken place in the border regions of Afghanistan and Pakistan. Scores of civilians, including many women and children, have reportedly been killed or maimed in the strikes.[11]

Gottlieb went on to point out that while "there are tremendous costs to aggressive counterterrorism policies" without explaining to the public how such controversial assassinations fit into an overall plan, Obama risked being compared unfavorably to the Bush administration and suffering a loss of goodwill toward his administration.[12]

On October 9, 2009, the Norwegian Nobel Committee offered Barack Obama the opportunity to explain himself by awarding him the Nobel Peace prize for 2009 "for his extraordinary efforts to strengthen international diplomacy and cooperation between peoples, for his "vision of and work for a world without nuclear weapons," for creating a new climate in international politics in which "multilateral diplomacy has regained a central position." and for initiating a more constructive role for the United States.[13]

Given that he had not accomplished any of those things, it appeared that Obama's Nobel Prize was intended to be a down payment, a kind of moral guarantee to America's kingmakers from the international community that all would be forgiven if Washington would just remove the brass knuckles and return to a policy of shared consensus. But in those eight years since 9/11, Washington had crossed a threshold it had been driving toward since 1944, and Obama's White House was not about to turn back.

According to Stephen F. Cohen, professor of Russian studies and history at New York University and an expert on U.S.-Russia relations, the Obama foreign policy team had been packed from the start with a long list of triumphalist, Cold War–era thinkers, whose lifelong purpose was the containment of Russian influence and control over energy pipeline routes to and from Central Asia.[14]

> His vice president, Joseph Biden, was a longtime zealous proponent of the triumphalist policy, including NATO expansion and the U.S. projects in Georgia and Ukraine, and of 'direct confrontation' with the Kremlin. Accepting his nomination, Biden rededicated himself to those pursuits. Obama's secretary of state, Hillary Rodham Clinton, was the spouse of the president who originated that general policy and staffed her department with people who had implemented it. Robert Gates, Obama's secretary of defense, had a longer governmental involvement in the failed policy than anyone else in Washington.[15]

In Cohen's view, the addition of men such as General James Jones as national security advisor and even Lawrence Summers as Obama's economic advisor further proved his point. Washington simply could not correct the course it had been on for nearly 70 years and adapt to new global realities, "not even with the United States bogged down in wars in Iraq and Afghanistan and crippled by economic crisis."[16]

Accepting a "peace prize" while conducting a war on two fronts was itself broaching a dangerous contradiction. To advocate for a war of targeted execution of real or suspected opponents as a way of attaining peace, was a mind-bending philosophical conundrum that neither the president nor his new, conservative speechwriter, Ben Rhodes,[17] were up to. State-sponsored killing had preoccupied critical thinking since the foundation of the Catholic Church. The Cistercian abbot Bernard of Clairvaux attempted to indemnify killing for Christ in his famous twelfth-century treatise *De Laude Novae Militiae* (*In Praise of the New Knighthood*)[18] by redefining the very nature of murder itself.

> Christ's knight deals out death in safety, as I said, and suffers death in even greater safety. He benefits himself when he suffers death, and benefits Christ when he deals out death. "He does not wear a sword without cause; he is God's agent for punishment of evil-doers and for glorification of the good." Clearly, when he kills an evil-doer, he is not a homicide, but, if you will allow me the term, a malicide, and is plainly Christ's vengeance on those who work evil and the defense Christ provides for Christians.[19]

Bernard of Clairvaux's extensive rationalization, written expressly for the new breed of warrior monks[20] that sprang up following the first Crusade to Jerusalem, was a defining moment in the legitimization of modern warfare. Alongside the Just War Doctrine,[21] first enunciated by St. Augustine of Hippo (354–430 CE) and further developed by St. Thomas Aquinas (AD 1225–1274), it proved to be a foundation document on the uses of organized violence, opened the floodgates of recruits for future Crusades and established the legal authority of powerful, wealthy Catholic military orders that were independent of both church and state control.[22]

Despite its importance and its timeliness, Obama's Nobel message was no such defining moment. Far from being original, inspiring or vital, Obama's Nobel acceptance speech was a patchwork of ideological and philosophical contradictions that roamed from "the imperfections of man and the limits of reason,"[23] to new ways to think "about the notions of just war and the imperatives of a just peace."[24]

Part rationale for a "just war" because "evil does exist in this world," part sales pitch for keeping NATO—"Peace requires responsibility. Peace entails sacrifice. That is why NATO continues to be indispensable"[25]—and part chastisement of "the ambivalence of the broader public" to the need for war, Obama's message left the world wondering whether he or Washington even understood that it was not the evolution of human nature and its ability to reason that was on trial but the increasingly privatized institutions of government itself, which had advanced and prolonged the need for war as a solution.

As brought forward in the prologue to this book, the Catholic doctrine of "just war" was refined and adapted in the sixteenth century as a legal defense against an all-out war of genocide waged by the soldiers of Walter Raleigh. Far from being a war over ecclesiastical principles, this "holy war" fought between the Catholic Geraldines and their Protestant "others" was above all a war against economic domination and colonization by London. From London's perspective, the war was a "just war" because it was a struggle to the death against the Papal forces of the Counter-Reformation, which were encircling it militarily and economically and rolling back Protestant reforms.

In the end, the war depopulated the Irish countryside, shifted the balance of power from local landowners to mercantilists in London and instilled a lasting fear and anger between Protestants and Catholics. As an experiment in colonization, Ireland set the standards of behavior that marked the beginnings of Britain's empire and live on as much today in the neighborhoods of Kabul, Kandahar and Peshawar as they do in Derry and Belfast. But it also marked a turning point in the Holy Roman Empire's ability to control events through military force and a shift from the ecclesiastically sanctioned violence of "just war" to the secular-state sanctioned violence of "just war." The Obama administration came to power at an equally important turning point for American empire and for the world. When the United States began its direct military intervention in the Hindu Kush to help provoke the Soviet invasion in 1979, it marshaled the forces of reaction and ignited an Islamic holy war that continues to spread throughout Central Asia. Instead of advancing rational democratic principles that promoted the cause of human rights, the United States helped the most backward elements of society restore a feudal order and force its agenda on an unwilling population. Today, the United States faces the consequences of that process. But instead of acknowledging a profoundly flawed policy and demanding accountability from the institutions responsible, the President continues to deny responsibility[26] while fostering a new social order for the AfPak region that rewards the very people, both here and there, who created the problem.

Over the last century, the United States built a reputation as a leader in science, technology, justice and individual human rights. With the Japanese attack on Pearl Harbor on December 7, 1941, the United States embarked on a massive military expansion. That expansion became permanent with the beginning of the Cold War and the designation of both the Soviet Union and the People's Republic of China as threats to U.S. security. But not everyone agreed on the necessity of a permanent Cold War or on catering to the dark forces that lay behind it. On May 21, 1948, Henry Wallace, Franklin Roosevelt's former vice president and, at the time, a candidate for president of the United States on the Progressive Party platform, warned of a dangerous element in U.S. foreign policy that was not fully appreciated at the time.

> If we recognize the fundamental fact that American foreign policy today is based on serving private corporations and international big business, rather than on serving great masses of

people—when we recognize this fact we can understand their unwillingness to reach agreement with Russia. Conflict with Russia is the excuse, it is the alibi for using the resources of our country to back up the same kind of cartels which contributed so greatly to the start of World War II.[27]

Since that time, the United States has vastly expanded the interests of private corporations across the globe and built the largest military establishment in history to protect them. Through the power of its economy and technology it has acquired the ability to target enemies anywhere in the world without regard to law, morality or justice. But in crossing Zero, the United States has crossed a threshold where its capacity for violence undermines its own standards of justice and individual rights without which the violence has no meaning. In other words, the United States has come to a turning point at which the purpose of the force it has created has become its own undoing.

The significance of this moment in time was not lost on the rest of the world or even the U.S. military itself. U.S. military thinkers were more than aware of the approaching crossover in global consciousness as well as their own growing powerlessness in the face of it. Nathan Freier of the Army's Strategic Studies Institute writes:

> Imagine, "a new era of containment with the United States as the nation to be contained," where the principle tools and methods of war involve everything but those associated with traditional military conflict. Imagine that the sources of this "new era of containment" are widespread; predicated on non-military forms of political, economic, and violent action; in the main, sustainable over time; and finally, largely invulnerable to effective reversal through traditional U.S. advantages.[28]

In a CFR speech on May 14, 2010, Zbigniew Brzezinski, President Jimmy Carter's national security advisor, Trilateral Commission co-founder and Eurasia strategist, spoke of the profound consciousness-altering changes occurring worldwide. "For the first time in human history, mankind is politically awakened. That's a total new reality. Total new reality. It has not been so for most of human history until the last hundred years. And in the course of the last hundred years the whole world has become politically awakened. And no matter where you go, politics is a matter of social engagement, and most people know what is generally going on in the world . . . and are consciously aware of global iniquities, inequalities, lack of respect, exploitation. Mankind is now politically awakened and stirring."[29]

Yet, instead of moving to correct its policies for an awakened world in which the United States is increasingly viewed as responsible for the iniquities, inequalities, lack of respect and exploitation, the Obama administration continues to forge ahead as if it were in a dream.[30] According to a recent Congressional Research Service report, the "war on terror" is the costliest war in U.S. history with the exception of World War II.[31] It now exceeds the costs of the Korean War, Vietnam or the Cold War at its peak. Currently, the Obama administration has requested an increase in total war spending in 2011 to $708 billion, a figure that is 6.1 percent higher than the peak under the Bush administration.[32] As the U.S. military profile expands, the country's technological, economic and educational base falls precipitously,[33] with urgent calls from all quarters for the country to come to its senses before it's too late. But for Afghans, as well as a growing number of Americans, it is already too late. Priyamvada Gopal writes in the *Guardian*,

> The truth is that the U.S. and allied regimes do not have anything substantial to offer Afghanistan beyond feeding the gargantuan war machine they have unleashed. And how could they? In the affluent west itself, modernity is now about dismantling welfare systems, increasing inequality (disproportionately disenfranchising women in the process), and subsidising corporate profits. Other ideas once associated with modernity—social justice, economic fairness, peace, all of which would enfranchise Afghan women—have been

relegated to the past in the name of progress. This bankrupt version of modernity has little to offer Afghans other than bikini waxes and Oprah-imitators. A radical people's modernity is called for—and not only for the embattled denizens of Afghanistan.[34]

America's national security is no longer an issue of the politics of left versus right or conservative versus liberal. It is not even an issue of good versus evil. It is simply at the point where war and the endless preparations for it do more harm than good, where they destroy what they claim to protect, where they are neither just nor unjust but add up to nothing more than zero.

Afghanistan has given us a mirror with which to understand this truth about ourselves and to see what we have become as a nation and a democracy. Our future will depend on whether we can accept the challenges that it portends.

NOTES

INTRODUCTION

1. Paul Fitzgerald and Elizabeth Gould, "Apocalypse of the American Mind," *boilingfrogs*, January 22, 2010. www.boilingfrogspost.com/2010/01/22/apocalypse-of-the-american-mind/
2. Paul Fitzgerald and Elizabeth Gould, "In Afghanistan: Embracing Gulbuddin Hekmatyar Is No Method at All," *Huffingtonpost*, January 25, 2010. www.huffingtonpost.com/elizabeth-gould/in-afghanistan-embracing_b_435239.html
3. Nick Grono and Candace Rondeaux, "Dealing with brutal Afghan warlords is a mistake," *Boston Globe*, January 17, 2010.
4. Executive Order for the purpose of "Blocking Property and Prohibiting Transactions with Persons Who Commit, Threaten To Commit, Or Support Terrorism." www.ustreas.gov/offices/enforcement/ofac/programs/terror/terror.pdf
5. Thom Shanker and Carlotta Gall, "U.S. Attack on Warlord Aims to Help Interim Leader," *New York Times*, May 5, 2002. www.nytimes.com/2002/05/09/world/us-attack-on-warlord-aims-to-help-interim-leader.html
6. "Warlord claims French ambush," RFI, September 29, 2008. www.rfi.fr/actuen/articles/105/article_1719.asp
7. "Biography, Gulbuddin Hekmatyar," *Afghanistan Online*, www.afghan-web.com/bios/today/ghekmatyar.html. Muhammed Tahir, "Gulbuddin Hekmatyar's return to The Afghan Insurgency," Jamestown Foundation Terrorism Monitor, Volume 6: Issue 11: May 29, 2008, www.jamestown.org/programs/gta/single/?tx_ttnews%5Btt_news%5D=4951&tx_ttnews%5BbackPid%5D=167&no_cache=1
8. Authors' email correspondence with Daoud M. Abedi, Especial Envoy of Brother Hekmatyar for the United States, Representative of HIA in the USA (Hesb-i-Islami Afghanistan, Hekmatyar), Los Angeles, California, February 9, 2010.
9. Christina Lamb and Jerome Starkey, "Karzai in move to share power with Hekmatyar, warlord wanted by US," *Sunday Times* (UK) May 10, 2009.
10. Nick Grono and Candace Rondeaux, "Dealing with brutal Afghan warlords is a mistake," *Boston Globe*, January 17, 2010.
11. Henry Kamm, "Afghan Rebel Opposes Talks; Vows Battle for Islamic State," *New York Times*, March 1988.
12. Steve Coll, *Ghost Wars* (New York: Penguin, 2004), p. 120, citing an interview with Graham Fuller, 1992.
13. Henry Kamm, "Afghan Rebels Opposes Talks; Vows Battle for Islamic State," *New York Times*, March 1988.
14. Ibid.
15. Nick Grono and Candace Rondeaux, "Dealing with brutal Afghan warlords is a mistake," *Boston Globe*, January 17, 2010.
16. Carlotta Gall, "Insurgent Faction Presents Afghan Peace Plan," *New York Times*, March 23, 2010.
17. Ibid.
18. Ahmad Masood, Wasiq Mahwash, *Water resource development in Northern Afghanistan and its implications for Amu Darya Basin* (Washington DC: World Bank Publications, 2004), p. 7.
19. East Pakistan seceded from the union with West Pakistan in 1971 and was renamed Bangladesh.

20. Encyclopedia Britannica Online http://britannica.com/bps/additionalcontent/18/9629172/The-Invention-of-Pakistan

21. "Will the Obama Administration Occupy Pashtunistan or All of Pakistan?" *Macro Viewpoints*, April 29, 2009. http://cinemarasik.com/2009/04/25/will-the-obama-administration-occupy-pashtunistan-or-all-of-paksitan.aspx

22. Ibid.

23. Ibid.

24. Ann Scott Tyson, "Pentagon Budget Devotes More to Afghanistan War Than to Iraq," *Washington Post*, May 8, 2009.

25. Trudy Rubin interview with Bruce Riedel: "Is Pakistan our biggest threat?" Posted to the *Philadelphia Inquirer* Web site September 9, 2008. www.philly/podcasts/28052589.html accessed June 12, 2009.

26. Malcolm Rifkind, "If we ignore Pakistan, we won't solve Afghanistan," *The Independent*, June 11, 2007.

27. Bernard Gwertzman interview with Bruce Riedel, "Riedel: U.S. Needs to Tread Carefully in Pakistan," Council on Foreign Relations, September 12, 2008. www.cfr.org/publication/17191/riedel.html accessed June 12, 2009.

28. See video and transcript: Pakistan's Zardari and Afghanistan's Karzai on *Meet the Press*, May 10, 2009. http://enduringamerica.com/2009/05/10/video-and-transcript-pakistans-zardari-and-afghanistans-karzai-on-meet-the-press-10-may/

29. M.K. Bhadrakumar, "Taliban wake-up call for India," *Asia Times*, October 9, 2008.

30. Sebastian Abbot, "US looks for Saudi help in Afghanistan, Pakistan," Associated Press, June 3, 2009.

31. Ahmed Rashid, *Descent into Chaos, The United States and the Failure of Nation Building in Pakistan, Afghanistan, and Central Asia* (New York: Viking, 2008), p. 140.

32. See video and transcript: Pakistan's Zardari and Afghanistan's Karzai on *Meet the Press* (May 10, 2005). http://enduringamerica.com/2009/05/10/video-and-transcript-pakistans-zardari-and-afghanistans-karzai-on-meet-the-press-10-may/

33. Paddy Ashdown, "Just the man to bang heads together in Kabul," *The Times* (London), February 2, 2009.

34. Bruce Falconer, "Kabul's K Street Project," *Mother Jones*, June 9, 2009.

35. M.K. Bhadrakumar, "Sino-Russian baby comes of age," *Asia Times*, June 13, 2009.

36. See Alvin A. Snyder, *Warriors of Disinformation* (New York: Arcade Publishing, 1995).

37. John Blake, "He would have found bin Laden," cnn.com, May 27, 2009. http://cnn.com/2009/WORLD/asiapcf/05/27/massoud.afghanistan/

38. Nancy and Richard S. Newell, *The Struggle for Afghanistan* (Ithaca, NY: Cornell University Press, 1981), p. 47.

PROLOGUE

1. Benjamin Woolley, *The Queen's Conjurer: The Science and Magic of Dr. John Dee, Advisor to Queen Elizabeth I* (New York: Henry Holt, 2001), p.100.

2. Giraldus Cambrensis, *Expugnatio Hibernica: The Conquest of Ireland* (Dublin: Royal Irish Academy, 1978).

3. Richard Berleth, *The Twilight Lords: An Irish Chronicle* (New York: Knopf: distributed by Random House, 1978), p. 89.

4. Vinay Lal, "The East India Company," *Manas*. www.sscnet.ucla.edu/southasia/History/British/EAco.html

5. Nick Robins, "The East India Company: the future of the past," September 12, 2006, opendemocracy.net. www.opendemocracy.net/globalization-vision_reflections/east_india_company_3899.jsp

6. Ibid.

7. Lal, "The East India Company."

8. Ibid.

9. Vartan Gregorian, *The Emergence of Modern Afghanistan, Politics of Reform and Modernization, 1880–1946* (Stanford, CA: Stanford Univ. Press, 1969), pp. 21–22.

10. www.econlib.org/library/enc/bios/Smith.html

11. http://bbc.co.uk/history/historic_figures/burke_edmund.shtml

12. Colonel H.B. Hanna, *The Second Afghan War*, Vol I. (London: Westminster Archibald Constable & Co., 1899), p. 1, n. 1.

Chapter 1—CROSSING ZERO

1. Anthony Cordesman, Arleigh A. Burke, *Follow the Money: Why the U.S. Is Losing the War in Afghanistan*, Draft: September 19, 2008. Center For Strategic and International Studies. http://csis.org/files/media/csis/pubs/080919_afghanwarcosts.pdf

2. Ibid.

3. Abdul Samad Ghaus, *The Fall of Afghanistan: An Insider's Account* (Washington, DC: Pergamon-Brassey's International Defense Publishers, 1988), p. 15.

4. www.harrapa.com/har/indus-saraswati.html

5. Raja Murthy, "Indus Valley code is cracked—maybe," *Asia Times*, May 13, 2009.

6. Vartan Gregorian, *The Emergence of Modern Afghanistan: Politics of Reform and Modernization, 1880–1946* (Stanford, CA: Stanford Univ. Press, 1969), p. 345.

7. Ibid., p 43.

8. Ibid., pp. 118–119.

9. Ibid., p.119.

10. Ibid.

11. Peter Hopkirk, *The Great Game: The Struggle for Empire in Central Asia* (New York: Kodansha International, 1992), p. 192.

12. Richard F. Nyrop and Donald M. Seekins, *Afghanistan, a Country Study* (Washington, DC: Supt. of Docs., U.S. G.P.O.), 1986, p. 29.

13. John H. Waller, *Beyond the Khyber Pass* (New York: Random House, 1990), pp. 280–281.

14. Barnett R. Rubin and Abubakar Siddique, *Resolving the Pakistan-Afghanistan Stalemate*, Special Report 176, United States Institute for Peace, October 2006, p. 5.

15. Rubin and Siddique, *Resolving the Pakistan-Afghanistan Stalemate*, p. 5.

16. T.W. Moody and F.X. Martin, eds., *The Course of Irish History*, revised and enlarged edition (Ireland: Robert Rinehart Publishers, 1994), p. 155.

17. "Evolution of the FCR: Frontier Crimes Regulation," *Alaiwah*, November 28, 2008. http://alaiwah.wordpress.com/2008/11/28/evolution-of-the-fcr-frontier-crimes-regulation/

18. Rubin and Siddique, *Resolving the Pakistan-Afghanistan Stalemate*, p. 12.

19. Ahmed Rashid, *Descent into Chaos: The United States and the Failure of Nation Building in Pakistan, Afghanistan, and Central Asia* (New York: Viking, 2008), p. 266.

20. Rubin and Siddique, *Resolving the Pakistan-Afghanistan Stalemate*, p. 6.

21. Hopkirk, *The Great Game*, p. 520.

22. Gregorian, *The Emergence of Modern Afghanistan*, p. 127.

23. Ibid., p. 261.

24. David B. Edwards, *Before Taliban: Genealogies of the Afghan Jihad* (Berkeley: University of California Press, 2002), pp. 26–27.

25. Remarks by Selig S. Harrison at the seminar sponsored by the Carnegie Endowment for International Peace on the topic "Will Pakistan Break Up?" Washington, June 9, 2009. www.ciponline.org/asia/ceiptalk.html Accessed June 19, 2009.

26. Pete Takeda, *An Eye At The Top Of The World* (New York: Thunder's Mouth Press, 2006), p. 103.

27. Rubin and Siddique, *Resolving the Pakistan-Afghanistan Stalemate*, p. 7.
28. Ibid., p. 8.
29. Selig S. Harrison, Carnegie Endowment seminar for International Peace.
30. Ibid.
31. Haqqani, Husain. *Pakistan: Between Mosque and Military* (Washington, DC: Carnegie Endowment for International Peace, The Brookings Institution Press, 2005), p 174. Rubin and Siddique, *Resolving the Pakistan-Afghanistan Stalemate*, p. 8.
32. Rubin and Siddique, *Resolving the Pakistan-Afghanistan Stalemate*, p. 6.
33. Ibid., p. 8.
34. Diego Cordovez and Selig S. Harrison, *Out of Afghanistan* (New York: Oxford Univ. Press, 1995), p. 187.
35. Ibid., p. 38.
36. Charles G. Cogan, "Partners in Time," *World Policy Journal*, September 22, 2008.
37. Cordovez and Harrison, *Out of Afghanistan*, p. 256.
38. Rubin and Siddique, *Resolving the Pakistan-Afghanistan Stalemate*, p. 9.

Chapter 2—CREATING THE TALIBAN
1. M. K. Bhadrakumar, "Afghanistan's ball back in Pakistan's court," *Asia Times*, August 18, 2007.
2. Rachel Maddow interview with Zbigniew Brzezinski, *The Rachel Maddow Show*, February 18, 2009.
3. Charles G. Cogan, "Partners in Time," *World Policy Journal*, September 22, 2008.
4. "Who are the Taliban?" *BBC News*, Updated June 18, 2009. http://news.bbc.co.uk/2/hi/1549285.stm
5. *CNN Crossfire*, September 10, 2002–19:00 ET, http://transcripts.cnn.com/TRANSCRIPTS/0209/10/cf.00.html
6. "CIA Worked in Tandem with Pak to Create Taliban," *Times of India*, March 7, 2001.
7. See video and transcript: Pakistan's Zardari and Afghanistan's Karzai on *Meet the Press* (May 10, 2009) http://enduringamerica.com/2009/05/10/video-and-transcript-pakistans-zardari-and-afghanistans-karzai-on-meet-the-press-10-may/
8. Kamal Matinuddin, *The Taliban Phenomenon, Afghanistan 1994-1997* (Karachi, Pakistan: Oxford Univ. Press, 1999), p. 33.
9. Nicholas Barrington, Joseph Kendrick and Reinhard Schlagintweit, *A Passage to Nuristan: Exploring the Mysterious Afghan Hinterland* (London: I.B. Tauris & Co. 1988), p. 143.
10. Melanie Phillips, *Londonistan* (New York: Encounter Books, updated paperback edition, 2007), p. 3.
11. See Paul Fitzgerald and Elizabeth Gould, *Invisible History: Afghanistan's Untold Story* (San Francisco: City Lights, 2009), pp. 153–154. See also Robert Dreyfuss, *Devil's Game* (New York: Metropolitan Books, 2005), pp. 47, 106–107.
12. Diego Cordovez and Selig S. Harrison, *Out of Afghanistan* (New York: Oxford University Press, 1995), p. 16.
13. Paul Fitzgerald and Elizabeth Gould, *Invisible History: Afghanistan's Untold Story*, p. 190.
14. Alvin A. Snyder, *Warriors of Disinformation* (New York: Arcade Publishing, 1995), p. 210.
15. Kurt Lohbeck, *Holy War, Unholy Victory* (Washington, DC: Regnery Gateway, 1993), pp. 166–167.
16. Ibid.
17. Ibid.
18. www.rlf.org.uk/FELLOWSHIPSCHEME/profile.cfm?fellow=155&menu=3

Chapter 3—AFPAK: WHAT IS IT?
1. K. Alan Kronstadt, "Direct Overt U.S. Aid and Military Reimbursements to Pakistan, FY2002-2009," Congressional Research Service, April 15, 2009; Amy Belasco, "The

Cost of Iraq, Afghanistan, and Other Global War on Terror Operations Since 9/11," Congressional Research Service, October 15, 2008, p.6.

2. Ahmed Rashid, *Descent into Chaos: The United States and the Failure of Nation Building in Pakistan, Afghanistan, and Central Asia* (New York: Viking, 2008), p. 269.

3. Ibid., p. 274.

4. Catherine Philip, "Pervez Musharraf was playing 'double game,' with US," *TimesOnline*, February 17, 2009. http://www.timesonline.co.uk/tol/news/world/asia/article5747696.ece

5. White House white paper on U.S. policy to Afghanistan and Pakistan, March 27, 2009.

6. Andrew J. Bacevich, "Winning in Afghanistan," *Newsweek*, December 31, 2008.

7. "Focus and Exit: An Alternative Strategy for the Afghan War," with Gilles Dorronsoro, Ashley J. Tellis and David Barno, February 3, 2009, at the Carnegie Endowment for International Peace. www.carnegieendowment.org/events/?fa=eventDetail&id=1257&prog=zch

8. Daniel Markey, *From AfPak to PakAf: A Response to the New U.S. Strategy for South Asia*, Council on Foreign Relations, April 2009. www.cfr.org/publication/19125

9. Ibid.

10. Michael Moran, "The 'airlift of evil' Why did we let Pakistan pull 'volunteers' out of Kunduz?," MSNBC, Nov. 29, 2001. www.msnbc.msn.com/id/3340165

11. Rashid, *Descent Into Chaos*, p. 268–270.

12. Moran, "The 'airlift of evil.'"

13. Markey, *From AfPak to PakAf*, p. 9.

14. The Malakand Accord was imposed in Malakand, Swat, Shangla, Buner, Dir, Chitral and Kohistan. This region comprises more than one-third of the North West Frontier Province.

15. Bill Roggio, "Swat peace agreement collapses," *The Long War Journal*, April 9, 2009. www.longwarjournal.org/archives/2009/04/swat_peace_agreement.php

16. Michael Heath, "Pakistan Made No Concessions to Taliban in Swat, Envoy Says," *Bloomberg.com*, Feb. 20, 2009. www.bloomberg.com/apps/news?pid=20601087&sid=a7ech afFRh6w&refer=home

17. Jane Perlez, "Pakistan Makes a Taliban Truce, Creating a Haven," *New York Times*, February 16, 2009.

18. Ibid.

19. Ghulam Farooq, "Swat Taliban Enter Buner," *Daily Times* (Pakistan), April 6, 2009.

20. Mark Landler and Elisabeth Bumiller, "Now, U.S. Sees Pakistan as Cause Distinct From Afghanistan," *New York Times*, April 30, 2009.

21. Interview with Thomas Barfield, *Mother Jones*, May/June 2009.

22. Interview with Bruce O. Riedel by Bernard Gwertzman, "Pakistan's 'Existential Threat' Comes From Within," Council on Foreign Relations, May 6, 2009. www.cfr.org/publication/19321/pakistans_existential_threat_comes_from_within.html

23. Interview with Bruce O. Riedel by Bernard Gwertzman, "U.S. Needs to Tread Carefully in Pakistan," Council on Foreign Relations, September 12, 2008. www.cfr.org/publication/17191/riedel.html

24. Mosharraf Zaidi, "One Hundred Days in Obamistan," *The News*, May 5, 2009. www.thenews.compk/daily_detail.asp?id=175827

25. David Kilcullen and Andrew McDonald Exum, "Death from Above, Outrage Down Below," *New York Times*, May 17, 2009.

26. Fisnik Abrashi, "US denies killing 147 civilians in Afghan clash," Associated Press, May 9, 2009.

27. Ann Scott Tyson, "Top U.S. Commander in Afghanistan Is Fired," *Washington Post*, May 12, 2009.

28. CNN, "Admiral: Troops alone will not yield victory in Afghanistan," September 10, 2008. www.cnn.com/2008/POLITICS/09/10/mullen.afghanistan/index.html accessed July 29, 2009.

29. Ibid.
30. Gareth Porter, "Staring at the sun in Afghanistan," *Asia Times*, April 23, 2009.
31. Katrina Vanden Heuvel, "War Supplemental Narrowly Passes," *The Nation*, June 16, 2009.
32. Katrina Vanden Heuvel, "Smart Power in Pakistan/Afghanistan?" *The Nation*, May 8, 2009.
33. Seth G. Jones, *In the Graveyard of Empires* (New York: W.W. Norton, 2009), p. 119.
34. Ibid.
35. Milton Bearden, "Obama's War: Redefining Victory in Afghanistan and Pakistan," *Foreign Affairs*, April 9, 2009. www.foreignaffairs.org/node/64925
36. Porter, "Staring at the sun in Afghanistan."
37. Ibid.
38. Ward, "Countering the Military's Latest Fad: Counterinsurgency."
39. Celeste Ward, "Countering the Military's Latest Fad: Counterinsurgency," *Washington Post*, May 17, 2009.
40. Ibid.
41. Ibid.
42. Michael Hirsh and John Barry, "The Hidden General, Stan McChrystal runs 'black ops.' Don't pass it on," *Newsweek*, June 26, 2006.
43. Ibid.
44. Gareth Porter, "US choice hardly McChrystal clear," *Asia Times*, May 14, 2009.
45. Ibid.
46. Eric Black, "Investigative reporter Seymour Hersh describes 'executive assassination ring,'" March 11, 2009. www.minnpost.com/ericblackblog/2009/03/11/7310/investiga-tive_reporter_seymour_hersh_describes_executive_assassination_ring Minnpost.com
47. Carlotta Gall and David E. Sanger, "Civilian Deaths Undermine War on Taliban," *New York Times*, May 12, 2007.
48. Ibid.
49. Eric Schmitt and Jane Perlez, "Pakistan Objects to U.S. Plan for Afghan War," *New York Times*, July 22, 2009. www.nytimes.com/2009/07/22/world/asia/22pstan.html
50. Ibid.
51. Omar Waraich, "Why Pakistan Balks at the U.S. Afghanistan Offensive," *Time*, July 28, 2009.
52. Ibid.
53. Juan Cole, "Pakistan Crisis and Social Statistics," *Informed Comment*, April 26, 2009. www.juancole.com/2009/04/readers-have-written-me-asking-what-i.html
54. Nicholas Kristof, "Terror Creeps into Heartland," *New York Times*, July 22, 2009.
55. Salman Masood, "Attack in Pakistani Garrison City Raises Anxiety About Safety of Nuclear Labs and Staff," *New York Times*, July 5, 2009.
56. Clay Ramsay et al., "Pakistani Public Opinion on the Swat Conflict, Afghanistan and the US," *worldpublicopinion.org*, July 1, 2009.
57. Selig G. Harrison, "Pakistan: The State of the Union Special Report," Center for International Policy April 2009, citing *Denying the Undeniable: Enforced Disappearances in Pakistan*, Amnesty International, July, 2008.
58. Ibid.
59. Daphne Benoit, "Unclear if Pakistan offensive serves US," *Kuwait Times*, June 21, 2009.
60. Ibid.

Chapter 4—OBAMA'S VIETNAM?

1. Thomas H. Johnson and M. Chris Mason, "Saigon 2009: Afghanistan Is Today's Vietnam. No Question Mark Needed," *Foreign Policy*, August 20, 2009. www.foreignpolicy.com/articles/2009/08/20/saigon_2009

2. The Domino Theory of U.S. foreign policy after World War II stated that the "fall" of a noncommunist state to communism would precipitate the fall of noncommunist governments in neighboring states. It was also referred to as the Domino Effect: http://www.britannica.com/EBchecked/topic/168794/domino-theory

3. Robert M. Gates, *From the Shadows* (New York: Touchstone, 1997), pp. 144–147

4. Mark LeVine, "Pakistan's nut that won't crack," *Asia Times*, October 26, 2007.

5. Ibid.

6. For a detailed presentation of the complexities of the Afghan tribal structure and its unique relationship to Islam see "Muslim Politics and U.S. Policies: Prospects for Pluralism and Democracy in the Muslim World," Pew Forum, September 17, 2003. http://pewforum.org/events/?EventID=50

7. Remarks by Selig S. Harrison at the seminar sponsored by the Carnegie Endowment for International Peace on the topic "Will Pakistan Break Up?" Washington, June 9, 2009. www.ciponline.org/asia/ceiptalk.html Accessed June 19, 2009.

8. LeVine, "Pakistan's nut that won't crack."

9. Selig S. Harrison, Carnegie Endowment seminar for International Peace.

10. Jon Ward and Eli Lake, "White House: 'War on Terrorism' Is Over," *Washington Times*, August 6, 2009.

11. David Alexander, "How long will the U.S. be in Afghanistan? It's a mystery," Reuters, August 13, 2009. http://blogs.reuters.com/frontrow/2009/08/13/how-long-will-us-forces-be-in-afghanistan-its-a-mystery/

12. Dean Nelson, Alex Spillius and Ben Farmer, "Barack Obama abandons Afghan President Hamid Karzai," *Telegraph* (London), January 29, 2009.

13. Dexter Filkins, "Former Favorite, Karzai Slips in U.S. Eyes," *New York Times*, February 8, 2009.

14. Julian Borger and Ewen MacAskill, "US will appoint Afghan 'prime minister' to bypass Hamid Karzai," *Guardian* (London), March 22, 2009.

15. Joshua Partlow and Karen De Young, "With Karzai Favored to Win, U.S. Walks a Fine Line," *Washington Post*, August 14, 2009.

16. Correspondence with Jawied Nawabi, Adjunct Professor of Economics and Sociology, City University of New York (CUNY).

17. Syed Saleem Shahzad, "Politicians have their day in Afghanistan," *Asia Times*, August 21, 2009.

18. Ibid.

19. Ibid.

20. Jean MacKenzie, "Thursday's poll will likely hand victory to one well-known candidate," *GlobalPost*, August 18, 2009.

21. Richard A. Oppel Jr. and Sangar Rahimi, "Europe Says a Third of Votes Are Suspect," *New York Times*, September 16, 2009.

22. Mark Landler and Helene Cooper, "Afghan Vote Uncertainty Sparks Dilemma for U.S.," *New York Times*, September 18, 2009.

23. Paul Fitzgerald and Elizabeth Gould, *Invisible History, Afghanistan's Untold Story* (San Francisco: City Lights, 2009), p. 5.

24. Ahmed Rashid, *Descent into Chaos, The United States and the Failure of Nation Building in Pakistan, Afghanistan, and Central Asia* (New York: Viking, 2008), p. 140.

25. David B. Edwards, *Before Taliban: Genealogies of the Afghan Jihad* (Berkeley: Univ. of California Press, 2002), p. 26

26. William Pfaff, "There's a Solution in Afghanistan—but Not the Way We're Headed," *truthdig.com*, August 11, 2009. www.truthdig.com/report/item/20090811_theres_a_solution_in_afghanistan_—_but_not_the_way_were_headed/

Chapter 5—**METRICS**

1. Anthony Cordesman, *The New Metrics of Afghanistan: The Data Needed to Support, Clear, Hold, and Build*, Report: August 7, 2009. Center For Strategic and International Studies.
2. Ibid.
3. Seth G. Jones, "Going the Distance," *Washington Post*, February 15, 2009.
4. Magna Carta: "No freeman shall be taken, imprisoned . . . or in any way destroyed . . . except by the lawful judgement of his peers, or by the law of the land. To no one will we sell, to none will we deny or delay, right or justice." www.archives.gov/exhibits/featured_ documents/magna_carta/
5. Scott Shane, "A Dogged Taliban Chief Rebounds, Vexing U.S.," *New York Times*, October 10, 2009.
6. Anthony Cordesman, *Follow the Money: Why the U.S. is Losing the War in Afghanistan*, Draft: September 19, 2008. Center For Strategic and International Studies. http://csis. org/files/media/csis/pubs/080919_afghanwarcosts.pdf
7. Cordesman, *The New Metrics of Afghanistan*.
8. Ibid.
9. Paul Reynolds, "US foreign policy: 'No we can't?,'" *BBC News*, September 15, 2009.
10. General Henry H. Shelton, Chairman, Joint Chiefs of Staff, "Joint Vision 2020, America's Military Preparing for Tomorrow," U.S. Government Printing Office, Washington, DC, June 2000. www.dtic.mil/doctrine/jel/jfq_pubs/1225.pdf
11. Paul Reynolds, "US foreign policy: 'No we can't?,'" *BBC NEWS:* September 15, 2009.
12. Raphael G. Satter, "No we can't? UK think tank says U.S. power is fading," Associated Press, September 15, 2009.
13. "Global Trends 2025: A Transformed World," NIC 2008-003, November 2008,U.S. Government Printing Office. www.dni.gov/nic/NIC_2025_project.html
14. Ibid.
15. Michael T. Klare, "Welcome to 2025," *Asia Times*, October 28, 2009.

Chapter 6—**NATO**

1. Alison Smale, "A Somber Warning on Afghanistan," *New York Times*, September 14, 2009.
2. Ibid.
3. John D. Banusiewicz, "'National Caveats,' Among Key Topics at NATO Meeting," American Forces Press Service, February 9, 2005.
4. Paul Gallis, "NATO in Afghanistan: A Test of Transatlantic Alliance," Congressional Research Service Report for Congress, updated January 7, 2008. www.fas.org/sgp/crs/ row/RL33627.pdf (April 4. 2008)
5. Stephen Fidler and John W. Miller, "U.S. Allies Await Afghan Review," *Wall Street Journal*, September 25, 2009.
6. Spiegel Staff, "German Troops Beef Up Fight against Taliban," *Spiegel Online*, July 9, 2009. www.spiegel.de/international/germany/0,1518,635192,00.html
7. David Ljunggren, "NATO 'a corpse,' fumes former Canadian military boss," Reuters, October 20, 2009.
8. Ibid.
9. JR/HGL, "Occupiers involved in drug trade: Afghan minister," Press TV, November 1, 2009. www.presstv.ir/detail.aspx?id=110130&sectionid=351020403
10. M.K. Bhadrakumar, "US goofs the Afghan election," *Asia Times*, November 3, 2009.
11. Joshua Partlow, Karen De Young and Debbi Wilgoren, "Karzai agrees to runoff," *Washington Post*, October 20, 2009.
12. Ibid.
13. Dexter Filkins, Mark Mazzetti and James Risen, "Brother of Afghan Leader Is Said to Be on C.I.A. Payroll," *New York Times*, October 28, 2009.
14. Pamela Constable and William Branigin, "Afghan election commission declares Karzai

the winner," *Washington Post*, November 2, 2009.

15. M.K. Bhadrakumar, "US goofs the Afghan election."

16. Andrew Malcolm, "John Kerry's Afghan war speech; Foreshadowing Obama's decision," text of remarks by Sen. John Kerry to the Council on Foreign Relations, *Los Angeles Times*, October 27, 2009.

17. Daniel Markey, *From AfPak to PakAf: A Response to the New U.S. Strategy for South Asia*, Council on Foreign Relations, April 2009. www.cfr.org/publication/19125

18. Malcolm, "John Kerry's Afghan war speech."

19. Graham Allison, "In Afghanistan, Kerry keeps U.S. goals modest," *Boston Globe*, November 4, 2009.

20. Malcolm, "John Kerry's Afghan war speech."

21. Richard F. Nyrop and Donald M. Seekins, *Afghanistan: A Country Study* (Washington, DC: For sale by the Supt. of Docs., U.S. G.P.O., 1986), p. xxi.

22. Selig S. Harrison, "Afghanistan's Tyranny of the Minority," *New York Times*, August 17, 2009.

23. Ibid.

24. Nyrop and Seekins, *Afghanistan: A Country Study*, p.37.

25. Ralph Peters, "How a better Middle East would look," *Armed Forces Journal*, June 2006. www.armedforcesjournal.com/2006/06/1833899

26. Karin Brulliard, "Kerry visit underscores power still wielded by Pakistani army," *Washington Post*, October 23, 2009.

Chapter 7—U.S.-Pakistan: A HISTORY

1. K. Alan Kronstadt, "Pakistan-U.S. Relations," *Congressional Research Service*, February 6, 2009. www.fas.org/sgp/crs/row/RL33498.pdf

2. Ibid.

3. "Pakistan Nuclear Weapons: A Brief History of Pakistan's Nuclear Program," Federation of American Scientists, http://www.fas.org/nuke/guide/pakistan/nuke/

4. "Pakistan Nuclear Weapons," Global Security.Org http://www.globalsecurity.org/wmd/world/pakistan/nuke.htm

5. "Fall 1990: US Tells Pakistan to Destroy Nuclear Weapon Cores, but It Does Not Do So," History Commons. www.historycommons.org/context.jsp?item=a1090sanctions

6. Kronstadt, "Pakistan-U.S. Relations."

7. Karin Brulliard, "Kerry visit underscores power still wielded by Pakistani army," *Washington Post*, October 23, 2009.

8. Mark Mazzetti and Eric Schmitt, "Afghan Strikes by Taliban Get Pakistan Help, U.S. Aides Say," *New York Times*, March 26, 2009.

9. C.M. Sennott, "Taliban leaders report progress in secret talks withU.S. and Afghanistan," *GlobalPost*, June 17, 2009. www.globalpost.com/dispatch/afghanistan/090617/taliban-talks

10. Ahmed Rashid, *Descent into Chaos: The United States and the Failure of Nation Building in Pakistan, Afghanistan, and Central Asia* (New York: Viking, 2008), p. 138.

11. Yochi J. Dreazen and Peter Spiegel, "Taliban Now Winning," *The Wall Street Journal*, August 10, 2009.

12. Greg Miller and Julian E. Barnes, "Taliban leader plans to reclaim Afghanistan, U.S. says," *Los Angeles Times*, March 26, 2009.

13. Ibid.

Chapter 8—WARLORDS, THE TALIBAN AND AL QAEDA

1. Suzanne Presto, "Former Hostage: Afghan Taliban and Pakistani Taliban Work 'Seamlessly Together," VOANews.com, October 1, 2010. www.voanews.com/english/news/asia/Former-Hostage-Afghan-Taliban-and-Pakistani-Taliban-Work-Seamlessly-Together-104187274.html

2. Ziauddin Sardar, "Pakistan: The Taliban takeover," *NewStatesman*, April 30, 2007. www.newstatesman.com/asia/2007/04/pakistan-taliban-afghanistan

3. Imtiaz Ali, "The Father of the Taliban: An Interview with Maulana Sami ul-Haq," *Asia Times*, June 13, 2007. www.atimes.com/atimes/south_asia/if13df01.html

4. Sardar, "Pakistan: The Taliban takeover."

5. Ibid.

6. Bajoria cites Gunaratna at International Centre for Political Violence and Terrorism Research, www.pvtr.org/

7. Jayshree Bajoria, "Backgrounder: Pakistan's New Generation of Terrorists," *Council on Foreign Relations*, October 7, 2010. www.cfr.org/publication/15422/pakistans_new_generation_of_terrorists.html

8. Ibid.

9. Ibid.

10. "Afghanistan: Proliferation of armed groups threatens aid work," *IRIN*, UN Office for the Coordination of Humanitarian Affairs, November 1, 2010. www.alertnet.org/the-news/newsdesk/IRIN/e1e96c31f960fe2043fb2887564e20bf.htm

11. Ibid.

12. "Analysis: Doubts over new Afghan security strategy," *IRIN*, UN Office for the Coordination of Humanitarian Affairs, August 23, 2010. www.irinnews.org/Report.aspx?ReportID=90257

13. "FACTBOX: Insurgency in Afghanistan: who are they?" Reuters, September 25, 2009. www.reuters.com/article/GCA-Afghanistan-Pakistan/idUSTRE58O2F620090925

14. Ron Moreau, "America's New Nightmare," *Newsweek*, July 25, 2009. www.newsweek.com/2009/07/24/america-s-new-nightmare.html

15. Ibid.

16. Dexter Filkins, The Forever War (New York: Vintage Books/Random House, 2009; orig. ed. 2008), p. 30.

17. Norimitsu Onishi, "A Shrine, A Tale of the Mullah and Muhammad's Amazing Cloak," *New York Times*, December 19, 2001.

18. Scott Shane, "A Dogged Taliban Chief Rebounds, Vexing U.S.," *New York Times*, October 10, 2009.

19. Anand Gopal, "Who are the Taliban?" *The Huffington Post*, www.huffingtonpost.com/anand-gopal/who-are-the-taliban_b_148565.html

20. "Mullah Baradar: In His Own Words," *Newsweek*, July 25, 2009, from the magazine issue dated August 3, 2009.

21. Dr. Thomas Gouttierre, *Sourcewatch*. www.sourcewatch.org/index.php?title=Tom_Gouttierre

22. Shane, "A Dogged Taliban Chief Rebounds, Vexing U.S."

23. Trudy Rubin, "Commentary: Taliban remains a potent threat," *Philadelphia Inquirer*, October 18, 2009.

24. Authors' conversation with Jonathan S. Landay.

25. Jonathan Landay, John Walcott and Nancy A. Youssef, "Are Obama advisors downplaying Afghan dangers?" McClatchy Newspapers, October 11, 2009.

26. Anand Gopal, "The most deadly U.S. foe in Afghanistan," *The Christian Science Monitor*, May 31, 2009. www.csmonitor.com/World/Asia-South-Central/2009/0601/p10s01-wosc.html

27. Ibid.

28. Mathew Rosenberg, "New Wave of Warlords Bedevils U.S.," *The Wall Street Journal*, January 20, 2010.

29. Gopal, "Who are the Taliban?"

30. Steve Coll, *Ghost Wars* (New York: Penguin, 2004), p. 202, citing interviews with U.S. officials.

31. For a comprehensive list of Al Qaeda donors see Gerald Posner, *Secrets of the Kingdom: The Inside Story of the Saudi-U.S. Connection* (New York: Random House, 2005), notes pp. 221–224.
32. According to a report on the Haqqani Network by the Institute for the Study of War, Haqqani is fluent in Arabic and one of his two wives is from the United Arab Emirates— "assets that have helped him raise a great deal of money from Saudi Arabia and individuals in the Persian Gulf." http://understandingwar.org/themenode/haqqani-network
33. Coll, *Ghost Wars*.
34. Gerald Posner, *Secrets of the Kingdom: The Inside Story of the Saudi-U.S. Connection* (New York: Random House, 2005), p. 115, citing As Ad Abukhalil, *The Battle for Saudi Arabia: Royalty, Fundamentalism, and Global Power* (New York: seven Stories Press, 2004), p.195.
35. Gopal, "Who are the Taliban?"
36. George Crile, *Charlie Wilson's War* (New York: Atlantic Monthly Press, 2003), p. 473.
37. Ibid.
38. Gopal, "The most deadlyU.S. foe in Afghanistan."
39. Joshua Partlow, "17 killed by Blast In Afghan Capital," *Washington Post*, October 9, 2009.
40. Gopal, "Who are the Taliban?"
41. Steve Hynd, "Every major attack 'is planned in detail with the ISI,'" June 1, 2009, www.newshoggers.com/blog/afpak
42. Peter Lee, "Meet Gulbuddin Hekmatyar," *Counterpunch*, March 9, 2009. www.counterpunch.org/lee03092009.html
43. Paul Fitzgerald and Elizabeth Gould, *Invisible History: Afghanistan's Untold Story* (San Francisco: City Lights, 2009), pp. 114–115.
44. Authors' personal correspondence, April 2008.
45. Omid Marzban, "Gulbuddin Hekmatyar: From Holy Warrior to Wanted Terrorist," *Terrorism Monitor*, The Jamestown Foundation, September 21, 2006.
46. Kurt Lohbeck, *Holy War, Unholy Victory* (Washington, DC: Regnery Gateway, 1993), p. 12.
47. Alfred W. McCoy, *The Politics of Heroin: CIA Complicity in the Global Drug Trade* (Chicago: Lawrence Hill Books, 1991), p. 452.
48. Coll, *Ghost Wars*, p. 218.
49. Ibid., p. 263.
50. Syed Saleem Shahzad, "Holbrooke reaches out to Hekmatyar," *Asia Times*, April 10, 2009.
51. Peter Lee, "Taliban force a China switch," *Asia Times*, March 6, 2009.
52. "Pakistan's terrorist and extremist groups number in the dozens." See *South Asia Terrorism Portal*. www.satp.org/satporgtp/countries/pakistan/terroristoutfits/group_list.htm for a full listing.
53. Gopal, "Who are the Taliban?"
54. Carlotta Gall, "Pakistan's No. 1 Enemy: Ex-Ally Bent by Al Qaeda, *New York Times*, August 8, 2009.
55. Sadia Sulaiman, "Hafiz Gul Bahadur: A Profile," *Terrorism Monitor*, April 10, 2009.
56. Ibid.
57. Carlotta Gall, "Pakistan and Afghan Taliban Close Ranks," *New York Times*, March 27, 2009.
58. Sulaiman, "Hafiz Gul Bahadur: A Profile."
59. Ishtiaq Mahsud, "Pakistan Taliban Head Cracks Jokes, Vows Vengeance," Associated Press, October 5, 2009.
60. Gopal, "Who are the Taliban?"
61. Mukhtar A. Khan, "Pakistani Government Offensive in Swat Heading for the Taliban of Waziristan," *Terrorism Monitor*, June 18, 2009.
62. John Pike, Federation of American Scientists (FAS) profile, Lashkar-e-Taiba, Lashkar-e-Tayyiba (Army of the Righteous), http://ftp.fas.org/irp/world/para/lashkar.htm

63. Jayshree Bajoria, "Profile: Lashkar-e-Taiba (Army of the Pure), (a.k.a.) Lashkar e-Tayyiba, Lashkar e-Toiba; Lashkar-i-Taiba," *Council on Foreign Relations*, December 2, 2008.
64. Husain Haqqani, "The Ideologies of South Asian Jihadi Groups," Carnegie Endowment for International Peace. www.carnegieendowment.org/publications/index. cfm?fa=view&id=16922
65. "Lashkar-e-Toiba 'Army of the Pure,'" *South Asia Terrorism Portal*, www.satp.org/satporgtp/countries/india/states/jandk/terrorist_outfits/lashkar_e_toiba.htm
66. Bill Roggio, "Pakistan launches South Waziristan operation," *Long War Journal*, October 17, 2009.
67. Khan, "Pakistani Government Offensive in Swat Heading for the Taliban of Waziristan."
68. Kayani was trained at Fort Benning, Georgia and graduated from the Command and General Staff College at Fort Leavenworth, Kansas. See Rick Westhead, "How long will Pakistan's army chief sit on the sidelines?" *Indus Asia Online Journal*, March 19, 2009. http://iaoj.wordpress.com/2009/03/20/how-long-will-pakistans-army-chief-sit-on-the-sidelines/
69. Gareth Porter, "US shrugs off Pakistan-Taliban links," *Asia Times*, August 6, 2009.
70. Ibid.
71. David E. Sanger, *The Inheritance: The World Obama Confronts And the Challenges to American Power* (New York: Random House, 2009), pp. 247–248
72. Ishtiaq Mahsud, "Pakistan negotiates deal with militants," Associated Press, October 20, 2009.
73. Ibid.
74. Declan Walsh, "Refugee flood reveals human cost of South Waziristan's invisible war," *Guardian* (London), October 19, 2009.
75. Saeed Shah, "Pakistan army's South Waziristan battle fails to win hearts and minds of tribesmen," *Telegraph* (London), October 25, 2009.
76. Jane Perlez, "Pakistan Retakes Army Headquarters; Hostages Freed," *New York Times*, October 11, 2009.
77. "1 persons killed in suicide bombing in NWFP," South Asia Terrorism Portal, Pakistan, October 13, 2009.http://www.satp.org/satporgtp/detailsmall_news.asp?date1=10/13/2009&id=1
78. "11 persons killed in suicide bombing in NWFP," South Asia Terrorism Portal, Pakistan, October 16, 2009.http://www.satp.org/satporgtp/detailsmall_news.asp?date1=10/16/2009&id=3
79. Mark Landler and Ismail Khan, "Clinton Arrival in Pakistan Met by Fatal Attacks," *New York Times*, October 29, 2009.
80. Mark Landler, "Clinton Challenges Pakistanis on Al Qaeda," *New York Times*, October 30, 2009.
81. Robert Burns, "Pakistanis confront Clinton over drone attacks," Associated Press, October 31, 2009.
82. Ibid.

Chapter 9—DEATH FROM ABOVE

1. C.M. Sennott, "Life, Death and the Taliban: Counterinsurgency," *GlobalPost*, August 7, 2009. www.globalpost.com/taliban/coin?page=0,1
2. Ibid.
3. "COMISAF Initial Assessment (Unclassified) — Searchable Document," September 21, 2009. www.washingtonpost.com/wp-dyn/content/article/2009/09/21/AR2009092100110.html
4. Andrew J. Bacevich, "Let's Beat the Extremists Like We Beat the Soviets," *Washington Post*, September 27, 2009.
5. "Bacevich, The Arrogance of American Power," *Tomdispatch*, May 25, 2006, http://tom-

dispatch.org/post/85882/tomdispatch_interview_bacevich_the_arrogance_of_american_power (accessed November 25, 2009).

6. "COMISAF Initial Assessment (Unclassified)," September 21, 2009.

7. COMISAF, Ibid.

8. (1) Command: The functional exercise of authority, based upon knowledge, to attain an objective or goal. (2) Control:The process of verifying and correcting activity such that the objective or goal command is accomplished. (3) Communications: The ability and function of providing the necessary liaison to exercise effective command between tactical or strategic units of command. www.fas.org/man/dod-101/navy/docs/fun/part20.htm

9. Nathan Hodge, "Deadly Pakistan Drone Strike Provokes. . . . Silence?," *Wired*, June 25, 2009. www.wired.com/dangerroom/2009/06/deadly-pakistan-drone-strike-provokes-silence/

10. Robert A. Pape, "The True Worth of Air Power," *Foreign Affairs*, March-April 2004.

11. David Kilcullen, Andrew McDonald Exum, "Death from Above, Outrage Down Below," *New York Times*, May 17, 2009.

12. Ibid.

13. Anthony D. Romero, "ACLU Letter to President Barack Obama," April 28, 2010. www.aclu.org/files/assets/2010-4-28-ACLULettertoPresidentObama.pdf

14. Ibid.

15. Rob Crilly, "UN official: Drone attacks controlled away from battlefield may lead to 'PlayStation' mentality," *Telegraph* (London), June 3, 2010.

16. Ibid.

17. Gareth Porter, "Drone doubts strike CIA ranks," *Asia Times*, June 5, 2010. www.atimes.com/atimes/South_Asia/LF05Df02.html

18. Jeremy Scahill, "Blackwater's Secret War in Pakistan," *The Nation*, November 23, 2009.

19. Ibid.

20. Allison Stanger, *One Nation Under Contract*: *The Outsourcing of American Power and the Future of Foreign Policy* (New Haven and London: Yale University Press, 2009), p. 2.

21. Phillip Smucker, "Fighting the wrong fight in Afghanistan," *Asia Times*, June 3, 2009.

22. Author's Meetings with Congressional sources in Washington, October, 2009.

23. Rajiiv Chandrasekaran, "A softer approach to Karzai," *Washington Post*, November 20, 2009.

24. Ibid.

25. Daniel Dombey, "Afghan war divides Congress and a nation," *Financial Times*, October 2, 2009.

26. Ibid.

27. Joshua Partlow, Greg Jaffe, "Deadly Attack by Taliban Tests New Strategy," *Washington Post*, October 5, 2009.

28. Bill Roggio, "U.S., Afghan troops beat back bold enemy assault in Eastern Afghanistan," *Long War Journal*, October 4, 2009. www.longwarjournal.org/archives/2009/10/us_afghan_troops_bea.php

29. Syed Saleem Shahzad, "Taliban take over Afghan province," *Asia Times*, October 29, 2009.

30. "U.S. Zeros in on Chitral Pakistan in Hunt for bin Laden," *National Terror Alert*, March 16, 2009.

31. Bill Roggio, "Taliban commander involved in Nuristan attack thought killed," *Long War Journal*, October 11, 2009. www.longwarjournal.org/archives/2009/10/taliban_commander_in_1.php

32. "COMISAF Initial Assessment (Unclassified)," September 21, 2009. www.washingtonpost.com/wp-dyn/content/article/2009/09/21/AR2009092100110.html

33. Syed Saleem Shahzad, "Militants change tack in Pakistan," *Asia Times*, November 18, 2009.

34. Alex Rodriguez, "Pakistan Taliban regrouping outside Waziristan," *Los Angeles Times*, November 26, 2009.
35. Ibid.
36. Christopher Preble, "President Obama to Announce Troop Increase in Afghanistan," *Cato at Liberty*, December 1, 2009. www.cato-at-liberty.org/president-obama-to-announce-troop-increase-in-afghanistan/
37. Li Qinggong, "Afghan peace needs a map," *China Daily*, September 28, 2009. www.chinadaily.com.cn/opinion/2009-09/28/content_8743470.htm
38. Ibid.
39. Peng Kuang, Li Xiaokun and Cui Xiaohuo, "PLA adds anti-terror ops to cache," *China Daily*, July 31, 2009. www.chinadaily.com.cn/cndy/2009-07/31/content_8496016.htm
40. "Separatism to be Outlawed," *China Daily*, July 21, 2009. www.chinadaily.com.cn/china/2009-07/21/content_8451507.htm
41. Li Qinggong, "Afghan peace needs a map."
42. Dilip Ganguly, PRC-Trained Pakistanis Sent to Hit Afghan Troops, April 14, 1979, contained in *Foreign Broadcast Information Service*, (FBIS) Daily Report, April 18, 1979—pp. S6-7
43. Dev Murarka, "The Russian Intervention: A Moscow Analysis," *The Round Table*, No. 282, April, 1981.
44. Peter Ford, "Why China has clenched its fist in Xinjiang," *Christian Science Monitor*, July 8, 2009. www.csmonitor.com/2009/0708/p06s06-woap.html
45. Tim Johnson, "Tibetans see 'Han Invasion' as spurring violence," McClatchy Newspapers, March 28, 2008.
46. Andrew Small, "China's Af-Pak Moment," *Policy Brief: The German Marshal Fund*, May 20, 2009.
47. Syed Fazl-e-Haider, "China calls halt to Gwadar refinery," *Asia Times*, August 14, 2009.
48. Elizabeth Mills, "Pakistan's port in troubled waters," *Asia Times*, August 9, 2009.
49. Jonathan S. Landay, "China's thirst for copper could hold key to Afghanistan's future," McClatchy Newspapers, March 8, 2009. http://www.mcclatchydc.com/2009/03/08/63452/chinas-thirst-for-copper-could.html
50. Ibid.
51. India : a country study / Federal Research Division, Library of Congress ; edited by James Heitzman and Robert L. Worden. Edition Information:5th ed. Published/Created: Washington, D.C. : The Division : For sale by the Supt. of Docs., U.S. G.P.O, [1996] Related Names: Heitzman, James, 1950-2008. Worden, Robert L. Library of Congress. Federal Research Division. http://lcweb2.loc.gov/frd/cs/intoc.html
52. Elizabeth Mills, " Pakistan's port in troubles waters," *Asia Times*, August 9, 2006.
53. See, Kalbe Ali, "Govt urged to scrap port deal," *Dawn*, January 3, 2010. Also Syed Fazl-e-Haider, "China calls halt to Gwadar refinery," *Asia Times*, August 14, 2009.
54. Keith Bradsher, "China Losing Taste for American Debt," *New York Times*, January 8, 2009.
55. Anthony Faiola, "China Worried About U.S. Debt," *Washington Post*, March 14, 2009.
56. Ibid.
57. Peter Ford, "US-Chinese naval standoff the latest in a string of clashes," *Christian Science Monitor*, March 10, 2009. http://features.csmonitor.com/globalnews/2009/03/10/us-chinese-naval-standoff-the-latest-in-a-string-of-clashes/
58. "CIA Helped Afghan Mujahideen Before 1979 Soviet Intervention: Brzezinski," Agence France-Presse, January 13, 1998.
59. Samira Goetschel interview with Zbigniew Brzezinski, *Our Own Private Bin Laden*, Chaste Films, 2005.
60. Zbigniew Brzezinski, "The Group of Two that could change the world," *Financial Times*, January 13, 2009.

61. Henry C.K. Liu, "Obama, change and China," *Asia Times*, June 19, 2009.
62. Zbigniew Brzezinski, *The Grand Chessboard: American Primacy and Its Geostrategic Imperatives* (New York: Basic Books, 1997).
63. Zbigniew Brzezinski, "U.S. Policy in Afghanistan: Basic Choices—Strategic Questions," RAND Corporation conference, October 29, 2009. www.rand.org/pubs/conf_proceedings/CF274/#keynote_speaker
64. Ibid.
65. Emily Wax, "U.S. Eyes Bigger Slice of Indian Defense Pie," *Washington Post*, September 26, 2009.
66. Brzezinski, "U.S. Policy in Afghanistan: Basic Choices—Strategic Questions."
67. Peter Baker, "Bush Sign Nuclear Law," *Washington Post*, December 19, 2006.
68. Wax, "U.S. Eyes Bigger Slice of Indian Defense Pie."
69. Helene Cooper, Michael Wines and David Sanger, "China's Role as Lender Alters Obama's Visit," *New York Times*, November 15, 2009.
70. Alex Spillius, "Barack Obama cancels meeting with Dalai Lama 'to keep China happy,'" *Telegraph* (London), October 5, 2009.
71. Linda Feldman, "At White House, the Dalai Lama sidesteps trash," *Christian Science Monitor*, February 10, 2010.
72. Brzezinski, "U.S. Policy in Afghanistan: Basic Choices—Strategic Questions."
73. Zbigniew Brzezinski, "A Geostrategy for Eurasia," *Foreign Affairs*, 76:5 September/October 1997. www.comw.org/pda/fulltext/9709brzezinski.html
74. Ibid.
75. Brzezinski, "U.S. Policy in Afghanistan: Basic Choices—Strategic Questions."
76. Christopher J. Fettweis, "Eurasia, the 'World Island': Geopolitics and Policymaking in the 21st Century," *Global Research*, March 14, 2006. www.globalresearch.ca/index.php?context=va&aid=2095
77. Gearóid Ó Tuathail, "Understanding Critical Geopolitics: Geopolitics and Risk Security," in Colin S. Grey, Geoffrey Sloan ed. *Geopolitics, Geography and Strategy* (London: Frank Cass Publishers, 1999), p.113. www.nvc.vt.edu/toalg/Website/Publish/Papers/ToalUnderstandingCG.pdf
78. Editorial, "Assessing the China Trip," *New York Times*, November 21, 2009.
79. Edward Luce, "Singh backs U.S. mission in Afghanistan," *Financial Times*, November 24, 2009.
80. Shaun Tandon "Indian PM offers to work with Obama," Agency France-Press, November 23, 2009.
81. Luce, "Singh backs U.S. mission in Afghanistan."
82. M.K. Bhadrakumar, "India lays to rest a Bush-era Ghost," *Asia Times*, November 26, 2009.
83. Cristin Segura and Wu Zhong, "China's military struts its stuff," *Asia Times*, October 2, 2009.
84. Joshua Kurlantzick, "Nonstop Party: The surprising persistence of Chinese Communism," *Boston Sunday Globe*, November 22, 2009.
85. Address by President Bill Clinton at Johns Hopkins Univ. "Re: Permanent Normal Trade Relations Status for China," White House Office of the Press Secretary, March 8, 2000. www.techlawjournal.com/cong106/pntr/20000308sp.htm
86. Kurlantzick, "Nonstop Party."
87. Ibid.
88. Wu Zhong, "Tough times breed nostalgia for Mao," *Asia Times*, May 6, 2009.
89. Willy Lam, "Power struggle behind revival of Maoism," *Asia Times*, November 24, 2009.
90. Ibid.
91. Jim Yardley, "Maoist Rebels Widen Deadly Reach Across India," *New York Times*, November 1, 2009.

93. Sudha Ramachandran, "India takes off against 'Red Taliban,'" *Asia Times*, October 16, 2009.
94. Timothy R. Kreuttner, "The Maoist Insurgency in Nepal and U.S. Counterinsurgency Doctrine," *Small Wars Journal*, April 13, 2009. http://smallwarsjournal.com/blog/2009/04/the-maoist-insurgency-in-nepal/
95. James Robbins, "Free market flawed, says survey," *BBC News*, November 9, 2009. http://news.bbc.co.uk/2/hi/8347409.stm
96. "Remarks by the President in Address to the Nation on the Way Forward in Afghanistan and Pakistan," White House Office of the Press Secretary, December 1, 2009. www.whitehouse.gov/the-press-office/remarks-president-address-nation-way-forward-afghanistan-and-pakistan
   Dan Balz, "With speech, president makes the conflict truly his own," *Washington Post*, December 2, 2009.
97. Steve Coll, "The Case for Humility in Afghanistan," *Foreign Policy*, October 16, 2009.
96. Elisabeth Bumiller, Remembering Afghanistan's Golden Age, *New York Times*, October 18, 2009.
98. "Transcript: Obama's Address on the War in Afghanistan," *New York Times*, Dec. 1, 2009. www.nytimes.com/2009/12/02/world/asia/02prexy.text.html
99. Robert M. Gates, *From the Shadows* (New York: Touchstone, 1997) pp. 144–145.
100. Selig Harrison, "U.S. aid fuels dangerous deal in Pakistan," *Boston Globe*, June 29, 2010.
101. "Transcript: Obama's Address on the War in Afghanistan," *New York Times*, Dec. 1, 2009. www.nytimes.com/2009/12/02/world/asia/02prexy.text.htmlTranscript.
102. Bob Churcher, "Afghanistan and Pakistan: Anatomy of a Proxy War," *Huffington Post*, December 10, 2009. www.huffingtonpost.com/bob-churcher/afghanistan-and-pakistan_b_387574.html
103. Mark Mazzetti, "No Firm Plans for a U.S. Exit in Afghanistan," *New York Times*, December 7, 2009.
104. John King interview with General James L. Jones, "Obama advisor: Key date in new Afghan strategy 'not a cliff'" CNN, December 6, 2009. http://politicalticker.blogs.cnn.com/2009/12/06/obama-adviser-key-date-in-new-afghan-strategy-not-a-cliff/
105. Churcher, "Afghanistan and Pakistan: Anatomy of a Proxy War"
106. Tom Ashbrook, On Point, December 11, 2009, National Public Radio. www.onpointradio.org/media-player?url=www.onpointradio.org/2009/12/week-in-the-news-105&title=Week+in+the+News&pubdate=2009-12-11&segment=1
107. Julian Barnes, "Joint Chiefs chairman making his influence felt," *Los Angeles Times*, August 3, 2009.
108. Anup Shah, "World Military Spending," *Global Issues*, September 13, 2009. www.globalissues.org/article/75/world-military-spending
109. Mark Perry, "The day the general made a misstep," *Asia Times*, December 10, 2009.
110. Ibid.
111. Andrew J. Bacevich, "Obama's folly," *Los Angeles Times*, December 3, 2009.
112. Ibid.
113. James Risen and Mark Mazzetti, "Blackwater Guards Tied to Secret Raids by the CIA," *New York Times*, December 11, 2009.
114. Adam Ciralsky, "Tycoon, Contractor, Soldier, Spy," *Vanity Fair*, January 2010.
115. David Crawford, "Germany Investigates Blackwater-CIA Report," *Wall Street Journal*, January 8, 2010.
116. Dexter Filkins and Mark Mazzetti, "Contractors Tied to Effort to Track and Kill Militants," *New York Times*, March 14, 2010.
117. Allison Stanger, *One Nation Under Contract: The Outsourcing of American Power and the Future of Foreign Policy* (New Haven and London: Yale University Press, 2009), Preface.
118. Declan Walsh, "US forces mounted secret Pakistani raids in hunt for al-Qaida," *Guardian* (London), December 21, 2009.

119. Joby Warrick and Pamela Constable, "CIA base attacked in Afghanistan supported airstrikes against al-Qaeda, Taliban," *Washington Post*, January 1, 2010.
120. Joby Warrick and Peter Finn, "Suicide bomber who attacked CIA post in Afghanistan was trusted informant from Jordan," *Washington Post*, January 5, 2010.
121. Perspectives on Pakistan, "Attack on CIA in Afghanistan raises jitters in Pakistan," Reuters, January 5, 2010.
122. Rahimullah Yusufzai, "Waziristan war in critical stage," *The News*, Karachi, January 5, 2010. www.thenews.com.pk/daily_detail.asp?id=216857
123. Rasool Dawar, "Missiles rain again at Pakistan border," Associated Press, January 7, 2010.
124. Ibid.
125. Rasool Dawar, "Militants kill 6 Pakistanis for alleged U.S. spying," Associated Press, January 24, 2010.
126. Karen De Young and Joby Warrick, "Under Obama, more targeted killings than captures in counterterrorism efforts," *Washington Post*, February 14, 2010.
127. Mary Ann Roser, "Suit possible over baby DNA sent to military lab for national data base," *American-Statesman*, February 22, 2010.
128. Ibid.
129. Ishtiaq Mahsud and Rasool Dawar, "In Pakistan, U.S. strike kills key terrorist," Associated Press, January 16, 2010.
130. "US drone strike kills 20, Pakistan says," Associated Press, January 18, 2010.
131. Eric Schmitt, "Elite U.S. Force Expanding Hunt in Afghanistan," *New York Times*, December 27, 2009.
132. Amir Mir, "US drones killed 123 civilians, three al-Qaeda men in January," *The News*, Karachi, February 1, 2010. www.thenews.com.pk/daily_detail.asp?id=221847
133. Pamela Constable and Haq Nawaz Khan, "Pakistan investigating report that Taliban chief is dead," *Washington Post*, January 31, 2009.
134. Riaz Khan and Munir Ahmad, "Pakistan confirms death of Taliban chief," Associated Press, February 11, 2010.
135. Ibid.
136. Carlotta Gall, "Video Shows U.S. Attacks Did Not Kill Top Militant," *New York Times*, May 3, 2010.
137. "Hakimullah Mehsud," Biography, *New York Times*, Updated April 29, 2010.
138. "US awash in drone data," *Boston Globe*, January 11, 2010.
139. Steven Thomma, "Poll: Most Americans would trim liberties to be safer," McClatchy Newspapers, January 12, 2010.
140. Kristen Mack, "Full-body scanner arriving at O'Hare," *Chicago Tribune*, February 24, 2010.
141. Kimberly Kindy, "Chertoff accused of abusing public trust by touting body scanners," *Washington Post*, January 1, 2010. (Chertoff's clients include the manufacturer of full-body scanners.)
142. Eric Lipton, Eric Schmitt, and Mark Mazzetti, "Review of airliner plot shows more missed clues," *New York Times*, January 17, 2010.
143. See Chris McGreal, "The Nevada gambler, al-Qaida, the CIA and the mother of all cons," *Guardian* (London), December 23, 2009.
144. Major General Michael T. Flynn, Captain Matt Pottinger and Paul D. Batchelor, "Fixing Intel: A Blueprint for Making Intelligence Relevant in Afghanistan," *Center for a New American Security*, January 4, 2010.
145. Ibid.
146. Charlie Reed, "'Journalists' recent work examined before embeds," *Stars and Stripes*, August 24, 2009. www.stripes.com/article.asp?section=104&article=64348
147. Ibid.
148. Ibid.

149. Major General Michael T. Flynn, Captain Matt Pottinger and Paul D. Batchelor, "Fixing Intel: A Blueprint for Making Intelligence relevant in Afghanistan," Center for a New American Security, January 4, 2010.
150. Mark Lander and Helene Cooper, "U.S. Wrestling with Olive Branch for Taliban," *New York Times*, January 27, 2010.
151. Karen DeYoung, "Afghanistan offensive is key test of Obama's strategy," *Washington Post*, February 15, 2010.
152. Matthew Green, "McChrystal sees Taliban role," *Financial Times*, January 24, 2010.
153. Ibid.
154. Afghanistan: The London Conference. http://afghanistan.hmg.gov.uk/en/conference/
155. Gerhard Spörl, "The Afghanistan Conference: Is There a Way Out of the 'Graveyard of Empires'?", *Der Spiegel*, January 27, 2010.
156. "Karzai government invites Taliban to peace meeting," Reuters, January 28, 2010. www.reuters.com/article/idUSTRE60Q31W201100128
157. "Karzai offers Taliban government office," Associated Press, September 29, 2007. www.msnbc.msn.com/id/21045198/
158. Ahmed Rashid, "A Deal with the Taliban?" *New York Review of Books*, February 25, 2010.
159. "Hamid Karzai says bring Taliban to the table," *The London Sunday Times*, July 19, 2009. www.timesonline.co.uk/tol/news/world/asia/article6719241.ece
160. Gareth Porter, "US, Karzai split over Taliban talks," *Asia Times*, February 4, 2010.
161. Ahmed Rashid, "A Deal with the Taliban?" *New York Review of Books*, February 25, 2010.
162. Joshua Partlow, "Karzai's Taliban recognition strategy raises ethnic, rights concerns at home," *Washington Post*, February 4, 2010.
163. Ahmed Rashid, "A Deal with the Taliban?"
164. Mathew Rosenberg, "New Wave of Warlords Bedevils U.S." *Wall Street Journal*, January 20, 2010.
165. Ibid.
166. An international conference was held in London, hosted by British Prime Minister Gordon Brown, on January 28, 2010, to set a course for Afghanistan's future. http://afghanistan.hmg.gov.uk/en/conference/
167. Stephen F. Lynch, "The Price of Appeasing the Taliban," *Boston Globe*, February 17, 2010.
168. Ibid.
169. Karen DeYoung and Joshua Partlow, "In Afghanistan, Karzai's invitation to Taliban creates discord and confusion," *Washington Post*, March 3, 2010.
170. Ibid.
171. Terry Gross, "Ahmed Rashid Offers an Update on the Taliban," NPR's *Fresh Air*, February 17, 2010. www.npr.org/templates/story/story.php?storyId=123777455&ft=1&f=1008
172. Ibid.
173. Paul Marshal, "Taliban-Lite," *National Review Online*, November 7, 2003, citing the U.S. Commission for International Religious Freedom.
174. Phone conversation with Sima Wali, March 31, 2010.
175. See Paul Fitzgerald and Elizabeth Gould, *Invisible History: Afghanistan's Untold Story* (San Francisco: City Lights, 2009), p. 67.
176. Scott Shane, "The War in Pashtunistan," *New York Times*, December 5, 2009.
177. Maria Golovnina, "Analysis: Radical Islam cast shadow over Central Asia," Reuters, Feb 9, 2010.
178. M.K. Bhadrakumar, "The winner takes all in Afghanistan," *Asia Times*, February 13, 2010.
179. Ibid.
180. M.K. Bhadrakumar, "An AfPak star over Central Asia," *Asia Times*, March 2, 2010.
181. Dexter Filkins, "Afghan Offensive Is New War Model," *New York Times*, February 13, 2010.

182. Greg Jaffe and Craig Whitlock, "Battle for Marja not only militarily significant," *Washington Post*, February 22, 2010.
183. Ibid.
184. Dexter Filkins, "Afghan Offensive Is New War Model," *New York Times*, February 13, 2010.
185. Zoe Magee, "Afghan Flag Raised Over Marja After Battling Taliban for 12 Days," *ABC News*, February 25, 2010. http://abcnews.go.com/International/Afghanistan/afghan-flag-raised-marja-12-days-combat/story?id=9937234
186. Amir Shah and Deb Riechmann, "16 killed in Kabul attacks," Associated Press, February 27, 2010.
187. Thomas H. Johnson and M. Chris Mason, "Down the AfPak Rabbit Hole," *Foreign Policy*, March 1, 2010.
188. Ibid.
189. Mark Mazzetti and Dexter Filkins, "Secret Joint Raid Captures Taliban's Top Commander," *New York Times*, February 15, 2010.
190. Dexter Filkins, "Two Taliban Leaders Caught in Pakistan," *New York Times*, February 19, 2010.
191. Pir Zubair Shah and Dexter Filkins, "Taliban Leader Said to Be Taken in Afghanistan," *New York Times*, February 23, 2010.
192. Lyse Doucet, "Pakistan's Push for New Role in Afghanistan," *BBC News*, February 19, 2010.
193. Gareth Porter, "Pakistan holds onto its Taliban," *Asia Times*, March 2, 2010.
194. Syed Saleem Shahzad, "Islamabad ready to deal," *Asia Times*, February 26, 2010.
195. Gareth Porter, "Pakistan holds onto its Taliban."
196. Johnson and Mason, "Down the AfPak Rabbit Hole," *Foreign Policy*, March 1, 2010.
197. Ibid.
198. Dexter Filkins, "Pakistanis Tell of Motive in Taliban Leader's Arrest," *New York Times*, August 22, 2010.
199. Ibid.
200. M.K. Bhadrakumar, "Natural law brings AfPak crashing," *Asia Times*, March 6, 2010.
201. Lyse Doucet, "Pakistan's Push for New Role in Afghanistan."
202. Syed Saleem Shahzad, "Pakistan's military sets Afghan terms," *Asia Times*, February 10, 2010.
203. Khaleeq Kiani, "First secretaries' meeting chaired by army chief," *LetUsBuildPakistan*, March 17, 2010. http://criticalppp.org/ubp/archives/7253
204. Lyse Doucet, "Pakistan's Push for New Role in Afghanistan."
205. M.K. Bhadrakumar, "Natural Law Brings AfPak Crashing," *Asia Times*, March 6, 2010.
206. Jon Boone, "Hamid Karzai takes control of Afghanistan election watchdog," *Guardian* (London), February 22, 2010.
207. M.K. Bhadrakumar, "Natural law brings AfPak crashing," *Asia Times*, March 6, 2010.
208. Sayeh Hassan, "Abdulmalik Rigi's 'Capture' and Its Implications for Iranian Opposition Abroad," *Canada Free Press*, February 26, 2010.
209. "Jundullah Leader, Abdul MalikRigi Executed," *Hamsayeh.net*, June 20, 2010. www.hamsayeh.net/hamsayehnet_iran-international%20news1372.htm
210. "US Envoy Denies Attack Was Targeted at Indians," *Indiaserver.com*, March 4, 2010.
211. "Kabul attack not targeted at Indian facility: Holbrooke, India Surprised," *Indianexpress.com*, March 3, 2010.
212. M.K. Bhadrakumar, "India lays to rest a Bush-era ghost," *Asia Times*, November 26, 2009.
213. M.K. Bhadrakumar, "Natural law brings AfPak crashing."
214. "Dutch cabinet collapses in dispute over Afghanistan," *BBC News*, February 20, 2010.
215. Brian Knowlton, "Gates Calls Europe Anti-War Mood Danger to Peace," *New York Times*, February 2, 2010.

216. Nathan Freier, "Known Unknowns: Unconventional 'Strategic Shocks' in Defense Strategy Development," Strategic Studies Institute, November 2008, p. 24. www.strategicstudiesinstitute.army.mil/pdffiles/pub890.pdf

217. "Afghan war key to NATO's new Mission," Associated Press, May 18, 2010. www.boston.com/news/world/asia/articles/2010/05/18/natos_draft_mission_statement_keys_in_on_afghanistan/

218. William Pfaff, "World War III and Other Scenarios," May 18, 2010. www.williampfaff.com/modules/news/article.php?storyid=464

219. Adam Mynott, "Afghans more optimistic for future, survey shows," *BBC News*, January 11, 2010. http://news.bbc.co.uk/2/hi/south_asia/8448930.stm

220. Julian Borger, "Britain to Hamid Karzai: start Afghanistan peace talks now," *Guardian* (London), March 10, 2010.

221. Charles Bremmer and Michael Evans, "British envoy says mission in Afghanistan is doomed, according to leaked memo," *The Times* (London), October 2, 2008.

222. Alissa J. Rubin and Helene Cooper, "In Afghan Trip, Obama Presses on Graft," *New York Times*, March 28, 2010.

223. Ibid.

224. Sun Zhuangzhi, Afghanistan Reflects US' Self-Obsession, *China Daily* March 24, 2010. www.chinadaily.com.cn/opinion/2010-03/24/content_9632407.htm

225. Simon Tisdall, "Sir Sherard Cowper-Coles: a casualty of Afghan policy war," *Guardian* (London), June 21, 2010. www.guardian.co.uk/commentisfree/2010/jun/21/sir-sherard-cowper-coles-afghanistan

226. Ahmed Rashid, "Before the Endgame: America's Fatal Flaws in Afghanistan," *Der Spiegel*, May 26, 2010. www.spiegel.de/international/world/0,1518,696662,00.html

227. "Militants Attack as Afghan peace conference starts," Associated Press, June 2, 2010. www.independent.co.uk/news/world/asia/militants-attack-as-afghan-peace-conference-starts-1989247.html

228. Sayed Salahuddin and Hamid Shalizi, "Afghan Gathering Agrees Peace Moves with Taliban," Reuters, June 4, 2010.

229. Matthew Pennington and Rahim Faiez, "Karzai defends removal of Afghan security chiefs," Associated Press, June 7, 2010.

230. Ernesto Londono, "Karzai removes Afghan minister and spy chief," *Washington Post*, June 7, 2010.

231. Jon Boone, "Afghan president 'has lost faith in U.S. ability to defeat Taliban,'" *Guardian* (London), June 9, 2010.

Chapter 10—DECRYPTING THE AFGHAN/U.S. AGENDA

1. Ann Jones, "Afghan Women Have Already Been Abandoned," *The Nation*, August 12, 2010.

2. Thomas Ruttig, "The one thing you need to read about Afghanistan," *Afghanistan Analysts Network*, June 8, 2009. http://aan-afghanistan.com/index.asp?id=189

3. Daniel Schulman, "Dana Rohrabacher's War," *Mother Jones*, March/April 2010.

4. Michael Hughes, "Congressman Rohrabacher on Afghanistan: Start the Drawdown Now," *The Huffington Post*, May 19, 2010 www.huffingtonpost.com/michael-hughes/congressman-rohrabacher-o_b_581258.html

5. www.afs.org/afs_or/focus_on/high_school

6. "Profile: Albert J. Wohlstetter," *History Commons*. www.historycommons.org/entity.jsp?entity=albert_wohlstetter

7. Paul Fitzgerald and Elizabeth Gould, *Invisible History: Afghanistan's Untold Story* (San Francisco: City Lights, 2009), p. 140.

8. Robert M. Gates, *From the Shadows* (New York: Touchstone, 1997), pp. 144–147.

9. "Team B Strategic Objectives Panel," *RightWeb*, www.rightweb.irc-online.org/profile/Team_B_Strategic_Objectives_Panel

10. Author Sharon Ghamari-Tabrizi cites an exchange at RAND between Wohlstetter and Kahn in which Kahn is scolded by his mentor Wohlstetter for having "poached nearly every one of his major ideas." Sharon Ghamari-Tabrizi, *The worlds of Herman Kahn: The Intuitive Science of Thermonuclear War* (Cambridge: Harvard Univ. Press, 2005), p. 69.

11. Frances FitzGerald, *Fire in the Lake: The Vietnamese and the Americans in Vietnam* (Boston-Toronto: Little, Brown, 1972), p. 352.

12. Dexter Filkins, "US Investigates Alleged Bribing of Taliban," *New York Times*, June 7, 2010.

13. Ibid.

14. Ben Farmer, "Karzai family's wealth 'fuelling insurgency,'" *Telegraph* (London), August 7, 2009. www.telegraph.co.uk/news/worldnews/asia/afghanistan/5991447/Karzai-familys-wealth-fuelling-insurgency.html

15. Arthur Kent, "Cashing In on Karzai," *Options Politiques*, November 2007. www.irpp.org/po/archive/nov07/kent.pdf

16. Ibid.

17. Ibid.

18. Ibid.

19. Aram Roston, "How the U.S. Funds the Taliban," *The Nation*, November 11, 2009.

20. "Host Nation Trucking," Federal Business Opportunities, FedBizzOpps.gov

21. Dexter Filkins, "U.S. Said to Fund Warlords to Protect Convoys," *New York Times*, June 21, 2010.

22. Rostam, "How the U.S. Funds the Taliban."

23. "Warlord, Inc.: Extortion and Corruption Along the U.S. Supply Chain in Afghanistan," Report of the Majority Staff, Rep. John F Tierney, Chair, Subcommittee on National Security and Foreign Affairs, Committee on Oversight and Government Reform, June 2010. http://media.washingtonpost.com/wp-srv/world/documents/warlords.pdf

24. Ibid.

25. Roston, "How the U.S. Funds the Taliban."

26. "Warlord, Inc.," Committee on Oversight and Government Reform.

27. Rod Nordland, "Violence Up Sharply in Afghanistan," *New York Times*, June 19, 2010.

28. "Afghan civilian casualties rise 31 percent in first six months of 2010," United Nations Assistance Mission in Afghanistan Report, August 10, 2010. http://unama.unmissions.org/Default.aspx?tabid=1741&ctl=Details&mid=1882&ItemID=9955

29. James Dao and Andrew W. Lehren, "Grim Milestone: 1000 Americans Dead," *New York Times*, May 18, 2010.

30. Liz Goodwin, "Army suicides hit record number in June," *Yahoo News*, July 16, 2010. http://news.yahoo.com/s/yblog_upshot/20100716/us_yblog_upshot/record-number-of-u-s-soldiers-commited-suicide-last-month

31. Rob Crilly, "Pakistan spy agency controls Taliban and plans attacks," *Telegraph* (London), June 13, 2010. www.telegraph.co.uk/news/worldnews/asia/pakistan/7824865/Pakistan-spy-agency-controls-the-Taliban-and-plans-attacks.html

32. Rick Hampson, Afghanistan: "America's Longest War," *USA Today*, May 28, 2010. www.usatoday.com/news/military/2010-05-27-longest-war-afghanistan_N.htm

33. Fred Kaplan, "Fainting Spells: Gen. David Petraeus' collapse is a grim metaphor for the prospects of a Kandahar offensive," *Slate*, June 15, 2010.

34. James Carroll, "On the verge of collapse," *Boston Globe*, June 21, 2010.

35. Nancy A. Youssef, "Pentagon rethinking value of major counterinsurgencies," McClatchy Newspapers, May 12, 2010.

36. C.J. Chivers, "What Marja Tells Us of Battles Yet to Come," *New York Times*, June 10, 2010.

37. Rajiv Chandrasekaran, "Still a long way to go," *Washington Post*, June 10, 2010.

38. Karen DeYoung and Scott Wilson, "Weakening, possible firing of McChrystal compounds sense of peril in Afghanistan," *Washington Post*, June 23, 2010."

39. Michael Hastings, "The Runaway General," *Rolling Stone*, June 22, 2010.
40. Ibid.
41. William R. Polk, "What Now? Afghanistan Sitrep," *Counterpunch*, July 1, 2010.
42. Ibid.
43. Deb Riechmann, "Petraeus calls victory the goal in Afghanistan," Associated Press, July 5, 2010.
44. Jane Perlez, Eric Schmitt and Carlotta Gall, "Pakistan Is Said to Pursue a Foothold in Afghanistan," *New York Times*, June 24, 2010.
45. Crilly, "Pakistan spy agency controls Taliban and plans attacks."
46. Ibid.
47. Dana Priest and William M. Arkin, "Top Secret America: A hidden world, growing beyond control," *Washington Post*, July 19, 2010.
48. Ibid.
49. Federal Awardee Performance and Integrity Information System (FAPIIS) www.cpars.csd.disa.mil/FAPIISmain.htm
50. Perlez, Schmitt and Gall, "Pakistan Is Said to Pursue a Foothold in Afghanistan."
51. David Stringer, "Ex-British spy chief faults Iraq invasion, says war has taken focus off Al Qaeda," Associated Press, July 21, 2010.
52. Mark Mazzetti, Jane Perlez, Eric Schmitt and Andrew W. Lehren, "Pakistan Spy Service Aids Insurgents, Reports Assert," *New York Times*, July 25, 2010. www.nytimes.com/2010/07/26/world/asia/26isi.html
53. Ibid.
54. C.J. Chivers, Carlotta Gall, Andrew W. Lehren et al., "Inside the Fog of War: Reports From the Ground in Afghanistan," *New York Times*, July 25, 2010.
55. Mazzetti, Perlez, Schmitt and Lehren, "Pakistan Spy Service Aids Insurgents, Reports Assert."
56. Matt Viser, "Kerry under pressure as leak energizes war critics," *Boston Globe*, July 27, 2010.
57. Ibid.
58. Ibid.
59. Editorial, "Wikileaks' release of classified field reports on Afghan war reveals not much," *Washington Post*, July 27, 2010. www.washingtonpost.com/wp-dyn/content/article/2010/07/26/AR2010072604626.html
60. Greg Jaffe and Peter Finn, "WikiLeaks disclosures unlikely to change course of Afghanistan war," *Washington Post*, July 27, 2010.
61. James Ridgeway, "A Brief Refresher on the Taliban's Worst-Kept Secret," *Mother Jones*, July 30, 2010.
62. "Afghanistan: Sustaining West European Support for the NATO-led Mission—Why Counting on Apathy May Not Be Enough," (CIA) Red Cell Memorandum, March 11, 2010. www.nefafoundation.org/miscellaneous/CIA_westeurosupportNATOAfgh.pdf
63. The CIA Red Cell is an intelligence unit "charged by the Director of Intelligence with taking an 'out-of-the-box' approach that will provoke thought and offer an alternative viewpoint on the full range of analytic issues." CIA Red Cell Memorandum, www.nefafoundation.org/miscellaneous/CIA_westeurosupportNATOAfgh.pdf
64. "Afghanistan: Sustaining West European Support for the NATO-led Mission" Red Cell Memorandum.
65. Ibid.
66. Aryn Baker, "Afghan Women and the Return of the Taliban," *Time*, August 9, 2010.
67. Jones, "Afghan Women Have Already Been Abandoned."
68. Ibid.
69. Justin Elliot, "WikiLeaks: U.S. knew of contractor bribes to Taliban," Reuters/*Bob Strong*, July 28, 2010.
70. Andrew Higgins, "Officials puzzled over millions of dollars leaving Afghanistan by plane

for Dubai," *Washington Post*, February 25, 2010. www.washingtonpost.com/wp-dyn/content/article/2010/02/24/AR2010022404914.html

71. Daniella Peled, "Afghans believe U.S. is funding Taliban," *Guardian* (London), May 25, 2010.
72. Ibid.
73. Ibid.
74. "Congress OKs Funds for Afghan Troop Increase," *Reuters*, July 27, 2010.
75. Haroon Siddique and Lizzy Davies, "Zardari: International community is losing war against the Taliban," *Guardian* (London), August 3, 2010.
76. "US official says coalition forces not losing war in Afghanistan," *Press Trust of India*, August 7, 2010.
77. Eric Schmitt, Helene Cooper and David E. Sanger, "U.S. Military Seeks Slower Pace to Wrap Up Afghan Role," *New York Times*, August 11, 2010.
78. Editorial, "The State of War," *New York Times*, August 12, 2010.
79. Ibid.
80. Walter Pincus, "Air base expansion plans reflect long-term investment in Afghanistan," *Washington Post*, August 23, 2010.
81. Selig S. Harrison, "How to Leave Afghanistan Without Losing," *Foreign Policy*, August 24, 2010. www.foreignpolicy.com/articles/2010/08/24/how_to_leave_afghanistan_without_losing

Chapter 11—CLOSING ZERO

1. See Jonathan Beaty and S.C. Gwynne, *The Outlaw Bank: A Wild Ride into the Heart of BCCI* (New York: Random House, 1993).
2. Directorate for Inter-Services Intelligence [ISI], Federation of American Scientists, www.fas.org/irp/world/pakistan/isi/
3. Karl E. Meyer and Shareen Blair Brysac, *Tournament of Shadows* (Washington, DC: Counterpoint, 1999), p. 569.
4. Paul Fitzgerald and Elizabeth Gould, *Invisible History: Afghanistan's Untold Story* (San Francisco: City Lights, 2009), p. 92.
5. Ann M. Simmons, "Lancaster's crime-fighting plane puts focus on civil rights," *Los Angeles Times*, November 27, 2009.
6. D.C. Denison, "Showcasing Mass. and the military," *Boston Globe*, October 20, 2009.
7. Ibid.
8. "Predator drones set to watch U.S.-Mexico border," *Reuters*, August 30, 2010.
9. W.J. Hennigan, "The changing face of aerial reconnaissance," *Los Angeles Times*, November 11, 2010.
10. Andy Greenberg, "Full-Body Scan Technology Deployed in Street-Roving Vans," *Forbes*, August 24, 2010.
11. Noah Shachtman, "Exclusive: Google, CIA Invest in 'Future' of Web Monitoring," *Wired*, July 28, 2010. www.wired.com/dangerroom/2010/07/exclusive-google-cia/
12. Eric Bland, "Software Predicts Criminal Behavior," *ABC News*, August 22, 2010. http://abcnews.go.com/Technology/software-predicts-criminal-behavior/story?id=11448231
13. Declan McCullagh, "House votes to expand national DNA arrest database," *News.cnet.com*, May 19, 2010. http://news.cnet.com/8301-13578_3-20005458-38.html
14. Paul Lewis, "CCTV in the sky: Police plan to use military-style spy drones," *Guardian* (London), January 23, 2010.
15. Ibid.
16. Rob Evans, Paul Lewis and Mathew Taylor, "How police rebranded lawful protest as 'domestic extremism.'" *Guardian* (London), October 25, 2009.
17. Cecilia Kang, "Broadband carriers speak out against FCC regulation," *Washington Post*, February 23, 2010.

18. Sir Charles Fawcett, "The Striped Flag of the East India Company, and its Connection with the American 'Stars and Stripes,'" *The Journal of the Society For Nautical Research*, October 1937. www.crwflags.com/FOTW/flags/gb-eic2.html
19. Ibid.

Chapter 12—**ISSUES, ANSWERS AND RECOMMENDATIONS**

1. Ann Jones, "What Are They Smoking? The Bush War on Afghan Drugs," *TomDispatch. com*, October 29, 2006. www.tomdispatch.com/post/134004/
2. Carlotta Gall, "Rights Groups Reports Afghanistan Torture," *New York Times*, December 19, 2005.
3. Asim Qureshi, "The 'Obama doctrine': kill, don't detain," *Guardian* (London), April 11, 2010. www.guardian.co.uk/commentisfree/cifamerica/2010/apr/11/obama-national-security-drone-guantanamo
4. Gian P. Gentile, "A Strategy of Tactics: Population-centric COIN and the Army," *Parameters: The U.S. Army's Senior Professional Journal*, Autumn 2009. www.public.navy. mil/usff/Documents/gentile.pdf
5. Raymond A. Millen, "Time for a Strategic and Intellectual Pause in Afghanistan," *Parameters: The U.S. Army's Senior Professional Journal*, Summer 2010. www.carlisle.army. mil/usawc/Parameters/Articles/2010summer/Millen.pdf
6. Jonathan S. Landay and Warren P. Strobel, "U.S. officials, experts: No high-level Afghan peace talks underway," McClatchy Newspapers, October 21, 2010. www.mcclatchydc. com/2010/10/21/102428/us-officials-experts-no-high-level.html
7. Timothy Williams and Duraid Adnan, "Sunnis in Iraq Allied with U.S. Quitting to Rejoin Rebels," *New York Times*, October 16, 2010. www.nytimes.com/2010/10/17/world/ middleeast/17awakening.html
8. Ben Farmer, "Afghan warlords prepare to rearm as Taliban arrive for peace talks," *Telegraph*, October 24, 2010.
9. Farmer, "Afghan warlords prepare to rearm as Taliban arrive for peace talks."
10. Email correspondence with McClatchy Newspapers' Jonathan Landay, October 22, 2010.
11. S. Frederick Starr, "A Federated Afghanistan?" *CACI Analysts*, Central Asia Caucus Institute, November 7, 2001. www.cacianalyst.org/?q=node/167
12. Robert D. Blackwill, "A de facto partition for Afghanistan," *Politico*, July 7, 2010. http:// dyn.politico.com/printstory.cfm?uuid=AACEE164-18FE-70B2-A8E30566E50DFB3A
13. Ibid.
14. Thomas Ruttig, "Empire Going Mad," *Foreign Policy*, September 28, 2010. http://afpak. foreignpolicy.com/posts/2010/09/28/empire_going_mad
15. George Friedman, "US hope lies in Pakistan," *Asia Times*, September 30, 2010. www. atimes.com/atimes/South_Asia/LI30Df02.html
16. M.K. Bhadrakumar, "Uncle Sam, energy and peace in Asia," *Asia Times*, October 30, 2010. www.atimes.com/atimes/Central_Asia/LJ30Ag01.html
17. "Islamabad votes in favor of TAPI pipeline," UPI.com, October 28, 2010. www.upi.com/ Science_News/Resource-Wars/2010/10/28/Islamabad-votes-in-favor-of-TAPI-pipeline/ UPI-78641288267136/
18. M.K. Bhadrakumar, "Uncle Sam, energy and peace in Asia."
19. Ibid.
20. Mohammed Osman Tariq, Najla Ayoubi and Fazel Rabi Haqbeen, "Afghanistan in 2010, A Survey of the People," *Asia Foundation*, November 9, 2010. www.asiafoundation.org/re-sources/pdfs/Afghanistanin2010survey.pdf
21. Katharine Houreld, "Most Afghans would accept talks with Taliban, survey says," Associated Press, November 10, 2010.
22. Timothy Williams and Duraid Adnan, "Sunnis in Iraq Allied With U.S. Quitting to

Rejoin Rebels," *New York Times*, October 16, 2010. www.nytimes.com/2010/10/17/world/middleeast/17awakening.html

23. Authors' interview with Matthew Hoh, of the Afghanistans Study Group, a joint project of the New America Foundation and the Center for International Policy. November 5, 2010.

24. Ibid.

25. Ibid.

26. Greg Miller, "U.S. military campaign to topple resilient Taliban hasn't succeeded," *Washington Post*, October 27, 2010.

27. Dion Nissenbaum and Saeed Shah, "Pakistan closes critical border after confused U.S. attack," McClatchy Newspapers, September 30, 2010.

28. White House Afghan-Pakistan Report September, 2010. www.humansecuritygateway.com/documents/WhiteHouse_Afghan_pakistan_Report_09_2010.pdf

29. Ravi Nessman, "Obama urges India, Pakistan to cooperate," Associated Press, November 8, 2010. www.boston.com/news/world/asia/articles/2010/11/08/obama_urges_india_pakistan_to_cooperate/

30. Selig Harrison, "Pakistan divides U.S. and India," *Los Angeles Times*, November 8, 2010.

31. Ravi NessMan and Ashok Sharma, "Indian gov't: Pakistan spies tied to Mumbai siege," *Washington Post*, October 19, 2010. www.washingtonpost.com/wp-dyn/content/article/2010/10/19/AR2010101900655.html

32. Ibid.

33. Ginger Thomson, Eric Schmitt and Souad Mekhennet, "D.E.A. Deployed Mumbai Plotter Despite Warning," *New York Times*, November 7, 2010. www.nytimes.com/2010/11/08/world/asia/08terror.html

34. Ibid.

35. "Sources: David Headley's 2 Wives Spoke to Authorities," Associated Press, October 17, 2010. www.bostonherald.com/news/us_politics/view/20101017sources__david_headleys_2_wives_spoke_to_authorities/

36. Ibid.

37. Joby Warrick, "'Systemic failures' led to attack, CIA says," *Washington Post*, October 19, 2010.

38. Ibid.

39. Phil Gast, "Growing backlash against TSA body scanners, pat-downs," *CNN.com*, November 12, 2010. http://articles.cnn.com/2010-11-12/travel/travel.screening_1_body-scanners-pat-downs-travel-companies?_s=PM:TRAVEL

40. Paul Richter, "U.S. gives details of Saudi Arms deal," *Los Angeles Times*, October 21, 2010.

41. Stephen Kinzer, *RESET: Iran, Turkey, And America's Future* (New York: Henry Holt, 2010), p. 169.

42. Julian Borger, "Pakistan nuclear weapons at risk of theft by terrorists, US study warns," *Guardian*, April 12, 2010.

43. Kevin Sieff, "Afghan troops overrated, audit to show," *Financial Times*, June 6, 2010.

44. Rod Nordland, "Showcase Afghan Army Mission Turns to Debacle," *New York Times*, August 12, 2010.

45. Dexter Filkins and Sharifullah Sahak, "Afghan Police Unit Defects to Taliban, Leaving Burning Station Behind," *New York Times*, November 1, 2010.

46. Karen DeYoung, "U.S. and NATO allies to announce 'transition' strategy in Afghan war," *Washington Post*, November 13, 20010. www.washingtonpost.com/wp-dyn/content/article/2010/11/13/AR2010111303551.html

47. Elisabeth Bumiller, "U.S. Tweaks Message on Troops in Afghanistan," *New York Times*, November 10, 2010.

48. David S. Cloud, "U.S. appears ready to acknowledge a long haul in Afghanistan," Los Angeles Times, November 17, 2010.
49. Joshua Partlow, "Karzai wants to reduce military operations in Afghanistan," *Washington Post*, November 14, 2010.
50. Ibid.
51. Joshua Partlow and Karen DeYoung, "Petraeus warns Afghans about Karzai's criticism of U.S. war strategy," *Washington Post*, November 15, 2010.
52. Richard L. Armitage, Samuel R. Berger and Daniel S. Markey, "U.S. Strategy for Pakistan and Afghanistan, Independent Task Force Report No. 65, *Council on Foreign Relations*, November 12, 2010. www.cfr.org/publication/23253/us_strategy_for_pakistan_and_afghanistan.html
53. Jim Lobe, "AfPak strategy at critical point," *Asia Times*, November 16, 2010. www.atimes.com/atimes/South_Asia/LK16Df02.html
54. Kamran Shafi, "Defining 'strategic depth,'" *Dawn*, January 19, 2010. http://news.dawn.com/wps/wcm/connect/dawn-content-library/dawn/the-newspaper/columnists/14-defining-strategic-depth-910
55. Louis Dupree, *Afghanistan* (Oxford: Oxford Univ. Press, 1997), p. 426.
56. Ibid., p. 427.
57. Selig Harrison, "How to Leave Afghanistan Without Losing," *Foreign Policy*, August 24, 2010. www.foreignpolicy.com/articles/2010/08/24/how_to_leave_afghanistan_without_losing?print=yes&hidecomments=yes&page=full
58. Correspondence with Jawied Nawabi, adjunct professor of Economics and Sociology, City University of New York (CUNY).
59. Investopedia, NINJA loan, www.investopedia.com/terms/n/ninja-loan.asp
60. "The Monster that Ate Wall Street," *Newsweek*, September 27, 2010. www.newsweek.com/2008/09/26/the-monster-that-ate-wall-street.html
61. Morgan House, "Lehman Brothers Bankruptcy: The Greatest Hits," *The Motley Fool*, April 1, 2010. www.fool.com/investing/general/2010/04/01/lehman-brothers-bankruptcy-the-greatest-hits.aspx
62. Bob Woodward, "Obama: We need to make clear to people that the cancer is in Pakistan," *Washington Post*, September 29, 2010.
63. Ibid.
64. "West being out-manoeuvred by Islamic extremism, Tony Blair warns," *Telegraph* (London), October 6, 2010. www.telegraph.co.uk/news/newstopics/politics/tony-blair/8045717/West-being-out-manoeuvred-by-Islamic-extremism-Tony-Blair-warns.html
65. Email exchange with Khalil Nouri of the New World Strategies Coalition Inc., October 2010.
66. Ibid.
67. www.knowth.com/newgrange.htm
68. Christopher Preble, "CUT (REALLY CUT) MILITARY SPENDING," in "A Plan B for Obama," Foreign Policy, November 2010.http://www.foreignpolicy.com/articles/2010/10/11/a_plan_b_for_obama?page=0,8
69. "A Plan B for Obama," *Foreign Policy*, November 2010. www.foreignpolicy.com/articles/2010/10/11/a_plan_b_for_obama

EPILOGUE

1. Samira Goetschel interview with Jack A. Blum, *Our Own Private Bin Laden*, Chaste Films, 2005.
2. Karen DeYoung and Greg Jaffe, "U.S. 'secret war' expands globally as Special Operations forces take larger role," *Washington Post*, June 4, 2010.

3. Jeremy Scahill, "Obama's Expanding Covert Wars," *The Nation*, June 4, 2010.
4. Helene Cooper and Mark Landler, "Targeted Killing Is the New U.S. Focus in Afghanistan," *New York Times*, July 31, 2010.
5. Ibid.
6. Kevin Sullivan, "Jurists decry loss of rights, international panel says 'war on terror,' has diluted principles," *Washington Post*, February 18, 2009.
7. Ibid.
8. "Assessing Damage, Urging Action: Report of the Eminent Jurists Panel on Terrorism, Counter-terrorism and Human Rights," An Initiative of the International Commission of Jurists, Geneva, 2009. www.icj.org/IMG/EJP-report.pdf
9. Sullivan, "Jurists decry loss of rights, international panel says 'war on terror,' has diluted principles."
10. "Drones Are Lynchpin of Obama's War on Terror," *Der Spiegel*, March 3, 2010. www.spiegel.de/international/world/0,1518,682612,00.html
11. Stuart Gottlieb, "Obama's drone-strike counterterrorism policy," *Foreign Policy*, April 7, 2009. http://experts.foreignpolicy.com/posts/2009/04/07/obama_s_drone_strike_counterterrorism_policy
12. Ibid.
13. Nobel Peace Prize for 2009, http://nobelprize.org/nobel_prizes/peace/laureates/2009/press.html
14. Stephen F. Cohen, *Soviet Fates and Lost Alternatives: From Stalinism to the New Cold War* (New York: Columbia Univ. Press, 2009), p. 197.
15. Ibid.
16. Ibid, p. 193.
17. Jason Horowitz, "Obama speechwriter Ben Rhodes is penning a different script for the world stage," *Washington Post*, January 12, 2010.
18. Bernard of Clairvaux, "De Laude Novae Militiae," c 1128–1131, http://faculty.smu.edu/bwheeler/chivalry/bernard.html
19. Bernard of Clairvaux, "De Laude Novae Militiae", c 1128–1131, http://faculty.smu.edu/bwheeler/chivalry/bernard.html
20. J.M. Upton-Ward, trans., ed., *The Rule of the Templars* (Woodbridge, UK: Boydell Press, 1992).
21. Colin B. Donovan, STL, "What Is Just War?," http://ewtn.com/expert/answers/just_war.htm
22. Upton-Ward, trans., ed. *The Rule of the Templars.*
23. Barack Obama's Nobel Peace Prize speech: Remarks of the U.S. president in Oslo, December 10, 2009.
24. Ibid.
25. Ibid.
26. Obama's Nobel Peace Prize speech.
27. Graham White & John Maze, *Henry A. Wallace: His Search For A New World Order* (Chapel Hill & London: The University of North Carolina Press, 1995), p. 269, quoting from Curtis Daniel MacDougall, *Gideon's Army* p. 357.
28. Nathan Freier, "Known Unknowns: Unconventional 'Strategic Shocks' in Defense Strategy Development," Strategic Studies Institute, November 2008. p. 34. www.strategicstudiesinstitute.army.mil/pdffiles/pub890.pdf
29. "Council on Foreign Relations Meeting: Zbigniew Brzezinski Fears the Global Awakening," *Youtube*, May 14, 2010. www.youtube.com/watch?v=qawPPSxbrYw
30. Mark Mazzetti, "U.S. Is Said to Expand Secret Military Acts in Mideast Region," *New York Times*, May 24, 2010.
31. Stephen Daggett, "Cost of Major U.S. Wars," *Congressional Research Service*, June 29, 2010. www.fas.org/sgp/crs/natsec/RS22926.pdf

32. Thom Shanker and Christopher Drew, "Pentagon Faces Growing Pressure to Trim Budget," *New York Times*, July 22, 2010.

33. John Michael Lee Jr. and Anita Rawls, "The College Completion Agenda 2010 Progress Report, Executive Summary," *College Board*, 2010. http://completionagenda.collegeboard.org/sites/default/files/reports_pdf/Progress_Executive_Summary.pdf

34. Priyamvada Gopal, "Burqas and bikinis," *Guardian* (London), August 3, 2010.

INDEX

Paul Fitzgerald and Elizabeth Gould, a husband-and-wife team, began working together in 1979, co-producing a documentary for Paul's television show, *Watchworks*, called "The Arms Race and the Economy: A Delicate Balance." They found themselves in the midst of a swirling controversy that was to boil over a few months later with the Soviet invasion of Afghanistan. The first U.S. television crew granted visas to enter Afghanistan in the spring of 1981, they arrived in the middle of the most heated Cold War controversy since Vietnam. But the pictures and the people inside Soviet-occupied Afghanistan told a very different story from the one being broadcast on the evening news.

Following their exclusive news story for *CBS Evening News* with Dan Rather, they produced a documentary, *Afghanistan Between Three Worlds*, for PBS, and in 1983 they returned to Kabul for *ABC Nightline* with Harvard Negotiation Project director Roger Fisher. Next the two wrote a film script about Afghanistan for Oliver Stone. In 1998 Paul and Liz began collaborating with Afghan human rights expert Sima Wali. Along with Wali, they contributed to the book *Women for Afghan Women: Shattering Myths and Claiming the Future*. In 2002 they filmed Wali's first return to Kabul since her exile in 1978. The film they produced about Wali's journey home, *The Woman in Exile Returns*, gave audiences the chance to discover the message of one of Afghanistan's most articulate voices and Wali's hopes for her people.

Paul and Liz continue to research and write about Afghanistan. They have been published by *The Boston Globe*, *The International Herald Tribune*, *Boiling Frogs Post*, *Oped News*, *Huffington Post*, *Counterpunch*, *Middle East Institute's VIEWPOINTS*, and more. Their 2009 book, *Invisible History: Afghanistan's Untold Story*, chronicles their three-decade focus on Afghanistan and the media. They regularly post new content on their Web site, www.invisiblehistory.com.